AF560351

INDUSTRIAL ORGANIZATION AND MANAGEMENT

INDUSTRIAL ORGANIZATION AND MANAGEMENT

Editors
SHAGUN AHUJA
R.K. SHARMA

REGAL PUBLICATIONS
New Delhi

INDUSTRIAL ORGANIZATION AND MANAGEMENT

ISBN 978-81-8484-546-4

Typeset by
RAHUL COMPOSERS
New Highway Apartments, Lakshmi Niwas
760, Pocket-D, Lok Nayak Puram, New Delhi - 110 041

Printed in India at
NEW ELEGANT PRINTERS
A-49/1, Mayapuri Phase-I, New Delhi - 110 064

Published by
REGAL PUBLICATIONS
F-159, Rajouri Garden, New Delhi - 110 027
Phone : 45546396, 25435369
E-mail : regalbookspub@yahoo.com, regaldeepbooks@yahoo.com

Contents

Preface ix

List of Contributors xi

Part I

MARKETING MANAGEMENT

1. Green Marketing :
   Social and Environmental Accountability 3
   Vaibhav Manocha

2. Innovative Measures Towards Green Logistics 17
   Tanu Manocha and *Marshal Mukesh Sahni*

3. Marketing Plan for Exporters 26
   Mamta Verma

4. Growth, Challenges and Opportunities in
   Indian Retail Industry 43
   Jyoti Gupta

Part II

HUMAN RESOURCE MANAGEMENT

5. Impact of Globalisation on Human Resource
   Management and Industrial Relations 55
   Aarti Arora

6. Cross-National Transfer of HR Policies and Practices in Multi Polar World 71
Neeru Sharma

7. Emerging HR Trends and Challenges in 21st Century 78
Priyanka Kapoor and *Meenakshi*

8. Green HRM—An Effective Tool for Sustainable Development 89
Seema Pandey

9. An Empirical Study on Career Development, Advancement and Opportunities 96
Shivani Dawer

10. Electronic Human Resource Management 112
Monika Khanna and *Aarti*

11. Assessment of the Performance Appraisal Practice Among the Employees in Reliance Communication Limited : A Case Study of Zonal Office, Chandigarh 122
Promila Kanwar and *Anu Jasrotia*

12. Effect of Pay and Promotional Factors on Job Satisfaction of Insurance Personnel : A Study of New India Insurance Company Limited 136
Gaytri

13. Interpersonal Relationship in School Education : An Empirical Study based on Students' Perspective 152
Neelam Kumari

14. Pertinence of Human Resource Development Strategies : The Importance and Gingery Areas of Hassels in Service Sector Companies in India 166
Aakashdeep Sharma and *Rupender Aulakh*

PART III

FINANCIAL MANAGEMENT

15. Performance Evaluation of Central Cooperative Bank Panchkula : A Study 179
Manisha

16. An Analysis of Service Tax in India 189
Harvinder Singh and *Parveen Kumar*

17. Banking Sector Reforms : E-banking 196
Richa Lomas and *Prabjot Kaur*

18. The Impact on Financial Position of Indian Companies after Adoption and Convergence to IFRS 207
Kapil Aggarwal and *Karamvir Sheokand*

19. Role of Information Technology in Banking Sector 221
Rizwan Ul Zaman Dar

PART IV

CONTEMPORARY ISSUES IN MANAGEMENT

20. Development and Future of Copyright in India 229
Silvie Aggarwal and *Sanjana Walia*

21. Spirituality at Work Place 236
Harvandna

22. Whistle Blowing : The Necessity for New Corporates 244
Pooja

Index 256

Preface

Industrial organization and management is a branch of engineering that deals with the creation and management of systems that integrate people and materials and energy in productive ways. It is concerned with the workings of markets and industries, in particular the way firms compete with each other. The study of how markets operate is however the subject of micro economics; the industrial organization and management emphasis on the study of the firm strategies that are characteristic of market interaction: price competition, product positioning, advertising, research and development and so forth.

The book is a compendium of better written research papers by the various contributors on the important aspects of Industrial Organization and Management.

Vaibhav Manocha attempted to study the ecological or green marketing initiatives taken by various companies from automobiles to products to services provided by different group of companies. Tanu Manocha highlighted the impact of logistics on environment has called for increasing attention to control the environmental problems. Harvinder Singh in his study concluded that the main purpose of imposing various taxes like service tax on various services which are taxable under the service tax act to generate revenue and increases revenue collection for the economic development of the country. Silvie Aggarwal and Sanjana Walia highlighted that the Copyright Act provides various types of remedies such as civil, criminal and administrative remedies to copyright holders against infringement of copyright. Apart from the above the various papers on the aspects of industrial organization and management like banking sector reforms, green logistics, human resource practices etc. are dealt with by the contributors.

We are extremely thankful to all the contributors for their valuable research work and trust on us which has made possible to make this endeavor a great success.

Above all our head bows in respect for the Almighty God who gave us strength and kept our spirits high during all the pursuits of our life.

SHAGUN AHUJA
R.K. SHARMA

List of Contributors

Aakashdeep Sharma, Research Scholar, Centre for Police Administration, Panjab University, Chandigarh.

Aarti, Assistant Professor, D.A.V. College, Ambala City (Haryana).

Aarti Arora, Assistant Professor of Commerce, Government PG College, Ambala Cantt. (Haryana).

Anu Jasrotia, Research Scholar, Department of Public Administration, Panjab University, Chandigarh.

Gaytri, Assistant Professor of Commerce, Government P.G. College, Ambala Cantt. (Haryana).

Harvandna, Government College for Girls, Sector-14, Panchkula (Haryana).

Harvinder Singh, S.D. College, Ambala Cantt. (Haryana).

Jyoti Gupta, Assistant Professor, Chaudhari Devi Lal College, Jagadhri, Yamuna Nagar (Haryana).

Kapil Aggarwal, Research Scholar, Institute of Management Studies and Research, Maharishi Dayanand University, Rohtak (Haryana).

Karamvir Sheokand, Assistant Professor, Institute of Management Studies and Research, Maharishi Dayanand University, Rohtak (Haryana).

Manisha, Extension Lecturer, G.C., Naraingarh, Ambala (Haryana).

Mamta Verma, 50, Dinesh Nagar (Near Babyal Power House), Ambala Cantt (Haryana).

Marshal Mukesh Sahni, HOD (MBA Telecom), Amity University, Sector 125, Noida (U.P.).

Meenakshi, Asst. Professor, D.A.V. College (Lahore), Ambala City (Haryana).

Monika Khanna, Assistant Professor D.A.V. College, Ambala City (Haryana).

Neelam Kumari, M.A., Ph.D., Department of Public Administration, Panjab University, Chandigarh.

Neeru Sharma, Assistant Professor, Arya Girls College, Ambala Cantt. (Haryana).

Parveen Kumar, S.D. College, Ambala Cantt. (Haryana).

Pooja, Assistant Professor (Commerce), Government College for Girls, Sector 14, Panchkula (Haryana).

Prabjot Kaur, Assistant Professor, Government P.G. College, Ambala Cantt (Haryana).

Priyanka Kapoor, Asst. Professor, D.A.V. College (Lahore), Ambala City (Haryana).

Promila Kanwar, Research Scholar, Department of Public Administration, Panjab University, Chandigarh.

Richa Lomas, Research Scholar, University School of Management, Kurukshetra University, Kurukshetra (Haryana).

Rizwan Ul Zaman Dar, Net, Set, Toffle (Economics).

Rupender Aulakh, Research Scholar, Centre for Women's Studies and Development, Panjab University, Chandigarh.

Sanjana Walia, Assistant Professor, Kamla Nehru Colleger for Women, Phagwara (Haryana).

Seema Pandey, Assistant Professor, Dr. B.R. Ambedkar Government College, Kaithal (Haryana).

Shivani Dawer, Department of Commerce, D.A.V. College, Ambala City (Haryana).

Silvie Aggarwal, Associate Professor, Arya Girls College, Ambala Cantt. (Haryana).

Tanu Manocha, Research Scholar, Amity University, Sector 125, Noida (U.P.).

Vaibhav Manocha, Undergraduate Student, NSIT, New Delhi.

Part I
MARKETING MANAGEMENT

1

Green Marketing

Social and Environmental Accountability

VAIBHAV MANOCHA

ABSTRACT

The present study is an attempt to study the ecological or green marketing initiatives taken by various companies from automobiles to products to services provided by different group of companies. As resources are limited and human wants are unlimited, that is why, it is an imperative to make a judicious use of resources available, as well as to achieve the desired objectives of organization. So green marketing is quite inevitable, so that may make the best use of available natural and man-made resources. Growing interests among the consumers all over the world, regarding protection of environment which tends to establish a reciprocal relationship between man and environment. As a result, green marketing notion has been given a third dimension to man and environment relationship. It includes sustainability and socially responsible products and services, rendered for human being, living on this earth. That is why green marketing has been widely adopted by the firms world-wide. Corporations are increasingly recognizing the benefits of green marketing, although there is often a thin line between doing so for its own benefit and for social responsibility reasons. The term "greenwashing" refers to all industries that adopt outwardly green acts with an underlying purpose to increase profits. From LCDs to clothing, every brand is giving an opportunity to ride the green wave. One challenge green marketers are likely to face as green products and messages become more common is confusion in the marketplace. Consumers do not really understand a lot about these issues, and there's a lot of confusion out there. Marketers sometimes take advantage of this confusion, and purposely make false or exaggerated "green" claims. So an act or law must be enforced to regulate such practices.

Keywords: Green marketing, Green-washing, Sustainable marketing, Consumer.

INTRODUCTION

The term Green Marketing came in the late 1980s and early 1990s, began in Europe in the early 1980s when certain products were found to be harmful to the environment and society as a whole. Consequently new types of products were created, called "Green product" that would cause less damage to the environment. According to Peattee (2001), the evolution of green marketing can be divided into three phases; first phase was termed as "Ecological" green marketing, to help solve the environment problems through remedies. Second phase was "Environmental" Green Marketing with focus on clean technology that involved designing of innovative new products, when take care of pollution and waste issues. Third phase was "Sustainable" where it becomes essential for companies to produce environment friendly products as the awareness for such products in on the rise as customers are demanding eco-friendly products and technologies. In this context, Narayan Lakhmi Vermuri (2008) has discussed multifaceted views on 'Green Marketing' its new hopes and challenges in the current scenario. Green marketing is the marketing of products that are presumed to be environmentally preferable to others. Thus green marketing incorporates a broad range of activities, including product modification, changes to the production process, sustainable packaging, as well as modifying advertising. Yet defining green marketing is not a simple task where several meanings intersect and contradict each other; an example of this will be the existence of varying social, environmental and retail definitions attached to this term. Other similar terms used are environmental marketing and ecological marketing. Green marketing refers to the process of selling products and/or services based on their environmental benefits. Such a product or service may be environmentally friendly in itself or produced and/or packaged in an environmentally friendly way. The obvious assumption of green marketing is that potential consumers will view a product or service's "greenness" as a benefit and base their buying decision accordingly. The not-so-obvious assumption of green marketing is that consumers will be willing to pay more for green products than they would for a less-green comparable alternative product—an assumption that, in my opinion, has not been proven conclusively. While green marketing is growing greatly as increasing number of consumers are willing to back their environmental consciousnesses with their money, it can be dangerous. The public tends to be skeptical of green claims to begin with and companies can seriously damage their brands and their sales if a green claim is discovered to be false or contradicted by a company's other products or practices. Presenting a product or service as green when it's not is called green-washing. Green marketing can be a very powerful marketing strategy though when it's done right. According to the American Marketing Association, green marketing is the marketing of product that are presumed to be environmentally safe. Thus, green marketing in corporate abroad range of activities, including product modification, changes to the production process, packaging changes, as well as modifying advertising. It is a complex combination which includes varying social, environmental and retail definitions attached to this term. Thus, "Green Marketing" refers to holistic marketing concept wherein the production, marketing consumption that is detrimental to the environment with growing awareness about the implication of global warming, non-biodegradable solid waste, harmful pollutants etc. Necessity of Green Marketing: Growing deteriorating environment due to air and water which has given rise to given pernicious effects on people, crops and wildlife in the developed as well as developing countries of the world. More than 12 other studies in the US, Brazil, Europe, Mexico, South Korea and Taiwan have tried to correlate between air pollutants and low weight premature birth still birth and infant death." As resources are limited and human wants are unlimited, that is why, it is an imperative to make a judicious use of resources available, as well as to achieve the desired objectives of organization. So green marketing is quite inevitable, so that may make the best use of available natural and man made resources. Growing interests among the consumers all over the world, regarding protection of environment which tends to establish a reciprocal relationship between man and environment. As a result, green marketing notion has been given a third dimension to man and environment relationship. It includes sustainability and socially responsible products and services, rendered for human being, living on this earth. That is why green marketing has been widely adopted by the firms would wide and the following are the reason for widely adoption of this conception. The basic five reasons for which a marketer should go for to adoption of green marketing are opportunities or Competitive advantage, corporate social responsibility (CSR), government pressure, competitive pressure and cost or Profit issues. Green, environmental and eco-marketing are part of the new marketing approaches which do not just refocus, adjust or enhance existing marketing thinking and practice, but seek to challenge those approaches and provide a substantially different perspective. Thus green marketing incorporates a broad range of activities, which cover product modification, change to the production processes, packaging changes as well as modifying advertising.

METHODOLOGY

The paper examines the notion of green marketing and the challenges which are associated with different aspects of green marketing in the present scenario. It also includes the strategies which are to be employed, so that the green marketing can be expedited and pave the way to make the 'green products' more 'ecological viable' as well as economical viable, for the consumers belong to different hierarchy. The green marketing strategies taken up by different industries and services were reviewed. Environmental initiatives of the industries like power industries, electronic goods, equipment-related, tyres, cement, clothing and services like hotel and celebration of days have been analyzed in this paper.

RESULTS AND DISCUSSION

With the rising concerns of global warming, people are becoming more and more aware of the dangers that will arise if they don't take the needs of mother earth into consideration. People are looking for environmentally friendly products that are good for the environment and their personal health. The green initiatives undertaken by various companies like power companies (Reliance, Tata), automobiles (Ford), electronics (LG, Hewlett-Packard, HCL, Haier, Voltas, Panasonic, Wipro, Siemens), products (MRF Tyres, ACC, Johnson & Johnson, Fevicol, Nike, Grassroot) and services (Vivanta, Disney and Rahgiri day).

RELIANCE POWER

The guiding principle for environmental initiatives is the 5

Rs: Reduce, Reuse, Recycle, Renew and Respect. The imperative is to use natural resources efficiently to leave a minimal carbon footprint and impact on biodiversity. Reliance Power strives to develop and promote processes and newer technologies to make all products and services environmentally responsible. Employees, the supply chain and other stakeholders are sensitized through personal interactions and other channels of effective communication. Strategies are in place for sustainable township development in various sites of Reliance Power by designing structures with minimum disturbance to the topography and ecology. Rainwater harvesting has been made mandatory for all sites, Solar heating for public buildings, Use of energy efficient building material, Minimum day lighting arrangements for over 75% of the area, Energy efficient electric fixtures within minimum 3 star BEE rating, Water efficient plumbing fixtures, Use of lead free paints, Treatment of sewage water and reuse for landscape and irrigation purposes. The company would be using super-critical technology and ultra super-critical technology that enables better combustion of coal and thereby reducing the emission levels apart from the Flue Gas-De-Sulphurisation plant that reduces sulphur dioxide emissions in flue gas. For some sites of Reliance Power, imported coal with low ash content is being used. Moreover to limit ground level concentration of pollutants, the chimneys are being made taller at all plant sites. The rest of the land resource is utilized for strengthening the green belt around the plants. Water being another precious natural resource, Reliance Power endeavors that in all plant sites the design and the technology will use only minimum required amount of water and further employ 100 per cent recycling too. The company is also involved in implementing green steps like the fly-ash collected from the plants which is further recycled for use by using it in manufacture of concrete bricks. Events and days of ecological importance are celebrated to raise awareness for conservation of natural resource. Environmental sanitation with special emphasis on solid waste management, waste segregation and vermin-composting is practiced at site locations. Some of the projects implemented are Switchover to Variable Frequency Drive from constant speed drive in large pumps across the power plant, Switchover the energy efficient lighting likes CFLs and standardizing the AC temperatures to 24°C, Replacing the electric water heaters with solar water heaters at canteens, Solar based LED lighting in selected areas; LED-based street lighting, Electric Vehicles for internal transport within plant premises, Recycle of paper and biomethanation of canteen waste, Rainwater harvesting in various location to tap the rain water and utilize for service purposes

TATA POWER

Tata Power along with other electricity distribution companies of Mumbai, few years back had launched an awareness campaign through advertisement to educate consumers about power conservation measures. The campaign—"I Will, Mumbai Will" was focused on shifting power usage away from the peak consumption period, more intelligent use of high power using devices such as air-conditioners, responsible electricity consumption behaviour (such as switching-off devices at the plug point when not in use) and encouraging consumers to use energy efficient devices. Now the Company focuses on year round education of its consumers in the area of energy efficiency.

Tata Power began an Energy Conservation Programme for school children in the academic year 2007-08. This initiative has evolved into an informal club called Tata Power Club Enerji comprising schoolchildren, teachers and families who not only practice but advocate energy conservation in their sphere of influence. Club Enerji has saved more than 3.4 million units of energy, sensitized more than 2.5 million citizens and saved more than 3300 tonnes of carbon emissions. Green Manufacturing Index (GMI) has been introduced as a new parameter for monitoring environmental parameters for operating divisions. Apart from statutory emission-based parameters, the non-statutory parameters are water conservation, efficiency of the operating plant, waste recycling and CO_2 intensity.

Corporate Sustainability Protocol (CSP), which addresses issues on environment and community has also been developed. Today, in the quest to deliver clean energy, the Company is focusing on building a robust renewable energy portfolio, scouting for clean sources of power, reducing carbon footprint and investing in cleaner technologies and global resources. The name Greenolution is a fusion of two concepts—'Green' and 'Evolution'. The objective of conceiving this concept is to traverse this journey and make green living our 'way of living'. The key programs that will run under Greenolution by Green Heroes are Implementation of 100% recycled paper usage in office, Tree plantation at all plants and site locations, Saving water at plants, Office and site locations, Saving fuel through carpooling and other initiatives, Waste Management at offices,

Energy conservation and efficiency initiatives at all locations and outside, Reducing air travel and using webcast/video conferencing facilities, Participation in 'Clean your city' drives and campaign. A communication pack comprising of a website, audio visual film and collaterals were launched to engage external stakeholders like customers, shareholders and youth across the country.

FORD MOTOR COMPANY

Automotive manufacturers used to be one of the heaviest polluters around, but Ford Motor Company is turning its image around with a ten part environmental policy that has been in force for years. Ford uses sustainable fabrics in its vehicles, and both the Escape and Focus vehicles are 80 percent recyclable. Ford is also an innovator in fuel efficiency, especially in the six speed transmission category, and offers a clean diesel heavy-duty pickup truck. In the Michigan Ford truck plant, paint fumes are recycled as fuel. Its factories also employ geothermal cooling systems, and the Crown Victoria Interceptor distributed to police has flexible fuel capacity, able to run on either gas or ethanol. Ford is also the proud owner of the world's largest green roof, and is the only company to win the EPA Energy Star Award two times in a row.

HEWLETT-PACKARD

Hewlett-Packard was the first company to come forward and report its own greenhouse gas emissions. Since then, they have initiated plans to reduce those emissions and have also cut back on the toxic substances it used to use in manufacturing its products, such as ink cartridges. Hewlett-Packard also uses an aggressive recycling program that helps keep much of its manufacturing waste out of landfills. It also spread the word about the importance of environmental responsibility through its ads promoting its green initiatives.

LG INDIA

South Korean consumer durables major LG Electronics recently introduced LG LED E60 and E90 series monitors in the Indian market. The LED E60 and E90 series monitors are packed with the eco-friendly features such as 40 per cent less energy consumption than the traditional LCD monitors. Also, the use of hazardous materials such as halogen or mercury is kept to minimal in this range. Globally, LG launched a range of eco-friendly products 'Eco-Chic' such as the platinum coated two-door refrigerator and washing machine with steam technology.

HCL

HCL launched its range of eco-friendly notebooks, HCL ME 40. HCL claims that this was India's first PVC free and eco-friendly notebook. This notebook is completely free from polyvinyl chloride (PVC) material and other harmful chemicals. Further, Bureau of Energy Efficiency has given HCL eco-friendly products a five-star rating, and they also meet REACH (REACH is the European Community Regulation on chemicals and their safe use) standards and are 100 per cent recyclable and toxin free.

HAIER

Haier India launches the green initiative with its 'Eco-Life' series, as a part of its global rebranding exercise. This is aimed at designing smart products which not only meet customer needs, but also adhere to environmental norms. The company's eco-friendly offerings include refrigerators, semi and fully automatic washing machines, split and windows air conditioners, a wide range of LED & LCD TVs and the Spa range of water heaters. Haier India launches the green initiative with its 'Eco-Life' series, as a part of its global rebranding exercise. This is aimed at designing smart products which not only meet customer needs, but also adhere to environmental norms.

VOLTAS

Air-conditioners, refrigerators and plasma or LCD TVs are going green with a vengeance. Next in the line is, Voltas from the Tata Group. In 2007, Voltas initiated the 'Green' range of air-conditioners, following which the government made it mandatory for home appliances to have energy star ratings. Energy Star is an international standard for energy efficient consumer products that originated in the US. Thus, devices carrying the star logo, such as computer products and peripherals, kitchen appliances and other products, use about 20-30 per cent less energy than the set standards.

PANASONIC

Panasonic has an Econavi range of air conditioners and LCD screens which is once again based on energy conservation. Econavi home appliances use sensor and control technologies to minimise energy consumption, based on a family's lifestyle. For instance, a door-opening sensor and lighting sensor allows the refrigerator to learn the time periods when the family typically doesn't use—when they're sleeping or away from home. The refrigerator goes into sleep mode accordingly. Globally, Panasonic is aiming to become top green innovation company in the electronics industry by 2018 and is laying a lot of emphasis on eco-friendly products.

NOKIA

Nokia has always takes steps to develop eco-friendly initiatives. It has also won the Greenpeace Award. The Finnish mobile company scored won this award mainly because of its back take-back program in India. It is also known for launching models free of PVC, brominated flame retardants and antimony trioxide. Now, it has launched a Nokia Bicycle Charger Kit (DC-14) in India. The bicycle charger kit works at walking speed (6 km/h) and when the speed reaches 50 km/h it stops charging. The charger is compatible with Nokia phones that have a 2mm charging interface, which includes most mid-range Nokia phones. The Nokia bicycle charger has an ergonomic design to make installation easier to suit different types of bicycles. The phone holder also has a rubberised design to hold the phone securely and protect it from shocks and vibrations.

WIPRO

The other company to launch wide range of eco-friendly desktops is Wipro. Introduced under the Wipro Green Ware initiative, these products aim to cut down e-waste in environment. The systems launched are toxin free and operate under a total recycling policy. With the removal of the toxins, recycling of the electronic products would be safer. Wipro has 17 e-waste collection centres in India where products are collected and recycled. Also, 12 Wipro campuses in the country have been certified as green buildings.

SIEMENS

Sustainability is a key pillar of the corporate strategy at Siemens, with the three areas—environment, economy and society—governing all the activities at the organization. In India, Siemens has put in place various initiatives for creating a sustainable environment.

This includes not only making employees, suppliers, business partners and customers environmentally-conscious but also encouraging all stakeholders to choose approaches that support sustainable environment. A few initiatives in the area of Sustainability are Green building initiative under the Energy Efficiency Program, Corporate citizenship program that promotes social development by creating a viable economic future, Rain water harvesting at factories, Sewage Treatment Plants, Environment Portfolio with energy efficient (green products), Recycling and Reuse. Siemens' expanding environmental portfolio offers relevant answers to the nation's energy and sustainability challenges. Apart from allowing customers to enjoy the benefit of lower energy costs, higher productivity and profitable businesses, the society benefits through improved environmental care and living standards.

MRF TYRES

Next in the line to join the eco-friendly product wagon is the Indian tyre manufacturer MRF with its ZSLK series. The premium eco-friendly tubeless tyres MRF ZSLK are made from unique silica-based rubber compounds and promises to offer fuel efficiency for vehicle owners. The tyres had been tested extensively on Indian road conditions with emphasis on endurance, wet and dry braking. At present, the ZSLK series are available for models including Honda City/Civic, Ford Fiesta, Hyundai Santro, Maruti SX4, Wagon R, Skoda Octavia, Tata Indica, Nissan Micra.

ACC

India-based cement manufacturer ACC has recently launched its eco-friendly brand, 'Concrete+'. This brand uses fly ash (a hazardous industrial waste) to help conserve natural resources, thus making it an eco-friendly product. The new product has been designed exclusively to ensure high durability and resistance of structures under extreme climate. This new product is a result of continuous feedback from customers, influencers and dealers.

FEVICOL

Fevicol, a leading brand of adhesive in India, has introduced environment-friendly synthetic resin adhesive. Claiming to be India's first eco-friendly adhesive, Fevicol AC Duct King Eco Fresh, boasts of being an all-in-one adhesive. The company says that this water-based adhesive has exceptional bonding strength and spreads smoothly at room temperature without emitting any toxic fumes. It is an ideal adhesive for AC Duct insulation for all residential and industrial projects. This brand is always concerned and worked towards developing and offering adhesives that contributed immensely to the betterment of health, safety and environment. As market leaders, it becomes our responsibility to take lead in caring and conserving our planet by using strong and secure adhesives.

JOHNSON & JOHNSON

Johnson & Johnson is leading the way in the arena of environmentally responsible personal care products, and has for more than 20 years. Its initiatives reduce the waste its manufacturing and distribution practices create, and it uses sustainable products and packaging methods whenever possible. Johnson & Johnson also owns and operates the single largest fleet of hybrid vehicles on earth. Its strong environmental goals just keep getting stronger year after year.

NIKE

Nike is another company that highlights the importance of green initiatives in its advertising, yet goes one step further by actually putting those great ideas into practice. Nike makes an entire line of sustainable sporting goods and equipment, including a basketball shoe made of "environmentally preferred materials," which includes recycled polyester. Nike also uses renewable energy sources for its manufacturing facilities. In addition to its environmental efforts on U.S. soil, it has pressed 650 of its contracted suppliers in 52 other countries to develop and carry out written environmental policies. This helps the environment all over planet earth.

GRASSROOT

Eco-friendly line of clothing is fast growing fashion trend. Though it had a slow take-off, it now has many takers. The eco-friendly brand Grassroot is a 100 per cent environment-friendly brand. They use certified eco-friendly and organic fabrics; have partnered with number of NGOs who are engaged into providing and promoting the work of local artisans. For the uninitiated, eco-fashion is a process of creating garments with environment friendly techniques and processes which are non-hazardous to the environment. Largely, eco-clothing uses organic cotton, bamboo jersey, viscose and linen, etc.

VIVANTA BY TAJ HOTEL RESORTS AND PALACES

Earth friendliness is the hallmark of the Vivanta line, just as it is at all Taj hotels. The parent company follows guidelines established at a United Nations Earth Summit and endorsed by nearly 200 countries. These green benchmarks are monitored by a leading worldwide certifier, Green Globe. Taj aims to bring the total of its Vivanta hotels to 30-plus in the coming years, totalling 5,000-plus guest rooms.

DISNEY

Striving to please the families that have made it the giant it is, Disney uses a zero net direct greenhouse gas emissions policies at all its facilities, and is working to reduce the indirect greenhouse gas emissions by reducing electrical consumption. It also has a zero waste policy, meaning none of its refuse ends up in landfills. Disney also uses water savings technologies and is lowering the footprint of its product manufacturing and distribution. Combine this with its policy of having a net positive impact on the environment, and Disney is a clear leader in environmental responsibility.

RAAHGIRI DAY

Raahgiri day is a weekly street event which provides citizens with the opportunity to reclaim their streets, connect with their community, celebrate their city and therefore reclaim their lives. The event started on all Sundays starting on 17 November 2013. Streets of Gurgaon, Delhi, Chandigarh are set aside for citizens to come together in large numbers to use the street for recreation that promotes health, well being, fitness, togetherness and joy. The name RaahGiri communicates that this is about taking charge of our own journey, of our own streets, of our lives. It has a mystic appeal, creates a sense of curiosity and will connect with today's children and youth. The concept is inspired by "Ciclovia" held weekly in Bagota, Columbia and now popular all over the world known by different names viz. Open Streets, Summer Streets, etc. The key objectives of Raahgiri Day are Promote Cycling, Walking and use of Public Transport as envisaged in the National Urban Transport Policy and

Integrated Mobility Plan, Re-state and remind its citizens that the streets belong to the people, Promote Healthy living by encouraging an active lifestyle, Create an inclusive community and promote and facilitate social integration and Promote and highlight the environmental issues/concerns. The streets identified for Raahgiri Day will be cordoned off for motorized transport and made safe for the citizens to cycle, walk, run, skate, play and enjoy the streets. The events will be on between 07:00 a.m. and 12:00 noon on all Sundays. On the full event days, stages will be set-up at intervals along the route in order to instruct for Zumba, Aerobics and Yoga, etc.

CONCLUSION

So, from LCDs to clothing, every brand is giving an opportunity to ride the green wave. Go ahead, make a choice and join the green revolution. One challenge green marketers—old and new—are likely to face as green products and messages become more common is confusion in the marketplace. "Consumers do not really understand a lot about these issues, and there's a lot of confusion out there," says Jacquelyn Ottman (founder of J. Ottman Consulting and author of "Green Marketing: Opportunity for Innovation"). Marketers sometimes take advantage of this confusion, and purposely make false or exaggerated green claims. Corporations are increasingly recognizing the benefits of green marketing, although there is often a thin line between doing so for its own benefit and for social responsibility reasons. The term greenwashing refers to all industries that adopt outwardly green acts with an underlying purpose to increase profits. The primary objective of greenwashing is to provide consumers with the feeling that the organization is taking the necessary steps to responsibly manage its ecological footprint. In reality, the company may be doing very little that is environmentally beneficial. The term greenwashing was first used by environmentalist Jay Westerveld when objecting to hotelier's practice of placing notices in hotel rooms which asked their guests to reuse towels to "save the environment". Westerveld noted that there was little else to suggest that the hoteliers were interested in reducing their environmental impacts, and that their interest in washing fewer towels seemed to be motivated by a concern to save costs rather than the environment. Since then greenwashing has become a central feature of debates about marketing communications and sustainability, with "awards" for greenwashing established and numerous campaigns, law and advices developed in an attempt to reduce or curb it. So an act or law must be enforced to regulate such practices. Corporations turn to greenwashing to make themselves look more environmentally friendly so that they can keep their customers coming back. If corporations were up front with their environmental wrongdoings, customers would most likely take their business elsewhere. It is a way for corporations to make themselves more marketable by hiding behind a mask and concealing their true colors. Not only has greenwashing fooled the general public, but it has made many corporations extremely prosperous.

References

Singh, Satpal, 2012. Green Marketing: Challenges and Strategy in the Changing Scenario, *International Journal of Advanced Research in Management and Social Sciences.* Vol. 1, No. 6.

Jacquelyn A. Ottaman (2006), 'Avoiding Green Marketing Myopia', Environment-Heldref Publication, Science and Policy for Sustainable Development, Washington, DC-5.

Narayan Lakshmi Vermuri and S. Dhinesh Babu (2008), Green Marketing—New Hopes and Challenges. Paper presented on Sept. 15, 2008, at Mohamad Sathak Engg. College, Kilakarai.

Green Marketing—Wikipedia, the free encyclopedia. *en.wikipedia.org/wiki/* ***Green_marketing.***

What Is Green Marketing? Green Marketing Definition. s*binfocanada.about.com/od/**marketing/g/greenmarketing**.htm.*

Green Marketing strategies to earn consumer trust | GreenBiz. www.**green**biz.com/.../five-strategies-avoid-taint-**green**wash-your-business.

What is Green Marketing? Definition and meaning. *ww.businessdictionary.com/definition/**green-marketing**.html.*

Green Marketing Inc. www.**greenmarketing**.net/

Green Marketing Definition | Investopedia. www.investopedia.com/terms/g/**green-marketing**.asp.

Green Marketing · Environmental Leader · Environmental .*www.environmentalleader.com/category/**green-marketing/***

www.inc.com/encyclopedia/**green-marketing**.htm

www.**green**biz.com/.../five-strategies-avoid-taint-**green**wash-your-busine

www.**marketing**-schools.org/types-of-**marketing/green-marketing**.html

www.**greenmarketing**.com

2

Innovative Measures Towards Green Logistics

TANU MANOCHA AND MARSHAL MUKESH SAHNI

ABSTRACT

The impact of logistics on environment has called for increasing attention to control the environmental problems. Due to increased environmental problems, companies need to understand the concept of Green Logistics. The article focuses on the need for the implementation of green logistics to survive in the green competitive world and the innovative measures taken by various companies to go green which has positive impact on environment as well as on the industry.

Keywords : Green Logistics, Innovation, Green Innovation, Environmental Problems.

INTRODUCTION

Logistics is the term used to describe the transportation, storage and handling of products as they move from point of origin to point of consumption for the purpose of confirming the customer's requirement. Logistics involves various activities like transportation, warehousing, packaging, inventory management, overall materials handling and related information processing (Council of Logistics Management, 2007).

Logistics, in the current scenario can be considered as a customer-focused business strategy with the emerging new technolgies creating strategic opportunities for the organizations to build competitive advantages. The use of GPS, GPRS, and RFID technologies gives the user more transparency and more specific information in terms of traceability of shipments and delivery status and saves manual operation time. Tracking physical goods at real-time greatly improves logistics performance, cost efficiency and customer satisfaction (Bhandari, 2008).

The major activities of logistics have been the key to economic development, but the flip side has been that over all these years the social and environmental issues which are key components of logistics have been ignored. It has many side effects on environment like noise pollution, air pollution and improper waste disposal in production.

To reduce the environmental impact of the logistics operations, aims to reduce the pollutant emission, Implementation of logistics system through environmental management, an emerging market conditions designed for more competitive and environment-friendly logistics. An environmental conscious logistics is called as green logistics (Chittyal, 2013). Green Logistics can be considered as the environmental focus and customer focus business strategies with the emerging new technolgies creating strategic opportunities for the organizations to build competitive advantage.

Innovation refers to any practices that are new to organisations, including products, services, processes, policies and projects. (Kimberly and Evanisko, 1981; Damanpour, 1991). Eco-innovation can be defined as actions to create or apply new goods, processes, services, systems, procedure, design to create value to customers and business also help to reduce the negative impact on environment. (Rennings, 1998)

The purpose of this paper is to study the various innovative measures taken towards the implementation of Green logistics in various companies and the various challenges which are experienced by the organisation in the implementation of green logistics.

LITERATURE REVIEW

The concept of "Greenness" (Sugiyama, 2008) has gain the importance in the industry in late 1980's and 1990's. It was an emerging concept, creating a sense of awareness, that led to understand that a world has started suffering from a wide range of environmental issues like Ozone layer depletion, global warming and acid rain. The World Commission on Environment and Development Report (1987) gave a significant boost to green issues in political and economic areas. The transportation industry is a major contributor to environmental issues (Banister and Button, 1993). Transportation of goods has a negative impact on environment, as it causes air pollution, noise pollution, which makes a remarkable input to global warming. The impact of logistics called for increasing attention in recent years, partially because increasing controls on pollution and road safety improvements have alleviated the other environmental problems. In 1990 s it was considered as the "decade of the environment" (Kirkpatrick 1990).Green logistics was studied with respect to different perspectives focused on environmental friendly approach. (Murphy, 2000). The green logistics can be defined as to plan, control, management and implementation of logistics system through the advanced logistics technology and environmental friendly (Chang & Qin, 2008). In modern era there are different and alternative definitions of green logistics are defined but according to (Wu and Dunn, 1995) a logistics system focused on environment friendly approach not only includes the forward logistics process from acquisition of raw material, production, packaging transportation, storage, delivery to end users but it also includes the reverse logistics dealing with waste recycling and disposal. Green logistics is considered to be environmental friendly approach which includes lot of activities like: green purchasing, green material management, green manufacturing, green distribution and green marketing and reverse logistics. (Hervani, 2005). The various evaluations criteria of enterprise green logistics (Chang & Qin, 2008) which includes:

1. **Green transportation**: The green transportation refers to a kind of fuel used which generates less noise; air pollution reduces the fuel consumption and cut operating costs. The main challenge for implementing green transportation is high investment cost of alternative fuel vehicles.
2. **Green storage**: The green storage refers to adoption the mechanized operation in the process of goods-storing to save the manpower cost, adoption the environmentally-friendly products to reduce Waste and liability cost. The company-wide standards should be used to build a "green corporate image."

3. **Green packing**: The green package refers to a maximize environment friendliness through alternative packaging materials and techniques. The packing materials should reduce the packaging cost and solid waste. The packing material used should be recycled and regenerated after use.
4. **Reverse logistics**: The reverse logistics is contrary to the traditional supply chain, it includes reasonably disposal or recovering the value by planning, managing and controlling the raw materials, middle stock, final products and relative information from consumer place to start point.

The emergent, innovative and environmental-friendly technologies are considered as an important link in the logistic chain (Gonzalez and Trujillo, 2008) as it helps to improve the economic performance and co-operate competitiveness.

The automobile industry in China manages to initiate the green logistics practices, to improve both their economic and environmental performance. The study explains the various drivers, initiatives and performance of automobile industry by doing an empirical analysis of 89 automotive enterprises with China (Qinghua Zhu in 2006).

The green logistics in electronic industry is explained by Chung-Hsiao in 2008. The various approaches and practices used for implementing green logistics has been proposed and recognised. Investigation is done to identify the reliability and validity of approaches in electronic industry. The fuzzy Analytical Hierarchy process is used to identify the relative importance in four dimensions, twenty-four applications among nine electronic industries. The findings indicate that the electronic industries would pay emphasis on implementing green logistics as it plays a crucial role in improving the overall performance of electronic industry.

In another study Ninlawan & Tossapol in 2010 works on the Implementation of Green logistics in Electronics Industry in which aims to survey current green activities in computer parts manufacturers in Thailand. Case studies which provides in-depth interview about green procurement, green manufacturing, green distribution, and/or reverse logistics are considered. To evaluate green logistics practices, the questionnaire is used to measure performance, and to explore the various drivers. The suggestion helps to implement the green practices in the electronic industry.

The overall green strategy, amount of carbon emission resulting from a transportation element is growing concern in the industries. Robert and Benjamin, 2010, introduced about the green transportation costs and tries to review methods for quantifying the carbon emission and estimating the cost of going green in selected set of optimization models.

Present situation of green logistics in various companies, is to reduce the emission of green house gas as well as to save fuel consumption, United Parcel Service (UPS), a global logistics service provider uses a route planning software and internet matching system in their logistics service process.

DHL AND BLUE DART

DHL and Blue Dart are India's Logistics companies which give a new direction towards eco-friendly environment by adopting a number of successful innovative technologies which helps to improve service quality, reduces time, cut cost and carbon dioxide emissions in the emerging market. DHL, the world's leading logistics company, and Blue Dart, part of the DHL Group gives a new direction with the launch of smart truck in Bangalore, created by DHL solutions and innovations (DSI). DHL Smart Truck is an "intelligent" pick-up and delivery vehicle that combines a number of innovative technologies including a route-planner, reducing both fuel consumption and CO_2 emissions. The methodology followed in the company works on the principles of the Greenhouse Gas Protocol and the World Economic Forum (WEF). (www.dhl.com.sg;www.dpdhl.com;white paper2012)

HCL Info. Systems Limited. The main focus of HCL is on developing a sustainable eco-friendly environment by using green ICT technology. It has been recognized as one of the greenest companies among Indian ICT manufacturing companies. The company launched 'HCL Eco-Safe' program which ensures that all HCL products are environmental-friendly in all respects, free from hazardous chemicals and matching standards and compliances. This led to the introduction of Green desktops, equipped with the unique Dynamic Energy Saver (DES) technology, that cut overall power consumption by 20-35%. It also developed desktops, servers and laptops and enjoys being a leader in Green Integrated Circuit Technology (GICT) manufacturers.

TATA CONSULTANCY SERVICES (TCS) LIMITED

TCS Limited is one of the best Indian IT services, consulting and business solutions organizations. TCS is committed to minimize its ecological impact working to reduce Greenhouse Gas (GHG) emissions and carbon footprint and optimizing resource consumption. TCS has developed an environment policy that guides its key activities like Green procurement. Reduce, reuse, and recycle, Green infrastructure—green buildings. All TCS sites are compliant with all relevant environmental laws, acts, rules and guidelines.

Cognizant

The main focus is on the green initiatives taken by the company. Cognizant has developed an Enterprise Mobility solution framework enabling real time tracking and dynamic scheduling of pick-up and delivery jobs. It has helped the companies to reduce their resource consumption and achieve higher service level. Cognizant has also developed RFID solutions which has helped the organization from a variety of environmental perspective. It has also developed a web -based solution called "Waste-Trace "which helps in industrial waste management. Waste Trace tracks the waste data from product conception and shipment through waste disposal. It has helped the organisation in cost reduction as well as increased operational efficiency.

Accenture

Accenture is *multinational management consulting, technology services,* and outsourcing company which focuses on "green" infrastructure—green buildings and data centres at all global offices.

Hewlett-Packard

Company have come up with global suppliers code of conduct and partner programme which ensures the compliance with environmental Regulations. Company provides energy -efficient products and services and follows the energy efficient operating practices in its facilities.

Wipro Technologies

Wipro technologies provide with sustainable IT products and solutions, which help customers, achieve high productivity in energy, space and asset management through the lifecycle. Wipro technologies have launched green ware ranges of desktops are not only 100% recyclable, but also toxin-free.

CISCO Systems

Cisco systems partnered with San Francisco's Department of Energy to develop World's first Urban Eco Map Pilot. It provides information on carbon emissions which are caused by transportation, energy waste, etc. organised by Zip Codes. Cisco has taken initiative to minimize the ecological impact by implementing various operational programmes. It helps to reduce energy consumption across the company, reducing the green house gas emissions and ensure proper disposal of hazardous materials.

Infosys Technologies Ltd.

Infosys Technology Focused on "Green Engineering". It is a unit which works on new products as well as on existing products to make them more energy efficient. Infosys have taken initiative on green buildings, water conservation and harvesting, better transportation management by encouraging car pool for its employees and by increasing bio-diversity in its campuses.

IBM-India

IBM has developed Business process modelling software based on SCOR framework to enable efficient planning of logistics functions.

Implementing green logistics in the industry is very challenging task. There are various challenges that organisation could face are:

- Lack of information about the green logistics best practices:
  The organizations might be unaware of the best practices, which act as a major obstacle in re-thinking and redesigning a process.
- Lack of tools to optimize the logistics with environmental management:
  Though there are plenty of tools available for supporting Green logistics initiatives, the challenge lies in selecting the right tool for a particular initiative.
- Advent of global sourcing making tracing of carbon footprint difficult:
  Since the advent of global sourcing, tracking the carbon footprint of finished products has become difficult. However, the practice of requesting carbon footprints from suppliers is slowly progressing.

- *Cost Issue* : Implementation of green practices incurs huge investment as a green product requires renewable and recyclable material or elements which are expensive.

CONCLUSION

Due to increase consumption of hydrocarbons and deforestation, results into ecological imbalance. Exhaustion of natural resources and abrupt climatic change results in increasing environmental problems. To protect the environment organization needs to understand the concept of green logistics. Organisations need to put emphasis on redesigning and rethinking of the logistics operations. Green Logistics has an impact on network designing, transportation used, warehousing, selection of equipments; business process. Green logistics has become one of the major issues followed by most of the industries to sustain in today s competitive environment. A competitive efficient and environmental friendly logistics sector is vital for all the economies.

Environmental issues plays a critical role in the scope of logistics. It has a significant impact on the various issues such as globalization, increasing competitiveness, economic development, employment, pollution, green house emission and many more factors. All these factors have a significant impact on key performance of the organisation such as cost, delivery, service, responsiveness and reliability.

Innovation is gaining importance in the logistics industry. The continuous innovation in terms of vehicle technology and environmental fuel which contributes a lot in reducing the environmental impact. The rapidly changing market technology has played a key role in the growth of the economy.

Implementing new innovative and green technology has created a widespread consciousness which has helped to improve efficiency, network optimization, package reduction, sustainable procurement and warehouse layout optimization. It also helps in reducing the carbon foot prints, waste management, by using various standards, innovative, environmental-friendly techniques and processes like ROHS (Restriction on the use of certain hazardous substances), IPPC (Integrated Pollution Prevention and Control Directive), REACH (Registration, Evaluation, and authorization of Chemicals), Eu P (Eco-design of Energy using Products). Implementing sustainable processes and innovative green technologies helps in boosting the business performance.

The paper studies the various innovative measures implemented by various companies which are environmental-friendly and helps the organisation to boost up the business performances. The research paper concludes that many organisations have taken initiatives but there are many more which needs to move from traditional strategies to "go green" strategies in order to survive in the green competitive world which has positive impact on environment.

References

Benjamin, R. (2010). Introducing Green Transportation costs in Supply Chain Modelling.

Bhandari (n.d.). Impact of Technology on Logistics and Supply Chain Management, *IOSR Journal of Business and Management (IOSR-JBM)*, 19-24. March, 2013). Green Logistics. *Indian Journal of Research in Management, Business and Social Sciences (IJRMBSS)* .

Chung-Hsiao (2008). Green supply chain management in electronic industry. creating_ a_ green supply _ chain_Cognizant.pdf

Damanpour, F. (1991). Organizational Innovation:a Meta-analysis of Effects of Determinants and moderators. *Academy of management journal* , 555-590.

Hervani, A.A. (2005). Performance Measurement for Green Supply Chain Management. *Benchmarking: An International Journal*, 330-53.

Kimberly, J.E. (1981). Organizational Innovation: the influence of Individual, Organizational and contextual factors on hospital adoption of technological and administrative innovations. *Academy of Management Journal*, 689-713.

Management, C.O. (2007, June 12). Retrieved from http://www.cscmp.org/Website/About CSCMP/Definitions.asp

Manjunath, G., G.M. (July, 2013). Green Marketing and its Implementation In Indian Business Organizations, *Asia Pacific Journal of Marketing and Management* .

Murphy, P.P. (2000). Green logistics strategies:an analysis of usage patterns. *Transportation Journal*, 5-16.

Ninlawan, C.S.A. (2010). *The implementation of Green Supply Chain Management Practices.*

Qin R., C. (2008). Analysis on Dvelopment path of Tianjin Green Logistics, *International Journal of Business and Management*, 96-98.

Qinghua Zhu, J.S.H. (2006). Qinghua Zhu, Joseph Sarkis Green Supply Chain Management: Pressures, Practices and Performance within the Chinese Automobile Industry. *Journal of Cleaner Production*, 1041-52.

Rennings, K. (n.d.). Towards a theory and policy of Eco-innovation-neo classical and (Co) Evolutionary Perspectives, *ZEW-Discussion paper*, 98-124.

Srivastava, S. (2000). Green Supply Chain Management : A State-of-art Literature Review. *International journal of management Reviews*, 53-80.

Wu, H.D. (1995). Environmentally responsible logistics system, *International Journal of Physical Distribution and Logistics Management*, 20-38.

www.dhl.com.sg;www.dpdhl.com;white paper2012)

(Whitepaper_Green_Logistics_08_2010_TCS)

3

Marketing Plan for Exporters

MAMTA VERMA

ABSTRACT

Marketing plan for exporters means planning the strategy (plan of action) to be implemented for selling the goods and services in/to another country (importer) by exporters. It is a step by step guideline or the blue-print made for successfully selling the product (goods and services) in/to foreign country. In international trade, marketing plans are developed by exporters but are developed for and implemented in importing countries (importer country).

INTRODUCTION

Developing a sound and successful plan for exporters demands the sharp-intuitive, intellectual, pragmatic and analytical skills on the part of the individuals entrusted with the tasks of developing marketing plan. The development of exporters marketing plan requires a number of decisions to be taken on various important aspects which forms the contents of marketing plan like Marketing objectives, Marketing segmentation and positioning, Budgeting, Marketing mix, Action plan/programs, Environment analysis.

The process of developing marketing plan for exporters may vary for new exporters and existing exporters according to the various unique characteristics of exporter's product, goodwill, years of existence etc.

However, the basic steps in the process of developing marketing plan for exporters may involve the 3 stages which are as follows-stage 1 situation analysis, stage 2 development stage and stage 3 evaluation stage. A good marketing plan for exporter should have the essentials like comprehensiveness, futuristic approach, compatibility, realism, cost-benefit analysis and soundness. As it provides guidance, strategic advantage, risk cover against uncertainties, basis for future decisions, control to the exporter for achieving his objectives.

There is not any single country in this world which can fulfill all her needs by itself. To fulfill its various needs every country has to get involved (indulge) in trade or the exchange process with another country. This trading between two or more countries for fulfilling their various needs and objectives is what is known as international trade.

In international trade, this exchange process involves two aspects— import and export. While imports fulfills the deficit needs (needs in which one country is not self-sufficient) of a country, exports provide an opportunity to a country to make maximum use of its surplus resources by exchanging it with other countries for some rewards (and for achieving its various objectives like earning profits, expanding market share, making efficient use of its surplus resources available, etc.)

Purchases Goods and Services

(Import)

Country A **Country B**

Sells Goods and Services

(Export)

International trade—an exchange process

In international exchange process two parties are engaged. The party performing the activity/function of purchasing goods and services is known as importer and the one selling the goods and services is known as exporter.

The onus/responsibility of initiating this exchange process by performing the functions like identifying the buyer/customer, his needs and satisfying those needs by making available the solution of that need (by making the appropriate products or services) and satisfying customer lies with the seller, which in the above international trade is exporter.

So, arise the need for marketing plan for exporters, to compete for the buyers i.e. importers.

MEANING OF MARKETING PLAN FOR EXPORTERS

Marketing plan for exporters means planning the strategy (plan of action) to be implemented for selling the goods and services in/to another country (importer) by exporters. It is a step by step guideline or the blue-print made for successfully selling the product (goods and services) in/to foreign country.

It involves making decisions about the following:

1. What is to be sold? (product/good and services/capital)
2. Where it is to be sold? (place/country)
3. Why it is to be sold? (objective)
4. Whom it is to be sold? (customer/importer)
5. How it is to be sold? (distribution/promotion)

The key decisions involved in developing marketing plan for exporters involve allocation of resources, deciding on new markets, products, promotional tools to be used and distribution channels to be explored. The plan of action (action programs) are developed in marketing plan by providing due consideration to the

- Needs and development status/stage of the destination (importing) country.
- Environmental factors influencing the scope and future prospects of opportunities available (i.e. influencing demand of exporter's products and services).
- Economic considerations (cost and benefits analysis).
- Long-term opportunities (diversification, etc.).

Definition

1. Marketing plan for exporters may be defined as "The strategy/blue print/guidelines, structured by exporters for exploring the opportunities available beyond the geographical boundaries of his home country for achieving the mutual benefits of (his) exporter and importer countries."

2. Marketing plan for exporters can also be defined as "The plans or action programs related to marketing components, i.e. marketing research, objectives, mix (4 P's), budget, evaluation etc., which are developed by exporters (for achieving commercial and other objectives) for their implementation in importing countries."

In international trade, marketing plans are developed by exporters but are developed for and implemented in importing countries (importer country).

Developing a sound and successful plan for exporters demands the sharp-intuitive, intellectual, pragmatic and analytical skills on the part of the individuals entrusted with the tasks of developing marketing plan.

The marketing plan of exporters should possess the following characteristics :

1. Develops strategies—Developing strategies is the essence of marketing plan of exporters. Without developing strategies the exporters cannot survive in the long-term in the international trade. Strategies are developed for the various marketing components like market research, objectives, segmentation and positioning, marketing mix/4 P's, etc. strategies are developed to compete successfully for the buyers, i.e. the importers of the products and services in which the exporters deal.

2. Affected by complex and dynamic environment—Marketing plan of exporters is in constant exposure to/of complex environment. Which involves not only the social, political, legal, economic, etc. constraints present in importers country but also of exporters country. These factors/constraints keeps on changing very rapidly which makes them not only dynamic but also more complex because of their interdependent nature.

Example—the marketing plan of exporters for exports in European countries (in the period of depression in euro zone) is affected by the foreign exchange constraints (value of currencies of European countries (euro), political commitments, stage of trade cycle, consumers sentiments regarding prevailing environment, etc.) prevailing in the European countries.

The marketing plan of exporters is affected by national as well as international environment.

3. Provides guidance—Marketing plan provides the exporters the step-by-step guidelines and procedure to be referred to at times of perplexity and while actually performing the activities in the international trade. It enlightens them regarding the pricing strategies, to be followed for various markets, which distribution channels to be followed and which promotional tools to be followed, etc.

4. **Blue print**—Marketing plan is the blue print to be followed by exporters for successfully achieving their objectives. It provides structure to the exporters for building the exporter niche in the foreign destination.

5. **Explore opportunities**—Marketing plan of exporters is meant to explore the opportunities available for expanding export markets, diversification, increasing profits and future prospects for growth in foreign destinations for exporters. These opportunities are explored in the initial stages of developing and implementing marketing plan for exporters. For this situation analysis and SWOT analysis is also undertaken by exporters.

6. **Time consuming**—Developing marketing plan for exporters is a time consuming process as the developer has to perform comprehensive research and analytical studies regarding the various factors and constraints present in the environment. Any mistake done in the initial stages of the developing marketing plan can ruin the fortune of the exporters.

7. **Multiple constraints**—Marketing plan of exporters is affected by multiple constraints present in the exporting and importing countries. For the success of marketing plan of exporter coordination between the exporter business philosophy, objectives, management and marketing skills, etc. and opportunities and threats posed by various constraints is necessary constraints are posed by social, political, legal, economic, competitors, etc. environment prevailing at national and international level.

8. **Planned/developed in exporter country and implemented in importer country**—Exporters develop their marketing plan in their home country by considering the incentives, tax benefits and subsidies made available to them by government but it is implemented in the importer country by making the products and services adaptable according to their needs and prevailing environment.

The development of exporters marketing plan requires a number of decisions to be taken on various important aspects which forms the contents of marketing plan. **The important contents/ components** which find place in exporters marketing plan are as follows :

- Marketing objectives
- Marketing segmentation and positioning
- Budgeting
- Marketing mix
- Action plan/programs
- Environment analysis

The brief description of content is as follows :

1. Marketing objectives—The foundation stones of any marketing plan are its marketing objectives. Marketing objectives provides the reason why all the efforts are being undertaken by exporters. Marketing objectives provides the vision of end target to be achieved. It can vary from exporter to exporter. It can be to increase sales, form a niche in foreign market, expand business or diversification, etc.

As marketing objectives lays the foundation for carrying out the succeeding marketing activities it is utmost important to lay marketing objectives with due diligence and vigil on every aspect. While formulating marketing objectives the exporter should perform the detailed SWOT analysis which enables him to know his strengths, weaknesses and also the opportunities and threats posed/available from/in the environment. He should carefully match his strengths with opportunities and weaknesses with threats and should accordingly formulate his marketing objectives.

Marketing objectives formulated should be such that which helps exporter to exploit potential opportunities using strengths and at the same time help him reduce his weaknesses and protect him from threats. Some of the characteristics of marketing objectives are:

- The marketing objectives should be specific rather than general. As the central/core marketing objective will only assist in setting the specific objectives of the marketing mix components like what would be the characteristics of product, which export pricing strategy to be followed, what will be the mode of entry, etc.
- The objectives need to be stated with reference to the time perspective i.e. short-term and long-term. And at the same time must be realistic, communicable, prioritize goals and specify the degree of results sought.
- Marketing objectives should clearly state the specific description of target markets, expected sales, profit expectations, market penetration and coverage.

2. Marketing mix—Marketing-mix provides the set of tools in the form of products, place, price and promotion in the hands of exporters. By using which the exporters can achieve their marketing objectives.

The elements of marketing mix to be decided while developing marketing plan by exporters are as follows :

(a) **Product characteristics (adaption or modification)**—product will find place in the foreign market only when it is capable of satisfying the needs of the customers in foreign market. So, it is important for a exporter to accordingly modify and make the product adaptable by bringing necessary changes in the core component, packaging component and support services component of the product according to the tastes, preferences, lifestyle etc. of the customers in the destination market.

(b) **Price determination/export pricing**—While setting the product export price the exporter should consider the additional costs which will supplement with the basic price of the product. It involves the following—

- Cost of the shipment of goods
- Transportation costs
- Handling expenses (i) pier charges (ii) loading and unloading charges
- Insurance costs and customs duties
- Import taxes, VAT
- Wholesale and retail markups and discounts
- Profit margin, etc.

In addition to the above while deciding export pricing exporters should duly give weight age to those pricing strategies—penetration, skimming, etc. which go with the marketing objectives set by the exporters.

(c) **Distribution**—Distribution creates the place utility for the exporter. Distribution decisions has to be taken carefully as these only will decide how exporters product will reach the potential customer and through which medium the customer will get the real physical interaction with exporter product. The decisions to be consider under distribution are:

(1) Mode of transportation from origin to destination-

port selection, mode selection, packing, documentation, freight, warehousing etc.

(2) Channels of distribution—the channels of distribution available to exporters are :

- Exporting through a domestic exporting firm that finds sales outlets abroad.
- Services of warehouses abroad.
- Selling through representatives abroad.
- Setting own export organization or through owned subsidiaries.

(d) **Promotion**—The promotion function will provide the information about the exporter product to the customers abroad. In present times it forms an indispensable part of marketing mix. Due to which it becomes utmost important for the exporter to spend a huge amount on promotion for his product. The marketing plan for exporters should clearly state the promotional strategies to be followed, promotion mix-advertising, publicity, sales promotion—their tools, etc. and at the same time should also give due weight age (towards) to making provision for getting feedback and customer support services and after sales services. The exporter can also tie-up with the various Medias, brands already existing in the destination markets.

3. Marketing segmentation and positioning—Until and unless the marketing plan of exporter do not clearly provide information about the market segment which the exporter intends to capture all the marketing tools will not bear its fruits.

As tools needs the object to show their application, same way/ likewise marketing-mix needs the target market segment for its application. Marketing plan of exporters should also provide information about what strategy the exporter intends to use to position his product in the mind of his customers.

This, it will have its impact on what and how customers form their perception about the exporter product or offering, which will induce them to search for information about the exporter product.

Example—the U.S. citizens have positive positioning of (perception about) the artistic and ethnic items like jewellery, crafts products of India.

4. Budgeting—All the aspects of marketing plan of exporters are dependent on budget. Budget provides the premises in terms of resources for each component of marketing plan. Budget allocates the resources among the various components of marketing plan. And each component has to make itself efficient and effective by keeping itself in its boundaries.

Example—if the resources allocated for the distribution function are 100 lakhs. The exporter has to choose those alternatives of transportation and channels which are available to him within these (100 lakhs) monetary premises and at the same time which fulfills his objective of making the product available to his customers promptly and conveniently.

5. Action plans/programs—Action plans are the programs which are developed to help the exporters to deal effectively with any problem which arises in due course of implementing the marketing plan. Action plans helps the exporters to bring harmony and proximity between the marketing objectives planned and the actual results achieved. Action plans provides a step by step procedure to be followed in case of any difficulties as well as in bringing the marketing plan into action.

Marketing plan of exporters must make provision for unforeseen contingencies in the form of action plans to be implemented in the time of need. Example-1.Indian government had banned export of wheat in past years during which the supply of wheat was deficit in the domestic market. 2. U.S. parliament is proposing a bill for restricting outsourcing from India (at the time of depression period of trade cycle).

Action plans are developed for tackling/managing unforeseen events arising out of and legal issues, political issues and other environmental factors.

6. Environment analysis—The marketing plan of exporter should develop a mechanism which keeps the exporter informed about the changes occurring in the environment. The mechanism should be such that which timely/promptly provides the exporters information so that he can take timely action in case of any expected changes in the factors having direct impact on any of the component of marketing plan of exporter. Example—the GAAR (general anti-tax avoidance rules) proposed to be implemented can affect the export of Indian investment abroad as well as the exports of foreign investors in India (in each other markets).

Similarly, the policies like FDI in retail, multi-brand retail, aviation, etc. will also affect the marketing plan of the existing exporters to India.

THE PROCESS OF DEVELOPING MARKETING PLAN FOR EXPORTERS

The process of developing marketing plan for exporters may vary for new exporters and existing exporters according to the various unique characteristics of exporter's product, goodwill, years of existence etc.

However the basic steps in the process of developing marketing plan for exporters may involve the 3 stages which are as follows:

Stage 1—Situation analysis—This is the pre-planning stage in developing marketing plan for exporters. It involves basically the 3 steps which are as follows:

(a) Searching for avenues—This is the first step where the exporter searches for the various avenues/alternatives and opportunities (choices) available to him for undertaking the exports. Here the exporters search for the information about the locations/ countries where he can undertake/pursue the exporting activities. This information can be procured from various sources like—

- (i) Export promotion councils, commodity board, chambers of commerce, trade associations, etc.
- (ii) Through analyzing EXIM policies, international trade statistics publications, Indian trade bulletin, etc.
- (iii) The increase in mutual trade relationship among the various countries through various international forums like ASEAN, SARAAC, WTO, etc. also present various avenues to be explored to the exporters.

From the above sources the exporters can search for the prospective countries as well as the area for exporters, i.e. products categories, etc. in this stage the exporter makes a list of various viable prospects available.

(b) Screening/matching/selecting among the available avenues:Screening—After making the list of various prospective avenues available in terms of countries and products, the next step is to screen the various avenues available on the basis of various criterias. The criterias can be developed on the basis of following considerations:

- (i) The trade cooperation among the countries.

(ii) The environment suitability in the prospecting countries.
(iii) The cost-benefits analysis.
(iv) Future viability on the basis of commercial and political relationships among the countries.

Matching—Then after screening on the macro-level, analysis/ matching is done on the micro-level. It involves matching the exporter's needs with the opportunities available in the screened prospects.

Here, the list of various avenues searched are reduced to the few based on the fulfillment of the criteria's set by the exporters for undertaking export.

Selecting—The exporter for selecting the avenues undertake the research regarding the general market potential in the various countries and product categories on the basis of macro-level variables like economic statistics, social structure, geographical factors and political environment i.e. GDP, population size, availability of resources, political stability, climatic conditions, geographical distance, etc.

(c) **Market research**—After selecting the destination and product category the next activity undertaken by exporter is to do general market research related to product like the market size, growth trend for similar products, taxes and government policies, cultural acceptance of similar products, competition, cost of entry, profit potential, reliability of information etc. the exporter can either perform market research by himself or can also get the help from export market research agencies.

Stage 2: Development Stage—The next stage after performing the situation analysis is the development stage. It involves the following phases:

(a) **Setting marketing objectives**—The exporter after having the various macro and micro-level aspects through market research undertakes the SWOT analysis for setting his marketing objectives. The objectives set should be specific, realistic and should clearly present information/targets in terms of target markets, sales and profit expectations, etc.

(b) **Deciding market segmentation and positioning**—Here the exporter concentrate on deciding the market segments which he wants to cater for fulfilling his objectives. Market segment decision will have its impact on the other factors/components of marketing plan of exporters. As all the activities undertaken in marketing plan will focus on capturing the selected market segment. The exporter can choose market segment, i.e. his target market according to his objectives. For example—if the exporter objective is to sell his surplus product for maximum profit he can go for choosing concentrated market segment.

(c) **Developing strategies**—For converting the planned marketing objectives into reality/achievement the exporter develops the various strategies for different components of marketing mix, i.e. 4 P's strategies refers to the plan of action to be undertaken for making the objectives achievable. It involves deciding the way and action plans to be followed for entering into the destination markets and how the exporter will compete with his competitors for capturing his target market and for achieving his marketing objectives. It involves deciding about the tactics to be followed for following aspects—

1. Pricing strategies—skimming, penetration, etc.
2. Distribution strategy—direct, indirect, etc.
3. Product—luxury, convenience, speciality, etc.
4. Promotion—advertising, sales promotion, etc.

(d) **Developing marketing-mix**—Here the exporter develop his marketing-mix i.e. takes decisions how he will use his tools of product, price, place and promotion for capturing his target market. It involves decisions about—

1. Product—features, modifications, adaptability, core component, packing component, support services component.
2. Place—distribution channels, mode of transportation, warehousing, etc.
3. Price—export pricing, profit margin, pricing strategies, skimming, penetration, etc.
4. Promotion—media, advertising, sales promotion, publicity (promotion mix), etc.
5. Customer support services and after sales services, mechanism for redressal of consumer grievances.

Here, the specific objectives of the 4 P's are developed in consonance with the main marketing objectives of the exporters and the specific action plan/programs are developed for achieving the marketing objectives.

Stage 3: Evaluation stage—Having passed through the situation analysis and development stage the process of developing marketing plan for exporters enters the evaluation stage, it involves the following feature—

(a) **Evaluating marketing components on various parameters**—Here the components developed so far are evaluated on the parameters of :

(i) **Budget**—The components so developed must be within the purview of the budget available with the exporter. It's the exporter's resources only which will validate the undertaking various plans into actions. Budget can restrict the plan and can also motivate the planners to search for new innovative ways to get maximum by efficiently utilizing his resources.

(ii) **Action programs**—For making the marketing plan a success it is important to make provision of flexibility in the marketing plan for making it capable of meeting risks of dynamic environment. For this action action programs are developed in terms of plan of action to be undertaken in case of arising any issues out of legal, political, social, economic issues. So marketing plan developed should be such that which provides a mechanism for identifying the changes/risks available in the environment which can affect the original marketing plan developed by the exporter.

FACTORS AFFECTING THE DEVELOPMENT OF MARKETING PLAN FOR EXPORTERS

A well planned marketing plan is based on the sound considerations of various aspects which have deep-rooted impact on its various components. These various aspects are the various factors which have to be analyzed in detail while preparing marketing plan for exporters. These factors are present in both destination and home country of exporters. These factors can be categorized on the following basis—

1. Factors present in home country and destination country.
2. Macro and micro-level factors.
3. Internal and external factors.

The exporter has to analyse the combined effect of these factors won his marketing plan. These factors are as follows—

1. **Needs**—The needs of the exporters pave the way for deciding what type of export the exporter want to undertake and at the same time his needs have to coincide with the types of demand shown by his destination market. For example—if an exporter deals in the food grains items and he wants to export those at maximum price. In this case he will be able to export to those countries only where there is demand for the same quality of food grains items which exporter possess, i.e. the exporter possess those goods which the destination market demands. Example—Indian handicrafts items are in great demand in the western countries. So they are in the list of export items of exporters.

2. **Development stage of a country**—The exporter while choosing the destination market for his exports analyse the various macro level factors present in the destination market. These macro level factors include GNP, NI, economic structure, infrastructure development, standard of living, trade cycles etc. the exporter while preparing his marketing plan has to adjust his marketing components like product, place, price, promotion based on these macro factors.

3. **Social and cultural factors**—Social and cultural factors involves aspects related to the traditions, values, lifestyle, beliefs, festivals, thinking which the population of the destination market conform to. These factors will have great impact on the exporters marketing plan as these factors not only will decide how far the exporter product will be adaptable to the population of destination market. Example-the countries like Saudi-Arabia, Iran, Iraq impose a number of restrictions on their women population like women cannot wear western cloths, they are not allowed to drive, etc. then in that scenario that destination country will not be lucrative for exporters of western garments and vehicles meant for women.

4. **Legal**—The legal environment prevailing in the foreign countries also affect the exporters. As exporters has to conform to the various laws, acts if they want to sell their products in that destination country. Example—the beverages like coca-cola, Pepsi have to conform their product to the standards established for food items in different countries by their ministries. In addition to this, legalities related to obtaining permission from the various ministries of the destination markets are also to be conformed.

5. Demographic factors–Demographic factors like sex ratio, education level, attitudes, and beliefs of the population also affect the marketing plan of exporters. The exporter has to modify his marketing tools according to the characteristics borne by the population of his target market.

6. Competitors–The competitors, i.e. the firms dealing in the similar products and substitutes products also effect the marketing plan of exporters. There are various questions like why the population will buy exporter product when the same product is available in the destination market, how the exporter product is better, etc. which the exporter should get answered in advance before choosing the various elements in marketing plan. The exporter also has to formulate and analyse strategies to compete with the competitors based on SWOT analysis.

7. Market-related factors–Market size, market composition, market behavior, market dynamics are the aspects which affect marketing plan of the exporters. Is the market size large enough for the exporters' products, does it compose of the target customers for the exporters product, how much vulnerable and dynamic is market in response to the environmental changes, how market behave to changes like price, inflation, what is the elasticity of demand, supply factors prevailing in the market are the questions which the exporters cannot overlook.

8. Economic factors–The exporter will undertake exporting only when he sees some economic returns occurring to him. The cost and benefit difference is the reason why the exporter will undertake various pains in developing marketing plan. The cost and benefit factors will be decided by the factors like income level of the target market, disposable income, incentives available, cost occurring on product adaptability, procuring distribution, promotion, the revenue growth opportunities available in future in the destination markets, etc. the greater the scope of occurring economic benefits in terms of the more foreign exchange (currency value difference), increased sales revenue, profit margin, the more inclined will be the exporter to undertake the marketing plan more aggressively.

9. Future prospects–Exporter will be allured to capture only those destinations where he sees opportunities to grow in the long run. Otherwise there will be no need/objective of incurring initial cost on establishing foot in the destination markets. The future prospects will depend on various aspects like political stability, relationship among the countries, development and growth rate of economy of the destination market, competition arrival possibilities in the destination markets from exporter's home country as well as from other countries.

10. International environment—The international forums like WTO, SAFTA, SARAAC rules and regulations and developments also affect the exporters. The developments processed in these forums generate opportunities for exporters. Increase in mutual trade relationships among various countries generates avenues for exporters.

11. Interdependence among countries—The economic, political interdependence among various countries also affects the exporters. The scope of opportunities and threats will be decided by the degree of dependence of countries on each other for meeting their needs. Example-around 80% of India demand for petroleum products are met by countries like Iran and Iraq. As the number of countries possessing these resources is little so dependence of other countries on these countries increase. So the exporters of these countries can dictate their terms.

12. Possession of resources—More the possession of scarce resources in the hands of any country more it will be having opportunities for exports. The exporters can utilize these surplus resources for their benefits. Under this kind of scenario the exporters are in more advantageous stage for dictating their terms for undertaking exports in different countries. Example-about 90% of the resources of petroleum products are possessed by group of countries like Saudi Arabia, Iran and Iraq.

13. Political considerations—The government of both exporter and destination countries paves and dictates the direction of exports by controlling the various tools/aspects like EXIM policy, incentives, tax levies, subsidies, trade pacts with other countries, trade policies like FDI, implementing regulations related to trade like GAAR, investment policies, enacting laws like FEMA, etc., if the government is in favour of promoting exports it will do away with the restrictions and *vice-versa*. So the government can according to its needs decide the direction and degree of exports it wants to promote, which will have its impact on the exporters marketing plan by limiting or expanding avenues for exports. Example—the Indian government has allowed the FDI in multi-brand retail sector which have made India a destination country for exporters in other countries. (As under FDI rules in multi-brand retail sector 70% of requirements can be procured from outside sources).

A good marketing plan for exporter should have the essentials like comprehensiveness, futuristic approach, compatibility, realism, cost-benefit analysis and soundness. As it provides guidance, strategic advantage, risk cover against uncertainties, basis for future decisions, control to the exporter for achieving his objectives.

References

Export Management, P.K. Khurana, Galgotia Publishing Company, New Delhi.

International Marketing Management—An Indian Perspective, B. Bhattacharya, Sultan Chand & Sons.

International Marketing, P.K. Vasudeva, Excel Books, New Delhi.

Pepsi Handbook of India Exports, Global Business Press, New Delhi.

Export Management, T.A.S. Balagopal, Himalaya Publishing House, Mumbai.

www.google.com

4

Growth, Challenges and Opportunities in Indian Retail Industry

JYOTI GUPTA

ABSTRACT

This paper provides detailed information about the growth of retailing industry in India. It examines the growing awareness and brand consciousness among people across different socio-economic classes in India and how the urban and semi-urban retail markets are witnessing significant growth. It explores the role of the Government of India in the industries growth and the need for further reforms. In India the vast middle class and its almost untapped retail industry are the key attractive forces for global retail giants wanting to enter into newer markets, which in turn will help the India Retail Industry to grow faster. The paper includes growth of retail sector in India, strategies, strength and opportunities of retail stores, retail format in India, recent trends, and opportunities and challenges. This paper concludes with the likely impact of the entry of global players into the Indian retailing industry. It also highlights the challenges faced by the industry in near future.

INTRODUCTION

The India Retail Industry is the largest among all the industries, accounting for over 10 per cent of the country's GDP and around 8 per cent of the employment. The Retail Industry in India has come forth as one of the most dynamic and fast paced industries with several players entering the market. But all of them have not yet tasted success because of the heavy initial investments that are required to break even with other companies and compete with them. The India Retail Industry is gradually inching its way towards becoming the next boom industry.

The total concept and idea of shopping has undergone an attention drawing change in terms of format and consumer buying behavior, ushering in a revolution in shopping in India. Modern retailing has entered into the Retail market in India as is observed in the form of bustling shopping centers, multi-storied malls and the huge complexes that offer shopping, entertainment and food all under one roof.

A large young working population with median age of 24 years, nuclear families in urban areas, along with increasing workingwomen population and emerging opportunities in the services sector are going to be the key factors in the growth of the organized Retail sector in India. The growth pattern in organized retailing and in the consumption made by the Indian population will follow a rising graph helping the newer businessmen to enter the India Retail Industry.

In India the vast middle class and its almost untapped retail industry are the key attractive forces for global retail giants wanting to enter into newer markets, which in turn will help the India Retail Industry to grow faster. Indian retail is expected to grow 25 per cent annually. Modern retail in India could be worth US$ 175-200 billion by 2016. The Food Retail Industry in India dominates the shopping basket. The Mobile Phone Retail Industry in India is already a US$ 16.7 billion business, growing at over 20 per cent per year. The future of the India Retail Industry looks promising with the growing of the market, with the government policies becoming more favorable and the emerging technologies facilitating operations.

THE INDIAN RETAIL SCENE

India is the country having the most unorganized retail market. Traditionally it is a family livelihood, with their shop in the front and house at the back, while they run the retail business. More than 99% retailer function in less than 500 square feet of shopping space. Global retail consultants KSA Technopak have estimated that organized retailing in India is expected to touch Rs. 35,000 crore in the year 2005-06. The Indian retail sector is estimated at around Rs 900,000 crore, of which the organized sector accounts for a mere 2 per cent indicating a huge potential market opportunity that is lying in the waiting for the consumer-savvy organized retailer. Purchasing power of Indian urban consumer is growing and branded merchandise in categories like Apparels, Cosmetics, Shoes, Watches, Beverages, Food and even Jewellery, are slowly becoming lifestyle products that are widely accepted by the urban Indian consumer. Indian retailers need to advantage of this growth and aiming to grow, diversify and introduce new formats have to pay more attention to the brand building process. The emphasis here is on retail as a brand rather than retailers selling brands. The focus should be on branding the retail business itself. In their preparation to face fierce competitive pressure, Indian retailers must come to recognize the value of building their own stores as brands to reinforce their marketing positioning, to communicate quality as well as value for money. Sustainable competitive advantage will be dependent on translating core values combining products, image and reputation into a coherent retail brand strategy.

There is no doubt that the Indian retail scene is booming. A number of large corporate houses have already made their foray into this arena, with beauty and health stores, supermarkets, self-service music stores, newage book stores, every-day-low-price stores, computers and peripherals stores, office equipment stores and home/ building construction stores. Today the organized players have attacked every retail category. The Indian retail scene has witnessed too many players in too short a time, crowding several categories without looking at their core competencies, or having a well thought out branding strategy.

STRATEGIES, TRENDS AND OPPORTUNITIES

Retailing in India is gradually inching its way toward becoming the next boom industry. The whole concept of shopping has altered in terms of format and consumer buying behavior, ushering in a revolution in shopping in India. Modern retail has entered India as seen in sprawling shopping centres, multi-storied malls and huge complexes offer shopping, entertainment and food all under one roof. The Indian retailing sector is at an inflexion point where the growth of organized retailing and growth in the consumption by the Indian population is going to take a higher growth trajectory. The

Indian population is witnessing a significant change in its demographics. A large young working population with median age of 24 years, nuclear families in urban areas, along with increasing workingwomen population and emerging opportunities in the services sector are going to be the key growth drivers of the organized retail sector in India.

GROWTH OF RETAIL SECTOR IN INDIA

Retail and real estate are the two booming sectors of India in the present times. And if industry experts are to be believed, the prospects of both the sectors are mutually dependent on each other. Retail, one of Indias' largest industries, has presently emerged as one of the most dynamic and fast paced industries of our times with several players entering the market. Accounting for over 10 per cent of the country's GDP and around eight per cent of the employment retailing in India is gradually inching its way toward becoming the next boom industry.

As the contemporary retail sector in India is reflected in sprawling shopping centers, multiplex—malls and huge complexes offer shopping, entertainment and food all under one roof, the concept of shopping has altered in terms of format and consumer buying behavior, ushering in a revolution in shopping in India. This has also contributed to large-scale investments in the real estate sector with major national and global players investing in developing the infrastructure and construction of the retailing business. The trends that are driving the growth of the retail sector in India are:

- Low share of organized retailing
- Falling real estate prices
- Increase in disposable income and customer aspiration
- Increase in expenditure for luxury items (Chart 1)

Chart 1 : Predicted Mall Distribution Space in India

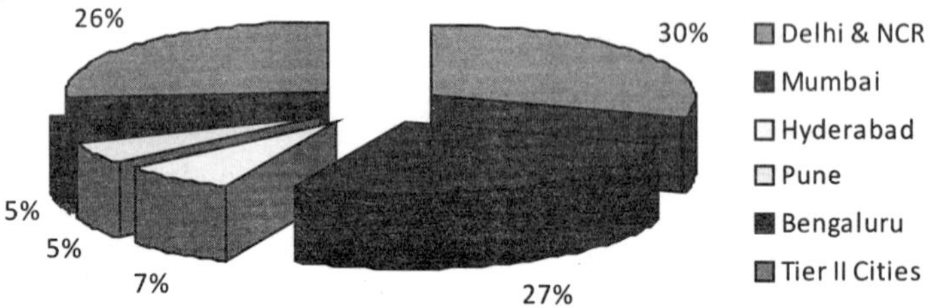

Another credible factor in the prospects of the retail sector in India is the increase in the young working population. In India, hefty pay packets, nuclear families in urban areas, along with increasing working-women population and emerging opportunities in the services sector. These key factors have been the growth drivers of the organized retail sector in India which now boast of retailing almost all the preferences of life—Apparel & Accessories, Appliances, Electronics, Cosmetics and Toiletries, Home & Office Products, Travel and Leisure and many more. With this the retail sector in India is witnessing rejuvenation as traditional markets make way for new formats such as departmental stores, hypermarkets, supermarkets and specialty stores.

The retailing configuration in India is fast developing as shopping malls are increasingly becoming familiar in large cities. When it comes to development of retail space specially the malls, the Tier II cities are no longer behind in the race. If development plans till 2007 is studied it shows the projection of 220 shopping malls, with 139 malls in metros and the remaining 81 in the Tier II cities. The government of states like Delhi and National Capital Region (NCR) are very upbeat about permitting the use of land for commercial development thus increasing the availability of land for retail space; thus making NCR render to 50% of the malls in India. (Chart 2)

Chart 2 : Retail Space Distribution in Delhi, NCR

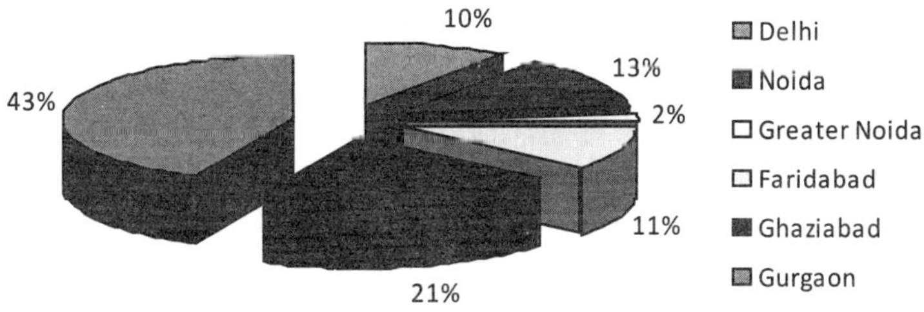

India is being seen as a potential goldmine for retail investors from over the world and latest research has rated India as the top destination for retailers for an attractive emerging retail market. India is vast middle class and its almost untapped retail industry are key attractions for global retail giants wanting to enter newer markets. Even though India has well over 5 million retail outlets, the country sorely lacks anything that can resemble a retailing industry in the modern sense of the term. This presents international retailing specialists with a great opportunity. The organized retail sector is expected to grow stronger than GDP growth in the next five years driven by changing lifestyles, burgeoning income and favorable demographic outline.

INDUSTRY EVOLUTION

- Traditionally retailing in India can be traced to
- The emergence of the neighbourhood Kiranaï stores catering to the convenience of the consumers,
- Era of government support for rural retail: Indigenous franchise model of store chains run by Khadi & Village Industries Commission,
- 1980s experienced slow change as India began to open up economy,
- Textiles sector with companies like Bombay Dyeing, Raymond's, S. Kumar's and Grasim first saw the emergence of retail chains,
- Later Titan successfully created an organized retailing concept and established a series of showrooms for its premium watches,
- The latter half of the 1990s saw a fresh wave of entrants with a shift from Manufactures to Pure Retailers,
- For e.g. Food World, Subhiksha and Nilgiris in food and FMCG; Planet M and Music World in music; Crossword and Fountainhead in books,
- Post 1995 onwards saw an emergence of shopping centers
- Mainly in urban areas, with facilities like car parking,
- Targeted to provide a complete destination experience for all segments of society,
- Emergence of hyper and super markets trying to provide customer with 3 V's—Value, Variety and Volume,
- Expanding target consumer segment: The Sachet revolution—example of reaching to the bottom of the pyramid,
- At year end of 2000 the size of the Indian organized retail industry is estimated at Rs. 13,000 crore.

RETAILING FORMAT IN INDIA

Malls

The largest form of organized retailing today located mainly in metro cities, in proximity to urban outskirts. Ranges from 60,000 sq.

ft. to 7,00,000 sq. ft. and above. They lend an ideal shopping experience with an amalgamation of product, service and entertainment, all under a common roof. Examples include Shoppers Stop, Piramyd, and Pantaloon.

Specialty Stores

Chains such as the Bangalore-based Kids Kemp, the Mumbai books retailer Crossword, RPG's Music World and the Times Group's music chain Planet M, are focusing on specific market segments and have established themselves strongly in their sectors.

Discount Stores

As the name suggests, discount stores or factory outlets, offer discounts on the MRP through selling in bulk reaching economies of scale or excess stock left over at the season. The product category can range from a variety of perishable/non-perishable goods.

Department Stores

Large stores ranging from 20000-50000 sq. ft. catering to a variety of consumer needs. Further classified into localized departments such as clothing, toys, home, groceries, etc.

Departmental Stores are expected to take over the apparel business from exclusive brand showrooms. Among these, the biggest success is K Raheja's Shoppers Stop, which started in Mumbai and now has more than seven large stores (over 30,000 sq. ft) across India and even has its own in store brand for clothes called Stop.

Hyper marts/Supermarkets

Large self-service outlets, catering to varied shopper needs are termed as Supermarkets. These are located in or near residential high streets. These stores today contribute to 30% of all food and grocery organized retail sales. Super Markets can further be classified in to mini supermarkets typically 1,000 sq. ft. to 2,000 sq. ft. and large supermarkets ranging from of 3,500 sq. ft. to 5,000 sq. ft. having a strong focus on food and grocery and personal sales.

Convenience Stores

These are relatively small stores 400-2,000 sq. feet located near residential areas. They stock a limited range of high-turnover convenience products and are usually open for extended periods during the day, seven days a week. Prices are slightly higher due to the convenience premium.

MBO

Multi-Brand outlets, also known as Category Killers, offer several brands across a single product category. These usually do well in busy market places and Metros.

CHALLENGES AND OPPORTUNITIES

Retailing has seen such a transformation over the past decade that its very definition has undergone a sea change. No longer can a manufacturer rely on sales to take place by ensuring mere availability of his product. Today, retailing is about so much more than mere merchandising. Its about casting customers in a story, reflecting their desires and aspirations, and forging long-lasting relationships. As the Indian consumer evolves they expects more and more at each and every time when they steps into a store. Retail today has changed from selling a product or a service to selling a hope, an aspiration and above all an experience that a consumer would like to repeat.

For manufacturers and service providers the emerging opportunities in urban markets seem to lie in capturing and delivering better value to the customers through retail. For instance, in Chennai CavinKare LimeLite, Maricoï Kaya Skin Clinic and Apollo Hospitals Apollo Pharmacies are examples, to name a few, where manufacturers/service providers combine their own manufactured products and services with those of others to generate value hitherto unknown. The last mile connect seems to be increasingly lively and experiential. Also, manufacturers and service providers face an exploding rural market yet only marginally tapped due to difficulties in rural retailing. Only innovative concepts and models may survive the test of time and investments. However, manufacturers and service providers will also increasingly face a host of specialist retailers, who are characterized by use of modern management techniques, backed with seemingly unlimited financial resources. Organized retail appears inevitable.

Retailing in India is currently estimated to be a US$ 200 billion industry, of which organized retailing makes up a paltry 3 percent or US$ 6.4 billion. By 2013, organized retail is projected to reach US$ 23 billion. For retail industry in India, things have never looked better and brighter. Challenges to the manufacturers and service providers would abound when market power shifts to organized retail.

CONCLUSION

The retail sector has played a phenomenal role throughout the world in increasing productivity of consumer goods and services. It is also the second largest industry in US in terms of numbers of employees and establishments. There is no denying the fact that most of the developed economies are very much relying on their retail sector as a locomotive of growth. The India Retail Industry is the largest among all the industries, accounting for over 10 per cent of the country's GDP and around 8 per cent of the employment. The Retail Industry in India has come forth as one of the most dynamic and fast paced industries with several players entering the market. But all of them have not yet tasted success because of the heavy initial investments that are required to break even with other companies and compete with them. The India Retail Industry is gradually inching its way towards becoming the next boom industry.

REFERENCES

http://www.fibre2fashion.com/services/featrued-article/featured_article.asp

A.T. Kearney's (2007): Global Services Locations Index.

Bhagwati J.N. (1978), "Anatomy and Consequences of Exchange Control Regime", Vol. 1, Studies in International Economies Relations, No.10, New York, ideas-repec.org/b/nbr/nberbk/bhag78-1.html.

Handbook of Industrial Policy and Statistics, Government of India.

Maitra, Ramtanu (2003): "Why India's Economy lags behind China's", *Asian Times.*

Part II
HUMAN RESOURCE MANAGEMENT

5

Impact of Globalisation on Human Resource Management and Industrial Relations

AARTI ARORA

ABSTRACT

The paradigm shifts in human resource management structure brought fundamental change in industrial relation institutions and structure. It is viewed that Globalisation provided free and deregulated environment to the business to operate which in turn resulted in severe competition and formulation of competitive strategies. These strategies demand for getting highest human resource productivity at lowest possible cost. The efficient implementation of human resource management strategies demanded a non regulative environment from the industrial relations. Institutions paving the way for a fundamental change in industrial relations systems. Thus globalisation tends to bring significant shift in human resource management, i.e. from collective to individual human resource management and thereby a fundamental change in industrial relations, i.e., from collective relations to individual relations.

Keywords : Challenges of Industrial Relations, Effectiveness of Industrial Relations, Industrial Relations Environment, Job Design, Collective Bargaining, Individual Bargaining, Participative

Management, Team Design, Soft Skills, Outsourcing, Employee Referrals, De-Layering

REVIEW OF LITERATURE

In their seminal thesis on the development of HR function, Jamrog and Overholt declare that over the past 100 years the human resource management professionals has been continuously evolving and changing, adding advantage by providing high quality people and by helping business managers strategically plan the functions of human capital within the organizations (Rowden, 1999). Aparna Ghosh on Chillibreeze discussed the evolution of HRM practices and challenges in HR practices after 1991. She observed that changes like emphasis on employees, upgradation of skills, progressive HR policies and entrepreneurship by employees. Dave MacKay; chief operating officer; Ceridian Canada Ltd. in his keynote presentation discussed 10 major trends that are changing the face of business. Anjali at citehr.com explained HR trends such as mobile culture, new technology impact on skills requirements, globalisation of business, demand for innovation through training/development. Shiny Nair in her article "Emerging trends in HRM" discussed changes in human resource management. K.V. Rao who is a management consultant, in his paper 'Recent trends in critical human resource management practices threw light on issues such as leadership management, work life balance, inclusion and diversity, health and wellness, right skilling. Samir R. Chatterjee in his paper "Human Resource Management in India: Where from and Where to" traced notable evidence of economic organizations and managerial ideas from ancient Indian sources and considers them in context of contemporary challenges.

The significance of relationship between employer and employee in India dates back to Kautilya's Arthshastra about 298 B.C. The factory system of industrial production came into existence in around 1880. The first Factory Act was enacted in 1881 and was subsequently amended in 1891 and covered a wider area such as weekly holiday, compulsory rest period, fixing maximum working hours, etc. A review of industrial relations reveal that the number of mandays lost decline to 210 million during 1991-2000 as against 402. 1 million during 1981-90. According to Report of National Commission on Labour (2002) it is noticed that trade unions do not normally give a call for strike and service sector workers are becoming disinterested in trade union activities. The attitude of government have undergone a change. Now permissions for closure or retrenchment are more easily granted. The labour adjudication machinery is more willing to entertain the concerns of industry.

INDUSTRIAL RELATIONS

Industrial relations is used to denote the collective relationships between management and the workers. Traditionally, the term industrial relations is used to cover such aspects of industrial life as trade unionism, collective bargaining, workers participation in management, discipline and grievance handling, industrial disputes and interpretation of labor laws and rules and code of conduct. In the words of Lester, "Industrial relations involve attempts at arriving at solutions between the conflicting objectives and values; between the profit motive and social gain; between discipline and freedom, between authority and industrial democracy; between bargaining and co-operation; and between conflicting interests of the individual, the group and the community".

The National Commission on Labor (NCL) also emphasize on the same concept. According to NCL, industrial relations affect not merely the interests of the two participants—labor and management, but also the economic and social goals to which the State addresses itself. To regulate these relations in socially desirable channels is a function, which the State is in the best position to perform. Institutions of industrial relations includes government, employers, trade unions, union federations or associations, government bodies, labor courts, tribunals and other organizations which have direct or indirect impact on the industrial relations systems.

The need for looking at Industrial Relations in a broader context has been recognized in academic as well as business circles. While absence of strikes, lockouts, indiscipline, individual and collective grievances and restrictive practices have been attributed to existence of Industrial Relations system in an enterprise, these constituted however the negative indicators of Industrial Relations environment. The positive indicators of healthy relationship amongst various internal stakeholders in the organization ought to be productivity, morale, commitment, constructive discipline and heightened sense of belongingness and identity with the vision and values of the organization amongst the employees. Challenges Concerns for Industrial Relations cannot be limited to the maintenance of industrial harmony at enterprise level but also to prevailing issues of socioeconomic conditions prevailing in the country at the macro level. Industrial Relations systems and practices therefore must be directed towards responding major challenges surfacing in the new economic order.

HUMAN RESOURCE MANAGEMENT

In todays dynamic business environment, every organization wants to be a successful organization. It cannot be possible without Human Resource (HR). The most important asset, i.e. Human Resource (man power) is known as life blood of any organization. The success of any organization depends upon the performance of their Human Resource. If question arises to find out the most important difference between ordinary organization and successful organization, the answer would be their HR. The organization also wants quality people. The greatest challenge before every organization is to recruit right people in right place. HR is the factors. Employee and Employer both are important. They are the two sides of the same coin. One cannot operate without the services of the other. The main purpose of this study is to observe the industrial relation operation and satisfaction level of the employees, to observe the different welfare schemes provided by the industry.

HR AND IR COORDINATED ACTIVITIES

Growing industrialization and the rapid expansion of the services sector resulted in the galloping demand for skilled labor after 50s. The emergence of the concept of human relations, human resource management and human resource development (HRD) contributed to the growing importance of labor. The issue of Industrial Relations arose from the issue of divorce of the workers from the ownership and management of the production process. Industrial Relations change with the times, generally keeping pace with the expectations of employees, trade union, employers associations, and other economic and social institution in a society.

The HRM approach can help in improving Industrial Relation. The HR Managers must create a motivating climate so that employees commit themselves to work. The HR managers can contribute to "Quality of Work Life" which includes fair remuneration, safe and healthy environment, opportunities for growth, etc. The contrast between industrial relations and human resource management lies in the collective focus of industrial relations and the individual focus of human resource management.

HRM is a strategic function and is more interested in policy within the organization and not the dynamic interplay between the state, employers, unions and employees. Whereas industrial relations has never been a part of strategic planning and has an approach that an enduring conflict of interests exists between employees and employers. Industrial relations is essentially pluralistic in outlook, in that it covers not only the relation between employer and employee (individual relations) but also the relation between employers and unions and between them and the state (collective relations).

GLOBALISATION

The objectives of managements, the ways in which enterprises are managed to achieve these objectives and the human resource management and industrial relations initiatives in this regard, are affected by pressures, many of which are exerted by globalization. Changes in IR practices (rather than in institutions and systems) such as increased collective bargaining at enterprise level, flexibility in relation to forms of employment as well as in relation to working time and job functions have occurred as a result of such factors as heightened competition, rapid changes in products and processes and the increasing importance of skills, quality and productivity. These factors have also had an impact on HRM policies and practices. As such, managing people in a way so as to motivate them to be productive is one important objective of HRM. The implications and consequences of globalization include the major shifts in HRM practices and industrial relations.

Better relationship between the employee and employer is very essential for successful running of any organization. Favorable relationship can avoid many adverse situations. One such impact of globalisation can be seen in case of Rourkela Steel Plant. With a huge manpower, Rourkela Steel Plant has taken every step to maintain a cordial relation. It has given a thrust on participation of employees through many forums—both traditional and revolutionary. Structured Communication as an important vehicle for carrying the employees and management together has been adopted nicely by RSP to facilitate the flow of information, ensure employees commitment and involvement in all critical aspects of the operation. Of course, there are many scopes for improvement. Both management and recognized union should come forward to restore the relationship of trust.

SHIFTS IN HUMAN RESOURCE MANAGEMENT : ORGANISATIONAL STRUCTURE

Companies traditionally designed and structured their organizations based on functional or departmental and matrix structures and also believed that strategy follows the structure. But organizations could not find appropriate to fit in these structures after globalisation. As such, companies started structuring flat structures, team based structures, strategic businessunit structures, empowered structures and virtual structures, flexible structures, decentralized structures in order to suit to the ever-changing global competition.

This situation is more dramatic in private sector. Coca-Cola (India) Limited followed the brown field strategy in entering the Indian Market and as such acquired the manufacturing facilities of the existing bottling companies throughout the country without the obligation of retaining all the employees of these bottling companies. This resulted in retrenchment, redeployment, re-training, salary-cut and/or demotion for poor performers and salary hike and/or promotion for high performers. Thus, Coca Cola India follows individualistic HRM approach as it was essential in the wake of severe competition from Pepsi-Cola. Tata Electricals and Locomotives Limited, Vishakhapatnam Steel Plant of SAIL also follows the individualistic HRM.

Revamping organizational structures and shifts in the structure are relatively more volatile in the software industry as its environment depends upon its cliental organizations, their structures, level of technology, etc.

Public sector banks like State Bank of India, Syndicate Bank, Indian Bank and Punjab National Bank formulated a strategy of low cost in order to meet the competition from the private sector banks. These banks de-layered their organizations by closing some regional offices and downsizing their operations as a part of implementation of low cost strategy. Organisations now believe that structure follows strategy.

JOB DESIGN

Traditionally jobs were designed based on engineering approach and later based on humanistic and job characteristic approaches. These approaches led to narrow job design which did not fit in the framework of post-globalisation business strategies. Globalisation resulted in significant shifts in job design to de-jobbing, multi-skilling, teams and employee empowerment. Team design and de-jobbing consequent upon employee multi skills lead to surplus of workforce and thereby resulted in retrenchment. Organisations also provided training and facilitation programmes and enabled the employees in acquiring multi-skills and to cope up with new demands of competitive strategies. Some Indian organizations like State Bank of India and LIC of India resulted in massive shifts from job design, job description and job specification to team design and structure. In addition, broadbanding replaced narrow jobs and team design replaced job design altogether. Changes in job design is quite normal in software industry and the young employees in this industry do automatically change their mindset and skills depending upon the requirements owing to the threat of loss of job or lower salary.

HUMAN RESOURCE PLANNING

Globalisation along with information technology enabled the production technology transferrable from country to country easily and at a fast rate. Consequently, manufacturing facilities dispersed geographically. This development, in turn led to the facility of outsourcing. Organisations like Satyam Computers, Wipro and Infosys shifted their human resource planning from number of and kind of employees to internal skill mobility planning. The traditional industries, like Indian Railways, Tata Iran and Steel Company Limited in India plan for outsourcing rather than plan for human resources exclusively for them. Thus, globalisation has been contributing to the shifts in human resource planning like planning for skill-mobility out sourcing plans and plan for candidates purely based on suitability to the job. In addition, globalisation either minimized or eliminated the influence of two actors of industrial relations viz., trade unions and government on human resource planning.

EMPLOYMENT PRACTICES

National business environment more volatile due to the foreign direct investment, techonogly, technology transfers, mobility of the human resources, dispersion of manufacturing facilities with the help of information technology and soft political and economic policies of the governments towards foreign companies owing to globalisation. These developments invariably reduce the gaps between national business environment and international business environment. The companies started developing appropriate techniques in employing right human resources at a fast rate rather than relying heavily on traditional techniques. The most important such recent techniques of recruitment followed by many sun-rising companies such as Zee Telefilms Limited, Global Trust Bank Limited, Satyam Computers Limited, and Bio-techniques Limited in India and Deltron, Datec and Global Techniques in Papua New Guinea is Employees Referrals rather than relying on formal qualifications and degrees. Other shifts in the recruitment practices include walk-in, consult-in, headhunting, body shopping e-recruitment and outsourcing. All the new practices help the companies to formulate and implement strategies fast and efficiently in the dynamic environment. According to the Regional Human Resource Manager, Andhara Pradesh Region of Coca-Cola India Limited such employees not only eliminate the unnecessary intervention of trade unions, but also reduce the amount of supervision and enhance productivity. The complex strategies let the organizations to select the candidates and employ them with multi-skills rather than expert skills in one area. Some of the companies like L&G in India, Larsen and Tourbo Limited's cement works divison in India realized that most of the company operations up to a certain level could be performed by majority of the employees, if required skills are provided through formal or informal training as, such these companies started selecting the candidates with basic multi-skills and developing them and empowering them.

PERFORMANCE APPRAISAL

Other significant area in human resource management is performance appraisal. Performance appraisal techniques were traditionally used to punish the employees and then trade unions used to interfere in the management's decisions and actions and protect the employees. 360 degree performance appraisal is another major shift in performance appraisal area that enables the employees to have all round feedback and to initiate the steps to correct themselves to contribute efficiently for strategy implementation as is the practice in Coca-Cola India and Larsen and Toubro Limited. Other performance appraisal shifts include: developing performance measures to assess the value addition of human resource contributions as adopted by Royal Dutch Shell. Most of the companies after globalisation use performace appraisal techniques for employee development. Thus shifts in performance appraisal also eliminated the influence of trade union and tend to follow individualistic approach to HRM.

HUMAN RESOURCE DEVELOPMENT

Traditionally industrial relations institutions were less concerned with training and development aspects of human resource development. But, the management during the post-globalisation era take interest in career planning and development of those employees whose skills are in demand. Thus, globalisation resulted in dependence of companies on contractual staff rather than regular staff that reduces the budget on human resource development as is the practice in Larsen and Toubro Limited in India. Contract staff to some extent takes care of their training and development by themselves. Furthur, they never become the members of company trade unions. Now there is decline in membership of trade unions and thereby their finances and activities.

SALARIES AND BENEFITS

Govt. of India before globalisation favoured socialistic pattern of society and consequently minimization of inequalities in the distribution of salaries. Globialisation set trends for adjustment of salaries based on performance as is the case with Coca-Cola India, Infosys, Satyam Computers and Wipro in India. Consequently individual bargaining displaced the collective bargaining paving the way for individualistic HRM. It results in higher salaries and benefits for those employees whose skills are in greater demand and lower salaries for those skills are in abundant supply. Indra Nooyi who is the chairman and chief executive officer of Pepsico started getting an annual package of $14.7 million.

SHIFTS IN INDUSTRIAL RELATIONS : TRADE UNIONS

Globalisation along with the deregulation of economies led to severe competition and placed the customer first by deregulating the position of employees. This situation led the employees to realize that they have to protect themselves and save the customers most efficiently by means of developing their skills. The able employees come out of the shadow of trade unions, acquired new skills, realized their capabilities and have grown beyond the expectations of their own as well as organizations through their individualistic approaches. It can be said that globalisation trends drive the trade unions in a reverse gear.

COLLECTIVE BARGAINING

Collective Bargaining played a vital role in settling the terms and conditions of employment, before globalisation.

The post-globalisation scenario tends to drive collective bargaining in reverse direction as terms and conditions of employment vary from employee to employee. Public sector organizations took a deviation in dealing with the issues of employment rather than discussing in collective bargaining. For Example, Vishakhapatnam Steel Plant of Steel Authority of India Limited, Hindustan Cables Limited and Bharat Heavy Plates and Vessels Limited adopted downsizing and turnaround strategies. Consequently, they retrenched redundant employees, outsourced certain employees' functions, trained and developed the partially redundant employees without negotiating the issues in collective bargaining. Thus, management tend to make unilateral decisions in these areas without negotiating in collective bargaining meetings.

INDUSTRIAL DISPUTES

The collective forms of industrial dispute like work-to-rule strikes by all group of employees, lay-offs and lockouts were common before globalisation. Globalisation reduced the scope for industrial conflicts. These trends have became more prevalent in various private sector organizations like Satyam Computers, Infosys, Larsen and Turbo limited, Coca-Cola India and Tata Consultancy Services Limited. However, public sector organizations like State Bank of India, Hindustan Cables Limited, and Hindustan Petrochemicals Limited introduced the voluntary retirement scheme and enabled the employees to quit the organization on their own.

PARTICIPATIVE MANAGEMENT

Some of the public sector organizations and a few private sector organizations adopted different schemes of workers participation in management like works committees, shop councils, joint councils and joint management council before globalisation. But, globalisation tends to drive the operation of, if not the theme of workers participation in management in a reverse direction. Competition, consequent upon globalisation forced the managements to realize that human resource offers them a distinctive competency. As such managements today encourage the employees to participate in decision-making, share their ideas and knowledge, disseminate the information they acquire at workplace and empower them by developing multi-skills to make decisions on their own. Globalisation led to optimum utilization of human resources through participative management idea.

THE FUTURE OF INDUSTRIAL RELATIONS IN INDIA

This is the dilemma being faced by nearly everybody in the industry today. To understand the importance of above topic, we would like to begin by talking about the 50 day long worker's agitation at the Bajaj Chakan plant, 2013. 950 workers of Bajaj Chakan plan went on strike, on 25-06-2013, in response to management's refusal to accept their demands. Though the management did not yield in to the demands of the workers, but the most striking feature of the strike was the 'Charter of Demands' raised by the union. The Union had bargained for 500 shares for Re. 1 for each worker, in its COD. The reasoning given by Mr. Dilip Pawar was that if the company could give 450% dividend to its shareholders, why can it not pay the same amount of rewards to its own workers? This demand would have been considered unimaginable in the past Industrial Relations Scenario but has become a reality now. Mr. Pawar suggests, "It's always the investors who benefits from our hard work, so we decided that we also want to be investors". The above scenario typifies our 'new worker', who has high aspirations and is also a lot more educated than his forerunners.

Factors Leading to decline in Institutional Industrial Relations in India

1. *Changing Contour of Industrial Relations in India*

As can be seen in the Figure 1, the numbers of strikes and lockouts have drastically reduced in India. There has been a progressive reduction in the cases of Industrial disputes, number of man-days lost (on account of strikes and lockouts) in India especially in the past two decades. Gone are the days of 'Institutional Industrial Relations' where violence (Ravindranath) due to political as well as the ideological rivalries dominated the industrial scene. The late 80's and early 90's industrial scenario was dictated by militant trade Unionism, with Datta Samant as its figurehead. Over the years, we have seen a greater democratization of work place in the form of increased prominence of 'Collective Bargaining' which is also now loosing it's sheen in the current scenario as discussed in the subsequent sections.

Figure 1 : Depicting the Changing IR Scenario in India

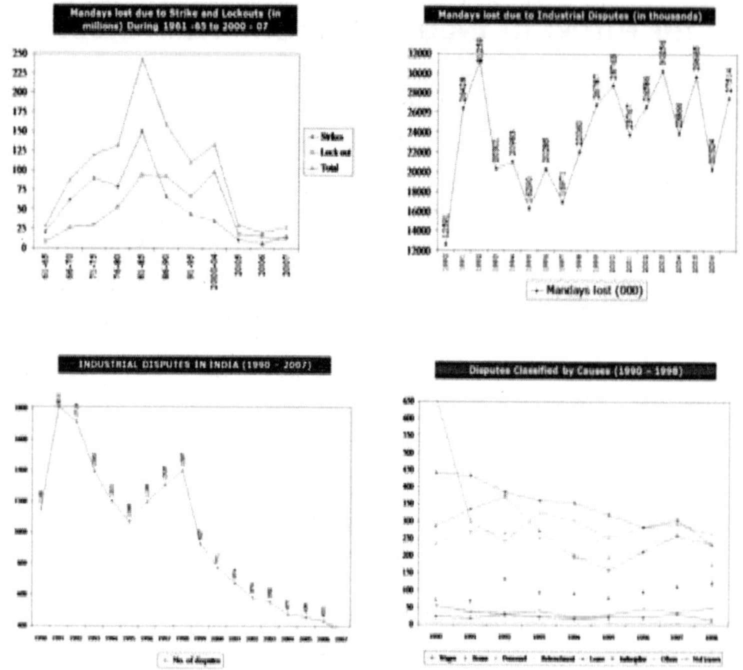

2. *Changing Demographics of Workforce in India*

ITC's Ranjargaon factory plant manager suggests that the average age of the workers working in their facility in Pune is 26 years. The oldest worker in the factory is 30 years. This has been the trend in most of the newly set up plants in the country. This has also been amply demonstrated by the studies in the past which clearly indicates that over a period of next 10-15 years we would have a relatively young population (18-35 years) as part of our workforce (Chandrashekhar, Ghosh and Roychowdhury, 2006). The employees in this workforce are referred to as the Gen-Y employees.

a) **Gen-Y characteristics:** Following are the basic characteristics which typifies a Gen-Y person, and have been a major factor in changing the workplace dynamics.

b) **Increased Aspirations:** "Two decades ago the retirement goal of a worker in India used to be, to become a supervisor. Today he wants to become a manager before he retires" which's an 80% jump in pay if nothing else says Sunil Ranjhan, VP HR, Hyundai Motors. Thus, they are very ambitious and have keen interest in being well aware of their surroundings.

c) **Self-Reliant and Independent**: "Gen-Y'ers are more self-confident than their previous generations—also called as latch-key generation" (Martin, 2005). Though, Gen-Y may be considered to be individualistic, but they also demonstrate a desire for being collaborative. Gen-Y demands clear instructions and directions from management but they also want flexibility and freedom to do their tasks. Moreover, Gen-Y workers are more technology savvy, enjoy being given responsibility and as a result are more productive at their work. They also have the ability to effectively communicate (Chesworth, 2013) and articulate their ideas and thoughts.

All the above factors of changing demographics and change in the age composition in the work-force is leading to diminishing segregation of workers such as white collar and blue collar. Another example to substantiate the above conclusion, The workers at the industrial establishments of Tata Motor's Jaguar-Land Rover assembly unit in Pune, wear jeans and t-shirts on Fridays, following the dress code of business casuals mandated for the white-collar employees. This was allowed very recently, only after the workers demanded equality of rights from the management.

3. *Role of Social Media in Changing Worker-Management Relationship*

"With the advent and proliferation of social media, the disconnect between the dressing, way of life and the language of the managers and workers is becoming immaterial"—Bino Paul, Chaiperson CHRMLR, TISS. Interactions with the member of Trade Union, ITC Ranjgaon plant, revealed that nearly all young workmen now have access to smart phones, majority of them are also on Facebook. He also suggested that there are some training activities organized by union for its workers to learn about the global practices and policies at work. As a result, he recalls a senior worker (who connects with his Japanese and European counterparts over facebook) in the plant complaining "if we can use global machinery, adopt their production methodologies, why can't we get the same level of facilities and recognition in our factories". Social media has thus been a major contributing factor to this awareness among workers.

Decline in the tenets of Collective Labor Power: One of the key issues of the strike at the Maruti Manesar plant was of recognition of new union there. The workers felt that they needed an independent body to represent their demands. "Independent unions (like the Manesar one) however mean that collective labor power is definitely on the decline" suggests Bino Paul, TISS. Dilip Pawar says that workers today even question the Union leaders. "Twenty years ago, if the leaders said do this, it got done, no questions asked. "It's not the same case today, they expect a logical explanation".

As a result of all the above factors, there has been a dramatic change in the supervisor-worker dynamics, since the young workers demand an explanation for doing any work which is outside the purview of the employment norms. The supervisor's still being driven by the old school of thought (IR) react by showing their authority. There might also be another source of conflict between the worker and the supervisor. The supervisor-subordinate relationships are greatly affected by the age composition of the workplace and the relational age difference between the two (Perry, Kulik and Zhou, 1999).

In the earlier scenarios, people generally had bosses/supervisors of much older age, and the workers used to have a sense of veneration for the superior which could be attributed to the patriarchal nature of our Indian society (Zandi, Mirle and Jarvis, 1990). This situation is increasingly changing at workplace now. We have many situations, where worker and supervisor are of similar ages and that veneration disappears once you're of the same age as your boss. The boss has to demonstrate now that he knows more. From an approach of veneration it has now transformed to an approach which says, prove me why should I listen to you?

Workers are prepared to deal with managers for their daily demands rather than routing it through the union. They are also ready to reach out to the very top management to get their demands fulfilled. HR manager of a reputed auto manufacturing firm states "factory workers approached the associate vice-president asking for access to the pantry, which was reserved for managers". This sounds like the end of the traditional labor union, because the capability of the workers to adequately communicate problems and confront the management without the involvement of trade unions goes against the ethos of 'Collective Bargaining'.

Changing Profile of Workers

A social wave is sweeping across our country. The declining power of trade unions, improving pay packets, the willingness of management to accommodate conflicting growing stature of workers in society, their increased levels of education and the emergence of process industries which has changed the very definition of work, have together caused a revolution of perception and aspiration. The social profile of industrial workers is changing rapidly. Unlike in the early years of our independence, not many come from a background of hardship and deprivation. Workers in the organized sector earn well and like to live well. Their aspirations for their children are no different from those of the middle class. Their eyes are set on upward mobility. Within industry itself, workers are pushing towards status equality. With a changing social profile, workers are becoming more assertive with their union bosses. They are also demanding more egalitarian treatment at the work place. Executive dining rooms are giving way to common canteens. There is growing demand that manager at least those who are compensated in some form for extra hours should punch the clock. The reluctance to perform lowly jobs. The search for fancy status giving designations—we have security guards and sanitary staff in place of chowkidars and sweepers. Our organizations are moving rapidly towards status equality. As a result we are seeing a huge paradigm shift, in the industrial workplace situations in day-to-day life. Thus, we also need to brace up for the change and move towards an approach which helps to maintain the workplace harmony and sanctity of the worker-management relationship. Therefore, we are seeing an increasing shift towards the approach of 'Employee Relations'.

References

A.S. Mathur, 'Labour Policy and Industrial Relations in India', Ram Prasad and Sons, Agra.

Aparna Raj; Worker-Management Relationship and Human Resource Development.

Ashwathapa, K. (2005), Human Resource Management', Tata McGraw Hills, Fifth edition.

C.B. Kumar, 'Development of Industrial Relations in India', Orient Longman and Co, Bombay.

International Human Resource Management; P. Subba Rao, Himalaya Publishing House.

K.V. Rao; Recent Trends in Critical HR Practices at www. herald. com

M.K. Singh, 'Industrial Relations in Maharashtra', *The Indian Journal of Society Work*, Vol. (1), April, 1983.

Managing Human Resources and Industrial Relations : Tapomoy Deb, Excel Books.

N. Kumar, R. Mittal, 'Personnel Management and Industrial Relations', First edition, 2001.

Preeti Naveen Yadav; Emerging Trends in Human Resource Department; *International Research Journal,* August 2010.

R. Ram Reddy, 'Industrial Relations in India', K.M. Mittal for Mittal Publications, 1990.

R.A. Lester, (ed.), Labour and Industrial Relations, Macmillian and Co., New York, 1964.

Ritiparna Banerjee, Emerging Trends in Human Resource Management at www. Chillbreeze.com

Sodhi, J.S., Industrial Relation and Human Resource Management.

Srivastava, K.B.L., Changing Power Dynamics in the Emerging Industrial Retions Scenario, *Management & Labour Studies,* Vol. 26, No. 4.

Strategic Human Resource Management: Rajesh Viswanathan, Himalaya Publishing House.

T.N. Kapoor, (Ed.), Personnel Management and Industrial Relations in India.

V.B. Singh, Climate for Industrial Relations: A Study of Kanpur Textile Industry, Allied Publishers, Bombay.

6

Cross-National Transfer of HR Policies and Practices in Multi Polar World

NEERU SHARMA

ABSTRACT

Human resource management is an aspect of management that has the goal of effective utilization of human resources of an organization. Managing people, human capital and culture-HRM is critical for business excess. International HRM is about the world-wise management of Human Recourses. The purpose of IHRM is to enable the Firms and MNCs to be successful globally. In this paper we discuss a key issue that dominates international HRM research, namely, the Global-Local question. The question concerns how multinational can or should balance the pressure to develop globally, standardized policies with the pressure to be responsive to the peculiarities of the local context. In my view, three important conceptual weaknesses have restricted research progress in this field, inadequate conceptualization of national effect, which results in culture being used as an unsatisfactory "catch all" for national differences, lack of attention to the influence of internal organizational policies and the absence of focus on the internal division of labor within the MNCs. We discuss the best policies, to pay the expatriates so that they can compete with the international-level work pressure.

INTRODUCTION

The business climate has clearly affected both the supply and demand of talent and company's ability to attract and hire talented employees. Many companies find themselves in a position of having to find new and innovative ways to entice and ultimately develop and leadership for the future. Human Resource Management is related to selection of workforce for various jobs, which have required skills for performing the job. In global HRM, first of all the MNCs determine the required number of workforce to be recruited. Then sources of recruitment are identified, which can be internal or external. Qualified persons are selected out of the applicants, who have offered to serve in the organization. Those people are selected, who fulfill the requirement of global workforce like good command over language, cultural toughness, mental and physical strength, confidence, flexibility in management style, etc. HRM is concerned with the procurement, development, compensation, integration and maintenance of personnel of organization of the purpose of contributing towards the accomplishment of the organization's major goals or objectives. As we enter the new millennium, more and more companies are recognizing the importance of managing their human resources as effectively as possible. They are also recognizing that doing do, however, cannot be done without recognition and incorporation of the global context. It is virtually impossible to read a business periodical or news paper, anywhere in the world, without seeing stories, detailing the success of a company, due to how effectively it manages its people. As the environment becomes more global, managing people also becomes more challenging, more unpredictable and uncertain and more subject to rapid change and surprise. And because of the importance of managing people effectively in the global context is so great, many companies are devoting a great deal more time, attention, skill and effort into doing it well.

GLOBAL STAFFING POLICIES

The rapid rise of MNCs from emerging economies has led to greater interest and urgencies in developing a better understanding of development and diffusion of managerial strategies from their perspective and without assuming the prevailing western ethnocentric orthodoxy. Taking international staffing decision is a complex task as human resource belongs to different countries, speak different languages, belong to different culture, have different work procedure, management styles, value systems, business ethics, etc. Global staffing policy is concerned with selection and appointment of employees for a particular job. These employees can be selected from home nation, host nation or from third country. And when an employee is selected in one country and is sent to work in the other country, such employee is termed as "Expatriate". Staffing policy can be classified as:

Ethnocentric Staffing Policy

In this policy, all key positions in foreign subsidiaries are filled by home country. This approach is based on the assumption that principles, management practices, core competence possessed by home country nationals are superior to competence possessed by host national. Moreover, home executives are well tested, trained and familiar with organizational policies, programs, management styles etc. So, they can better manage the foreign subsidiaries as compared to nationals of host nations. Further, these policies select senior executives, for key positions only from home nation, whereas the more competent executive may be available in host nation or in third nation. But this policy ignores local capabilities of host national.

Advantages: Helps to maintain unified corporate culture in the various subsidiaries of global company. Suitable when close control over core competence is required. Appropriate when qualified and competent personnel are not available in host nation.

Disadvantages: Ignores local caliber. This policy limits managerial development opportunities in the host nation, leading to resentment among employees. Decrease in moral and productivity, increase in workforce turnover in host nation. Increase in human resource cost as higher remuneration is to be paid to expatriates in comparison to local employees. At initial stage, expatriate may fail to understand culture, language, working style, marketing strategies, etc. of host nation.

Polycentric Staffing Policy

In this policy host country nationals are appointed at all positions including key positions in foreign subsidiary units. This policy assumes that sufficient local talent is available in host nation and they are better aware of local customs, market condition, government policies, management styles, work culture, business ethics, etc. Further they are presumed to competent enough to hold key position and take strategic decisions for example HSBC, Johnson and Johnson, Microsoft follow polycentric staffing policy. Local managers are readily accepted by subordinate staff as they prefer to work under person of their own nationality rather than foreign national. Human Resources Management course is also less in this policy as local managers are available at lower compensation in comparison to remuneration to expatriates. But, if local talent is not competent enough, then this policy is not effective. It is especially so when, global company is headquartered in developed nation and has its subsidiary units in least developed nations, then the local work force in host nation may not be competent enough to hold key position in subsidiary units. The subsidiary company becomes a separate unit rather than a well integrated global unit.

Advantages: Less human resources cost. Growth opportunities for staff of host nation leading to increase in morale and productivity of workforce. Easy acceptability of local managers by subordinates. Efficient management of subsidiary units as local managers are well acquainted with local suppliers, customers, financial institutions, government policies, competitor, etc.

Disadvantages: Less effective control on subordinates as compared to ethnocentric approach. Local managers may not be talented enough to hold strategic positions. Problem of co-ordinations and integration of subsidiary unit with headquarters.

Geocentric Staffing Policy

Under this policy best people are selected for key jobs, irrespective of their nationality. The key personnel can be from any nation of the world. This policy not tied to just home nation or host nation instead best people for key jobs are selected from any nation of the world. The management style is flexible which can adjust in any nation of the world, but human resources cost in this approach is high. Moreover, cultural conflict problems also arrive as personnel from different nations work together in same organization.

COMPENSATION PLAN OF EXPATRIATES

Designing and managing compensation plan for global workforce is a complex task as salary structure, tax structure, housing cost, purchasing power, etc. are different in different nations. The components of expatriate compensation package are—base salary, Foreign Service incentive, allowances, tax differentials, fringe benefits. Due to Foreign Service allowances and premiums the total compensation of expatriates is more than what they were getting in the home country. Expatriates must be suitably rewarded for their services. They can be retained in the organization only when they get adequate remunerations for their services. If the company pays them too much, it will overburden the organization as the cost of human resources will escalate. But if they are paid less, they will join some other organization. According to *Cundiff and Still*, "compensation is an essential part of total program for motivating workforce. A compensation plan should have three elements: (i) Provide living wage, (ii) Adjust pay scale to performance level, thereby relating job performance with remunerations, and (iii) Provide a mechanism for attaining company goals and individual goals."

ESSENTIALS OF A GOOD EXPATRIATE COMPENSATION PLAN

It should motivate the high performance for their good work. It must reward their efficiency and performance. It should provide fair salary to workforce, so that they must feel that they can lead a good life while working with the organization. Remuneration plan should be simple and easy to understand, so that expatriate can calculate their earnings at their own. It should be flexible too which can be adjusted according to changing circumstances, i.e. compensation in depression and in period of boom. The plan should be based on the principle of equality and should be linked with the paying capacity of the organization. It will remain economical for the organization as more compensation can easily be paid if profits are rising in the consequence to increase in sales. Hedge against inflations should be the feature of the compensation plan for technical jobs, which require technical skills and higher education, the compensation should be more. The compensation plan should provide effective control of management over workforce. It should be linked with their productivity and the top most, compensation plan should ensure timely payment of remuneration to the workforce. Whatever the period may be, the payment must be made well in time, so that the expatriate can plan their spending accordingly.

BALANCE SHEET APPROACH OF COMPENSATION PLAN FOR EXPATRIATES

There are two common methods for implementing balance sheet approach.

i) **Host-based method**: In this method expatriate compensation package is designed on the basis of salary structure for similar job in host nation. In this method, base salary for similar job in host nation is taken as basis for designing compensation plan. This method is adopted for long term assignments of expatriates.

ii) **Home-based method**: In this method expatriate compensation package is designed on the basis of what they are getting in their home nation. Under this method, expatriate will be given same compensation package as they are getting in home nation. This method is used for short-term assignment.

PERFORMANCE APPRAISAL/WORK FORCE CONTROL SYSTEM

Performance appraisal of employees in case of global companies is very complex as work-related practices, organizational culture, job dimensions, business ethics, discipline norms, etc. vary from country to country. Performance appraisal of employees of global companies should be done by managers who have deep knowledge of job contents, global work environment, organizational structure and standards of work performance expected from employees. The process includes four steps:

Establishing performance standards
Measuring actual performance
Comparing actual performance with standards
Taking necessary actions

LIMITATIONS OR DIFFICULTIES IN WORKFORCE CONTROL SYSTEM

For achieving maximum benefits from workforce control system, the business executive should know the limitations and difficulties of workforce control system. The main limitations are:

- **Human Problem**: It ignores the human element in workforce. Employees feel that control system is made just to criticize them, which turns into a source of frustration to them. And as a result employees fail to achieve the desired target.
- **Continues Change in External Environmental Factors**:

May render the standards fixed futile. In other words' the standards fixed may not be relevant in the changed environmental conditions.

- **Inefficient Controllers**: Sometimes business executives engaged in the process of workforce control themselves become hindrance in it, because they may not have sufficient information to set standards or they may not be expert in setting standards or they may make wrong assessment of actual performance level of employees. It may result in failure of workforce control system.
- **Difficulty in Fixing Individual Responsibility** As business activities are jointly performed by employees, i.e. group effort of employees is required to achieve certain standards.
- **Expensive Process**: Sometimes expenditure incurred on operating control system is more than the benefits received from it.

CONCLUSION

As the trend of globalization increased in HRM, the rate of failure of expatriates also increased day-by-day. In spite of selecting best people who are self-confident, mentally mature, culturally tough, have flexible management style etc., failure of expatriate is common. The failure rate varies from 10% to 40% for expatriate of different nations. Expatriate failure means premature return of workforce sent to other nation. Cost of expatriate failure proves very high to global business units. Main reasons of failure are: (i) climate conditions not suitable for expatriates or his family members, (ii) Lack of technical competence, (iii) cultural shock, (iv) inability to cope up with overseas responsibilities, (v) Difficulty in adjusting a new environment, and (vi) Excessive resistance of local workforce.

References

Harzing, A.W., Pudelko, M. Reiche, B.S. (2015), The Bridging role of Expatriates and Inpatriates in knowledge transfer in MNCs.

HRM Guides—www.hrmguide.net

International HRM and Staffing Policies—Harzing.com

International HRM, 3rd edition, London, Saga Publication.

International HRM: National Business System, Orgal. Politics and the International Division of Labor in MNCs—Tony Edwards, Kings College London, Sarosh Kuruvilla—Cornell University.

The International Journal of HRM—Tailor and Francis— www.tandfonline.com

7

Emerging HR Trends and Challenges in 21st Century

PRIYANKA KAPOOR AND MEENAKSHI

ABSTRACT

Human Resource Management has undergone a major transformation over the last two decades and experienced a drastic change in the form and function primarily in the 21st century. It is necessary for the management to invest considerable time and amount, to learn the changing scenario of the HR practices in the 21st century. In order to survive the competition and be in the race, HR department should consciously update itself with the transformation in HR and be aware of the HR issues cropping up. With high attrition rates, poaching strategies of competitors, there is a huge shortage of skilled employees and hence, a company's HR activities play a vital role in combating this crisis. Suitable HR policies that would lead to the achievement of the Organization as well as the individual's goals should be formulated. HR managers have to manage all the challenges that they would face from recruiting employees, to train them, and then developing strategies for retaining them and building up an effective career management system for them. Just taking care of employees would not be enough; new HR initiatives should also focus on the quality needs, customer-orientation, productivity and stress, team work and leadership building. The paper focuses on the HR trends and

the challenges which are emerging in the 21st century and also gives some of the suggestions to succeed in the present HR scenario.
Keywords: Management, human resource, talent management, skills, knowledge, HRM trends, policies, outsourcing, competency mapping.

INTRODUCTION

Human resource management is a process of bringing people and organizations together so that the goals of each other are met. The role of HR manager is shifting from that of a protector and screener to the role of a planner and change agent. The major purpose of HRM is to increase and improve the productive contribution of personnel to the organization in more ethical, social, and administratively responsible way. It is a well known reality that India is set to become one of the largest economies of the world over the next two decades. As business all over the world is changing at a fast pace, the major trends which are affecting industries and their HR departments are globalization, poaching strategies, technology, competency mapping, outsourcing and talent crunch. The biggest challenge being faced by the businesses all over the world is the shortage of skilled manpower. For many companies, lack of talented employees has adversely affected the profitability and growth of many businesses.

The 21st century brings with it enormous opportunities but also enormous pressure, if the companies will not improve the productivity of the people and treat them "human being' which are the vital objects of all the economic activities leading towards industrial development. Now there is worl-dwide consensus on human resource being one of the major means of increasing efficiency, productivity and prosperity of the firm. Over the years, highly skilled and knowledge based jobs are increasing while low skilled jobs are decreasing. This calls for future skill mapping through proper HRM initiatives. Role of HRM is becoming all the more important. With the increase in competition, locally or globally, organizations must become more adaptable, resilient, agile, and customer-focused to succeed. And within this change in environment, the HR professional has to evolve to become a strategic partner, an employee sponsor or advocate, and a change mentor within the organization. The paper focuses on emerging HR trends and challenges. This paper may be of great value for HR practitioners and also for those who have a keen interest in the area of Human Resource Management.

REVIEW OF LITERATURE

Aparna Ghosh discussed the evolution of HRM practices and changes in HR practices after 1991. She observed that changes like emphasis on employees, up-gradation of skills, progressive HR policies and entrepreneurship by employees.

Anjali at citehr.com explained HR trends such as mobile culture, new technology impact on skills requirements, globalization of business, business alignment, business innovation through training/development, its technology development, rise in per capita income, developing economies growth rate, major economic reforms and outsourcing opportunities.

K.V. Rao who is a management consultant, in his paper, "Recent trends in critical HR management practices" threw light on issues such as leadership development, work-life balance, inclusion and diversity, health and wellness, right skilling, managing solid citizen, instant rewards, managing aspiration and 360 degree feedback.

Cox (1993) suggests that in order to effectively manage workplace diversity, a HR manager needs to change from an ethnocentric view to a relative perspective. This shift in philosophy has to be ingrained in managerial framework of HR in his Planning, Organizing, Leading and Controlling of organizational resources.

Armstrony (2004) described HRM as the function within an organization that focuses on recruitment of management of and providing direction for the people who work in the organization.

Andries Du Plessis (2008) explained that HR manager will have to build or develop a framework that allows flexibility to develop a workforce for tomorrow.

The world Federation of personnel management association (2009) survey pointed out the most important HR challenges are Leadership development, Organizational effectiveness, Change management, Compensation, Health and Safety, Staff retention, Learning and Development, Succession Planning, Staffing, Recruitment and Skill labour.

Preeti Naveen Yadav (2010) in her research paper titled, "Emerging Trends in Human Resource Department" observed the trends such as shrinking talent pool, an increase in outsourcing, more intense focus on work/life balance, changing workplace demographics, greater need for talent management, ethics requirements and globalization.

Anurag (2011) discussed that managing the expectation of skilled workers are also going to be a major area of concern for all HR managers in the year ahead.

HR Managers today are focusing attention on the followings:

a) **Policies**—HR policies based on trust, openness, equity and consensus.
b) **Motivation**—Create conditions in which people are willing to work with zeal, initiative and enthusiasm; make people feel like winners.
c) **Relations**—Fair treatment of people for healthy work place relations.
d) **Change Agent**—Prepare workers to accept technological changes by clarifying doubts.
e) **Quality Consciousness**—Commitment to quality in all aspects of personnel administration will ensure success.

Due to the new trends in HR, the HR manager should treat people as resources, reward them equitably, and integrate their aspirations with corporate goals through suitable HR policies.

Changes in HRM

Some of the significant changes that are likely to take place in the human resource management are as follows:

1. **Increase in education levels**: Due to technological progress and the spread of educational institutions workers will increasingly become aware of their higher level needs; managers will have to evolve appropriate policies and techniques to motivate the knowledge of workers. Better educated and organized workforce will demand greater discretion and autonomy at the work place.
2. **Technological developments:** This will require retraining and mid-career training of both workers and managers. Rise of the international corporation is proving new challenges for personnel function.
3. **Changing composition of work force:** In future, women and minority groups, SCs and STs would become an important source of manpower in future on account of easy access to better educational and employment opportunities. Therefore, manpower planning of every

organization will have to take into consideration the potential availability of talent in these groups. Changing mix of the workforce will lead to new values in organizations.

4. **Increasing government role:** In India, personnel management has become much legalized. In future private organizations will have to co-ordinate their labour welfare programme with those of the government private sector which will be required increasingly to support government efforts for improving public health, education training and development and infrastructure.
5. **Occupational health and safety:** Due to legislative presence and trade union movement, personnel management will have to be more healthy and safety conscious in future.
6. **Organizational development:** In future, change will have to be initiated and managed to improve organizational effectiveness. Top management will become more actively involved in the development of human resources.
7. **New work ethic:** Greater forces will be on project and team forms of organization. As changing work ethic requires increasing emphasis on individual. Jobs will have to redesign to provide challenge.
8. **Development planning:** Personnel management will be involved increasingly in organizational planning, structure, composition etc. Greater cost-consciousness and profit-orientations will be required on the part of the personnel department.
9. **Better appraisal and reward systems:** Organizations will be required to share gains of higher periodicity with workers more objective and result oriented systems of performance appraisal and performance linked compensation will have to be developed.
10. **New personnel policies:** New and better polices will be required for the work force of the future. Traditional family management will give way to professional management with greater forces on human dignity.

Thus, in future personnel management will face new challenges and perform new responsibilities. Participative leadership will take the place of autocratic leadership. Creative skills will have to be redeveloped and rewarded emphasis will shift from legal and rule bound approach to more open and humanitarian approach.

Emerging Role of HRM

HRM is no more a system to follow norms and monitor guide lines. HRM now is all about:

- Bring new changes,
- Diversify process actions
- Invent new ideas
- Understand future needs
- Forecast problems and act
- Generate trust
- Value the deserving
- Enhance capabilities
- Respect the respectable

Major challenges and issues include:

1. ***Challenges of globalization***
   - Integration of economies
   - Global benchmarking
   - Change in the management style
   - Future of public enterprises
2. ***Technological advances***
   - In the competitive world of today, industry cannot hope to survive for long with the old technology.
   - Unemployment resulting from modernization will be solved by properly assessing manpower needs and training of redundant employees.
3. ***Challenges of Quality revolution***
   - Action Revolution which has been developed around customer satisfaction as the central focal theme.
   - Forced organizations throughout the world to become conscious about quality, productivity, pricing and consumer satisfaction.
   - Products are now available that are far more superior than the earlier ones in terms of quality given the same or even lower price.
   - E.g. 'Motorola', implemented six-sigma to attain 99.99997% defect-free manufacturing.

4. *Workforce Diversity*

- The increasing heterogeneity of organizations is an important challenge for HR managers.
- Includes workers from different groups.
- Employees don't set aside their values, beliefs, lifestyles, preferences, etc. when they come to work.

If it is managed properly, there would be better communication, human relations and congenial work culture in the organization.

5. *Empowerment of Employees*

- In future, the proportion of professional and technical employees will increase as compared to the blue collared employees.
- They will seek greater degree of participation in goal setting and decision making and also demands greater avenues of self-fulfillment.
- So, the organizations will have to be redesigned or restructured to empower the employees for their autonomy or freedom to take decisions while performing their jobs.
- The techniques of empowerment range from participation decision making to the use of self-managed teams.

HR professionals can't ignore these challenges, rather they have to design and execute innovative mechanisms of developing skills and competencies.

Emerging Trends in HRM

Some of the recent trends that are being observed are as follows:

Trends in Recruitment

Human Resource Outsourcing

- A company may draw required personnel from outsourcing firms.
- Outsourcing firms develop their human resource pool by employing people for them and make available personnel to various companies as per their needs.
- The outsourcing firms or the intermediaries charge the organizations for their services.

Poaching/raiding

- Means employing a competent and experienced person already working with another reputed company in the same or different industry.
- Company can attract talent from another firm by offering attractive pay packages and other terms and conditions.

E-recruitment

- E-Recruitment is the use of technology to assist the recruitment process.
- Use Internet as a source of recruitment.
- Social media networking is a new way to find employees.
- Job vacancies are advertised through WWW (World Wide Web) and applications are invited online.
- It is preferred source of recruitment due to many reasons like low cost, fast recruitment and efficiency in the recruitment process.

360-degree Feedback

- Also known as "multi-rater feedback," "multisource feedback," or "multisource assessment".
- It is a feedback that comes from all around an employee.
- Feedback is provided by subordinates, peers, and supervisors and external sources such as customers and suppliers or other interested stakeholders.

Leadership Development

- Creating a pipeline of leadership talent is a key to business future growth.
- Companies including *HUL, P&G* have been able to withstand attrition in key executives because they have always invested in developing leaders.

Competency Mapping

- Identify key competencies for an organization and/or a job and incorporating those competencies throughout the various processes (i.e. job evaluation, training, recruitment) of the organization.
- Process for measuring the strengths and weaknesses of an individual worker or organization.
- Focuses on the skills and strengths of the individual in

areas like team structure, leadership, and decision-making for doing a particular job.

- It is being used by many big organizations in one form or the other to understand the ways to use the strengths of workers most effectively.

Instant Rewards

- Recognizing and rewarding performers is one of the most effective tools to attract and retain the right talent.
- Include compensation in both cash and kind.
- Companies are also including work-life balance programmes; competency pay packages and career opportunities.

Six-sigma Practices

- It is a business management strategy.
- Initially implemented by Motorola.
- Seeks to improve the quality of process outputs by identifying and removing the causes of defects and variation in manufacturing and business processes.
- It uses a set of quality management methods including statistical methods and creates a special infrastructure of people within the organization.
- It improves organizational values and helps in creating defect free product or services at minimum cost.

Exit Policy

- Surplus manpower is a major problem in many industrial units.
- Exit policy refers to the policy regarding the retrenchment of the surplus manpower from restructuring of industrial units/the workers becoming unemployed by the closure of sick units.
- It covers the compensation for the employees who leave the organization and the measures for their rehabilitation also.

What HR Managers can do?

- Use workforce skills and abilities in order to exploit environmental opportunities and neutralize threats.
- Employ innovative reward plans that recognize employee contributions and grant enhancements.

- Indulge in continuous quality improvement through TQM and HR contributions (training, development, counseling, coaching, etc.).
- Utilize people with distinctive capabilities to create unsurpassed competence in an area (Xerox in photocopier, 3M in adhesives, Telco in trucks, Britannia in biscuits, Nestle in coffee, McDonald's in fast foods, etc.).
- Decentralize operations and rely on self managed teams to deliver goods in difficult times (Motorola is famous for short product development cycles. It has quickly commercialized ideas from its research labs).
- Lay off workers in a smooth way, explaining facts (IBM, Kodak, Xerox, AT&T, Steel and Textile firms in India etc.) to unions, workers and other affected groups. HR generally plays a key role, these days, in planning and implementing corporate downsizings, and then in maintaining the morale of the remaining employees.

SUGGESTIONS

The above mentioned trends pose significant challenges to organizations at national and international level with respect to work force recruitment, development and retention. To face the rapid changes, programs are needed to cater to development of young workers and encourage continuous training and education. Further, proper communication between cultures and management is required to ensure the awareness among HR people about the emerging trends and issues. HR managers will have to continuously refresh themselves to learn the use of new techniques and methods as six sigma and competency mapping. In the wake of emerging trends, greater discretion and autonomy at the work place is need of hour as workforce is becoming better educated and organized. HR managers will have to take more care of health and safety issues in future. As changing corporate cultures requires increasing stress on individual, the jobs will have to redesign to meet the emerging challenges and issues.

CONCLUSION

Trends in Human resource management have changed the way we work, as organizations are more depended on HRM to increase the success ratio in today's competitive global environment. So now we have companies looking to acquire the best talent and a growing workforce of talented individuals who are no longer attracted by compensation alone, but who require and value intangibles as well. In order to achieve professional growth and success in the next period of increased talent acquisition, technology professionals are going to have sleep out of their comfort zone and develop the holistic, relationship-focused business skills that companies are going to take more strategic and supportive approach to recruiting and retention if they want to find and keep the new breed of evolving talent.

References

Armstrong (2004), "A Handbook of Human Resource Management Practice," 9th Edition.

Anurag (2011), "How the Technological advancement affect the HRM," retrieved on 12/9/2013.

Aparna Bhattacharya; Evolution of HR Practices in Indian Corporate at www.Chillbreeze. Com.

Ashwathapa, K. (2005); "Human Resource Management", Tata McGraw Hills, Fifth edition.

Andries J. Du Plessis (2008), "The Changing Role of Human Resource Managers," International Review of Business Research Paper, Vol. 4, No. 5, pp. 166-81.

Anita Lettink (2009); 7 – key Trends influencing HR in 2009 and beyond.

Kothari, C.R., "Research Methodology: Methods and Techniques", Wishwa Prakashan, New Delhi, Edition 2nd , 2003.

Preeti Naveen Yadav, August 2010; Emerging Trends in Human Resource Department; *International Research Journal,* August 2010; ISSN-0975-3486 RNI:RAJBIL 2009/30097, Vol. 1.

Sims, Doris, December 2009, Debunking Ten Top Talent Management Myths; *Talent Management Magazines*.

Susan M. Heathfield; Top ten Human Resource Trends of the Decades, at www.about.com.

8

Green HRM—An Effective Tool for Sustainable Development

SEEMA PANDEY

ABSTRACT

Green Human Resource management is a new concept in today's scenario. Growing concern for Global environment has created a need for business to adopt environment strategies and programs. In this paper concept of Green HRM and sustainability is studied. Impact of industrialization on environment has discussed. Different types of green practices which should be followed in the organization are explained in details. Green HRM will help the employees and manufactures in changing the organization culture, thinking about waste management, pollution and helping the society and its own people those are getting affected by pollution. It makes employee and society members aware of the utilization of natural resource more economically and encourages them to go more for eco-friendly products.

Keywords: Green HRM, green practices, sustainability, environment.

INTRODUCTION

In the present scenario the organizations are more serious about the impacts of their production on environment. So all most all the organizations has carried forwarded the Go-Green concept worldwide because although the man has achieved economic development yet less importance has been given to the environmental issues. Misuse of natural recourses by man has brought many threats on our planet and our prosperity like Global warming, reduction in Ozone layer and melting of Ice Mountain and glaciers. For protection of environment and sustainable development business organization should adopt environment-friendly practices and products. Now HR department of an organization can become an active partner for achieving the objective of sustainable development by creating a Green HR Platform because many employees are not conscious for their responsibility to protect the environment while they are at work. If employees understand their role towards environment and sustainable development then they can experience high job satisfaction and being better engaged which ultimately results in higher productivity. The HR strategy must reflect and inspire the ambitions of the HR team and other employees, aligning with the company strategy, values and culture, deliver sustainable returns to investors, address customer needs, identify and respond to emerging societal trends, respond to governmental and regulatory expectations, and influence the public policy agenda. There is thus a growing need for the integration of environmental management into human resource management (HRM)–green HRM–research practice. Green HR is the use of HRM policies to promote the sustainable use of resources within business organizations and, more generally, promotes the cause of environmental sustainability through electronic filing, car-sharing, job sharing, teleconferencing and virtual interviews, recycling, telecommuting, online training, energy efficient office spaces etc.

LITERATURE REVIEW

Callenbach *et al.* [1993] has elaborated that in order to carry out green management employees must be inspired, empowered and environmentally aware of greening to be success. Collin & Clark [2003], Survey highlighted the link of HR practice and the organization outcomes such as productivity, flexibility and financial performance. Laursen & Foss [2003] have revealed that not much emphasis has been laid on relating these outcomes to innovating performance and environment management initiative . It of a recent origin, Lee (2009) elaborated that the green management was initiated as a part of business strategy during 1990 but was popular in 2000's.

Jobbour *et al.* [2013] studied the relationship between human recourse and environment management at 75 Brazilian companies and conducted that HRM relates positively to environment management. Margaretha and Saragin [2013] has highlighted that organization focuses on environmental sustainable business practices by initiative greener corporate culture resulting into greater efficiency, lower cost and creating an atmosphere of better employees engagement. GHRM also focuses on establishing green culture. Thus from the above literature review it can be seen that although many researchers has studied the GHRM concept related to various aspects. But there is more requirements of research in this area

OBJECTIVES

The objectives of this paper are:

- To indicate and study significance of Green HRM.
- To elaborate on various green practices that can be incorporated for building a Green Workplace.
- To what extent and how HR policies and practices can improve the environment performance of organization.

Green HRM

Activities involved in the development, implementations and ongoing maintenance of a system that aims at making employees of an organization green. It means transforming normal employees into green employees to achieve environment goal of the organization and finally to make a significant contribution to environment sustainability.

Sustainability

Sustainability has become a key focuses for many organization as climate changes, regulatory pressures and societal demand for greater environment and social responsibility has increased. "Sustainability is often defined as the ability to meet the need of the present without compromising the ability of future generation to meet their needs".

Three Pillars of Sustainability

- **Compliance** is the state of being in accordance with all national, federal, regional or local laws, regulations and government authority requirements. Not being in accordance with such regulations often incurs sanctions in the form of business limitations, fines or even legal proceedings. Compliance with labor regulations is a critical start point for sustainable HRM.

- **Corporate governance** is "the system by which companies are directed and controlled." Of particular relevance to corporate governance is the way the board of directors performs its duties to ensure corporate integrity, and in many cases, the way the BOD directs the organization's strategy regarding sustainability. For HRM, BOD direction on sustainability can provide a necessary, legitimizing and empowering framework for advancing sustainable HRM practices.
- **Business ethics** is a set of behavioral guidelines by which all directors, managers and employees of an organization are expected to behave to ensure appropriate moral and ethical business standards, typically beyond the letter of the law. Ethics usually includes guidelines relating to conflict of interest, corruption, bribery, maintaining business records, discrimination, showing respect for people and more.

Impact of Industrialization on Environment

Sl. No.	*Industry*	*Natural Resources used*	*Products*	*Impact /Effects*
1.	Paper	Plants and Trees	Paper	Forest
2.	Pharma	Plants and Animals	Medicines	Flora and Fauna
3.	Automobiles	Petroleum	Cars and Trucks	Air Pollution
4.	Food	Plants and Animals	Human Consumptions Product	Air, Water Pollution
5.	Chemicals	Soils and Minerals	Agriculture and Industrial Product	Soil, Air and Water Pollution

The above table shows the impact of different type of industries on environment. It can be seen that Paper industry has an adverse effect on forest because large number of plants and trees are cutting for making papers. Due to Pharma industry Flora and Fauna get affected. Automobiles industry generates air pollution which is hazardous to human beings. Food industry creates air/water pollution, whereas chemical used for Agriculture and Industrial product leads to soil/air and water pollution.

Green Practices

Operation requires a lot of consumables, such as paper, plastic, envelope and ink toner. Although there are both environmental and economical concerns, it is very hard to use less of those because they are integral part of our basic operations. Apart from general green office practices, here are some latest environmentally-friendly solutions to stay Green are:

- Use of both sides of paper while printing/photocopy.
- Use of local transport or by making car pool for coming to office.
- Use natural light when work.
- Use solar energy instead of electric energy.
- Use Plants in the working areas which helps in reducing air pollution through absorption.
- Switch of Air Conditioner 30 min-1 hour before ending to work.
- Provide mugs, glasses, and insulated drink containers to all employees for drinks such as coffee, water, and juice, and keep a few extra mugs around for office visitors and guests. If you need, then use ones made from recycled paper, not Styrofoam.
- Drink tap water, and avoid plastic water bottles. Tap water is much safer and more regulated than bottled water, and many bottled waters use municipal water as their source.
- Change all of your light bulbs to CFLs, LEDs, or other energy-saving alternative light bulb. Use minimum bulbs or tube while working or switch off unnecessary tubes or bulbs.
- Turn off and unplug all computers and electronic devices after use. Even when these devices are turned off, they will continue to use electricity unless the power cords to keep them from charging all night.
- Use recycled products in the office. Look for products with a high percentage of post-consumer recycled content, reduced chemical content, and biodegradable or compostable components.

- Reuse files folders, boxes and all other office supplies for as long as possible before purchasing any new ones.
- Avoid individual packaging by buying items such as coffee, sugar, and creamer in bulk.
- Whenever possible, use digital document delivery methods such as email or internal fax to avoid postage, printing, ink, and paper use.
- Practice on-screen reading and editing habits to save printing and view your document first using your application's print preview feature prior to printing to avoid mistakes
- Purchase computer software and download them to avoid packaging and shipping costs and materials.
- Report to the superior if you notice environment pollution caused by anything.
- Help and teach others to go Green e.g. Juniors or colleagues.

Outcomes of Green HRM

- It helps to reduce health hazards caused due to pollution.
- It maintains balance between Man-Animal-Plant and Environment.
- It ensures survival of human being and business organization for a longer period of time.
- It helps to reduces consumption of electricity.
- It saves resources for the future consumption.
- It teaches human resource how to Go-Green.
- It helps in avoiding or minimizing global warming.
- It helps in avoiding or minimizing natural disasters such as acid rains, red rains, tsunamis, flooding, hurricanes, droughts, etc. owing to informal, harmful and greedy usage of natural resources for production and consumption.
- It helps in avoiding or minimizing health diseases owing to pollution.
- It helps in avoiding or minimizing harms to animals and other natural creatures.
- It ensures appropriate balance of relationships among plants, animals, people, and their environment.

- It ensures survival of humans and business organizations for a prolonged period of time.

CONCLUSION

The future of Green HRM appears promising for all the stakeholders of HRM. The employers and practitioners can establish the usefulness of linking employee involvement and participation in environmental management programmed to improved organizational environmental performance, like with a specific focus on encouraging green practices and help green management evolve and develop. Unions and employees can help employers to adopt Green HRM policies and practices that help safeguard and enhance worker health and well-being. GHRM practices presented in this paper helps an organization to implement green HRM, thus highlighting the benefits of Green HRM and some practices associated with it.

REFERENCES

www. greenlivingideas.com
www.theglobaljournals.com
www.theglobaljournals.com
www. abhinavjournal.com
www. eminencejournal.com

9

An Empirical Study on Career Development, Advancement and Opportunities

SHIVANI DAWER

ABSTRACT

This paper looks at career opportunities, assessment, planning, and development, from the interest and perspective of the undergraduate students. It is the merger of student development and career development. Career counseling is seen within the parameters of developing the student's strengths and matching the student to a fitting career, while building a lasting relationship between the student and mentor-counselor. It consists of three core sections: theory, assessment, and relations. Long-term relationships between the student and mentor/counselor and the value of experiential learning and related and supporting experiences, are mentioned throughout. The theory and assessment section of this paper is not in-depth, but sets the foundation for counseling in a close and professional relationship with the student.

Student advising and student development involves many things working together for the good of the student. One element of student development is career counseling and development. Advisors and counselors play a role in helping students develop themselves, whether in classes, counseling sessions, extracurricular activities, job tasks, or elsewhere. Advisors assist students in many things, beyond mere academic, course, and degree planning. Likewise, a model counseling relationship or program should also exceed a four-year span of time. What happens in the college experience begins at recruitment and extends beyond graduation into the student's work career.

REVIEW OF LITERATURE

This paper aims to provide a synthetic review of the literature on the career development opportunities. Review of literature justifies the reason for our research.

"Literature Review" means to systematically read, critically appraise, and then synthesize the material into a coherent, structured, and logical review of the literature.

The first stage of the review involved the identification of papers, research reports and policy documents that were broadly concerned with career development interventions and learning for work. Potentially relevant papers were identified through electronic databases, websites and personal contacts. The research team, in conjunction with the Critical Reader, identified appropriate electronic databases and websites.

The research takes the form of a case study, and the findings are collated through qualitative interviews. A focus group was conducted, which framed the issues of concern, and these were explored in much more detail through semi-structured interview.

Various authors have explained their observations and experiments in detail regarding career-counseling programmes. Different reviews have been made, literature is being studied and findings and conclusion suggests that there should be proper and accurate system to be followed for career counseling and development of employees in organizations. According to various researches, clear confined methods are to be adopted for making to research work successful, effective and fruitful.

Keywords: Career growth, Knowledgeable counseling, Development and advancement, Opportunities.

RESEARCH METHODOLOGY

This section examines the two major traditions of research methods: qualitative and quantitative. It discusses the dominant effect that one of these traditions (quantitative research) has had on current careers guidance and counseling practice and considers the value of piloting research.

Objectives of the Study

- Distinguish between quantitative and qualitative research;

- Outline some key issues from current practice which link with research method;
- Describe the main features of qualitative research;
- Describe the main features of quantitative research;
- Pilot your research project.

Models of Research

The most common way of conceptualizing the diversity of approaches to research is to distinguish between quantitative and qualitative models. It is this distinction that will be adopted here, though it should be stressed that this is a rather crude distinction that can be misleading. In reality, much social scientific research combines methods from the two traditions. For example, quantitative research favors structured forms of data, which can consist of frequency counts or other types of measurements. In contrast, the data that qualitative researchers typically deal with are verbal descriptions in natural language often collected from an interview or some type of recorded conversation (for example, using audio tapes). They deal more in meanings, experiences and descriptions. This type of data cannot be directly subjected to counting or measuring, though, of course, they can subsequently be presented so that they can be analyzed quantitatively.

A quantitative approach requires that the researcher collects all the data before analyzing it. A qualitative approach requires that data collection and analysis are intertwined. One other important difference relates to views about the role of theory. These and other differences will be discussed in more detail later.

Methods of data collection are also varied. Some are clearly associated with quantitative research (for example, the scientific experiment) and other with qualitative research (for example, participant observation). Others are shared by both traditions (for example, questionnaires and interviews) though the precise design of the research instrument and the approach adopted by the researcher are likely to differ. The purpose of all research is:

> 'to understand and explain social phenomena, to focus attention on particular issues and to challenge conventionally held beliefs about the social and natural worlds'.

RESEARCH TRADITIONS IN GUIDANCE AND COUNSELING

A key assumption is that it is possible to measure both individual talents and the attributes required in particular jobs which can then be matched to achieve a 'good fit'. It is when individuals are in jobs best suited to their abilities, they perform best, and productivity is highest.

This theory of occupational choice has dominated careers guidance and counseling practice for nearly a century, partly because of its practical appeal. It provides careers guidance and counseling practitioners with a clear rationale and framework for practice. Additionally, the underlying philosophy has suited policy makers since it lends itself to the servicing of labor market requirements. Consequently, it has been embraced enthusiastically by policy makers and barely questioned by the majority of practitioners.

There was no viable theoretical alternative during the first half of this century to this 'best fit' theory of occupational choice, and it was not until the 1950's and 1960's that theories originating from other academic disciplines such as sociology, and other branches of psychology like developmental psychology emerged as serious alternatives. Theories, which were developed from these academic disciplines, emphasized the context in which occupational 'choice' occurred and the importance of the maturation process of individuals, respectively. Since this time, the theories careers guidance practitioners have used to inform their practice have expanded dramatically. Whichever theories actually inform current practice, there is emerging consensus around the inadequacies of these theories. In particular, researchers are questioning the relevance of current theory for particular sectors of society.

Quantitative or traditional experimental approaches set out to quantify and measure the contributions of different factors to phenomenon (for example, occupational choice behavior). It can be useful if you want to compare things, like test scores under different conditions or behavior under different conditions. However, this approach to research has certain disadvantages for small-scale studies. For example, you would need a large enough sample to ensure your data is statistically significant. Additionally, your sample must be representative so that you can be confident of getting the same pattern of results again when you repeat the same procedures on a different population. Only then would you be able to generalize your findings to a wider sample than the one you are testing.

So, adopting a quantitative approach to research involves searching for causal relationships which are conceptualized in terms of the interaction of 'variables', some of which (independent variables) are seen as the cause of other (dependent variables). It will invariably involve designing and using standardized research instruments (for example, tests, questionnaires, attitude scales) so that numerical data can be collected which will then be manipulated using statistical techniques.

Some suitable data for this research method already exists in the form of published or unpublished statistics. Often, though, researchers have to produce the data they need for analysis themselves. For example, from a laboratory experiment or from psychometric or personality tests which have been administered to relatively large groups of participants. As previously indicated, if responses to unstructured questionnaires can be coded and then counted in some way, this may also be a source of quantitative data.

CAREER DEVELOPMENT THEORIES

Career development includes an element of reflection, requiring a student to engage in self-reflection, self-realization, and self-awareness. Self-reflection occurs where the student looks back onto his interests, likes, and goals, rather than looking at those of his family and friends. Students must then develop vocational awareness. Then, the student should prove a match between their chosen career and their personality, self-efficacy, and self-concept. Students must be personally responsible for researching a career choice, and that requires them to be interested in the first place. However, students do not have full knowledge of careers or in matching themselves to careers. They need the help of advisors, mentors, or other facilitators in making that choice.

Career development theory implies that students choose their dream based on personality traits, sociological factors, and development variables. Students establish a dream, enlist the emotional support of friends and family, and set out on the journey. The goal is not merely to find a job that will result in the most money, but also a job that they will enjoy.

Socrates said, "He who enjoys what he does, never works a day in his life."

Students are consumer oriented, and as free agents, managing their own career. By building a resume, they are marketing themselves as the best thing for an organization. The focus is not on employment security, but rather on employability security. People have learned not to believe the old adage, "Take care of the company and the company will take care of you". To this extent, the students may see the faculty, staff, and administration as employees. Students may be skeptical of what an employee-advisor tells them. It is the challenge of the advisor and counselor to build a stronger and more trusting relationship with the student.

The consumer approach is seen where students demand something that serves their interests, rather than the interests of the board of trustees. *In charge* students complain of administrative hurdles, meaningless general education courses, unnecessary prerequisites, tuition increases, fewer services, or a lacking job placement statistic at a given college. Entrepreneurial students, in charge of their own career, may hit on problematic transfer requirements and may seek to fully understand degree-planning options at the very beginning. These students know what they want or need, they plot a course to get there, and they do not want a policy or the narrow thinking of a scheduling counselor standing in the way. They may see advisors as salesmen, trying to sell a class or a program that does not serve the student's interests. The challenge is to orient student services professionals toward their customers.

Individuals move through three stages of occupational choice in life. These are the fantasy stage, the tentative stage, and the realistic stage. A child looks at play as being work-oriented, reflecting initial preferences. Then, the individual identifies likes and dislikes, becomes aware of personal capacities, identifies perceptions of occupational styles, and the individual becomes aware of career choice and the responsibilities of that choice. Finally, career exploration ends in making a college choice and choosing a focused occupational goal. Super described career development as a life-long process. He defined a career is being more than a job. It is the culmination of all activities that take place in the various life roles. It develops from the collection of life's experiences. Super formalized the stages of vocational development in his life span, life-space approach..

Occupational choice results from an interaction of cognitive and affective processes. Career selection is a problem-solving activity. The capability of a career problem solver depends on his cognitive operations and knowledge. Career problem solving requires great memory and processing skills. He must have motivation, an internal and intrinsic drive. The development of a person's career requires continual growth and renewal of knowledge structures. Career identity depends on self-knowledge, and career maturity depends on one's ability to solve career problems. The goal of the career counselor is achieved by facilitating the growth of information processing skills, enhancing the student's abilities as a career problem solver and decision maker. The crux of this theory is that career counseling and development is a learning event.

Social cognitive career theory seeks to merge cognitive variables to other career theories, or at least to complement them. Individuals make career decisions based on their own self-efficacy, their belief in themselves and their abilities. Self-efficacy may be affected by social beliefs and expectations as part of the developmental process. Social cognitive theory blends cognitive, self-regulatory, and motivational processes into lifelong development.

Determinants of career development consist of self-efficacy, outcome expectations, and personal goals. The choice model consists of three components: establishing a goal, taking action, and attaining a level of performance that determines the direction of future career behavior. The path to career choice in the social cognitive career theory are: (1) self-efficacy and outcome expectations promote career interests; (2) interests turn influence goals; (3) goal-related actions lead to performance experiences; (4) the outcome determines future paths (per the change in self-efficacy); and (5) one establishes a career decision or career change. The big hurdle in the choice model is that of environmental variables. Individuals who have more resources, benefits, and opportunities are more likely to take their goals into the action stage. Not everyone may be able to accomplish the goals or experiences that they prefer to, such as in being able to get the desired jobs.

The values-based model of career choice has six basic elements. Individuals prioritize only a few key values. Highly prioritized values are the most important determinants of life-role choices. Values are acquired through learning from values-laden information. Life satisfaction depends on life roles that satisfy all-important values. A role's salience is directly related to the degree of satisfaction of essential values from those roles. Success in a life role depends on many factors, including learned skills and cognitive, affective, and physical aptitudes. Self-efficacy theory has been alluded to earlier. This results from an individual's belief that he can or cannot perform certain tasks. As such, he will seek or not seek an assignment based on these limitations that he imposes on himself. Self-efficacy involves an individual's thoughts, values, attitudes, and beliefs that influence psychological functioning.

Career counseling should consider personal goals, family needs, leisure interests, and geographical preferences, among other things. It should involve the coaching on personal responsibility and self-empowerment. Social constructivist theory suggests that the career development process is a result of an individual's actions and his interactions with others. Life-long career development is developed by career-growing experiences, such as education, training, multiple job opportunities, and more. A counselor may use context conceptualization by engaging the student to become aware of environmental conditions or social influences on his career development. A counselor should assist a student in drawing insight from the wealth of knowledge in his own life's experiences and applying that to career development.

CAREER EXPLORATION

Some messages given to students by a counselor may seem obvious. Students do not really need to be told that college graduates make more money and have greater promotion potential. However, students may not know specifics about a particular career, such as its job opportunities, promotion potential, qualifications required, or the amount of money that can be made. Career exploration is a stage and an action. A career may be explored and established. Career development is a life-long activity, but its stages are not fixed. A growing trend in educational settings is to bring work experience together with the academic programming. This can be in the form of entry-level jobs, internships, job shadowing, on-the-job training, or other connections for the benefit of students. Students who graduate with relevant work experience have a greater chance at landing a job. The counselor should encourage such activities, provided there is a practical way to do work and school. On a related note, colleges and counselors should provide training on job searching, interviewing, and resume-writing skills. Often, faculty or staff may participate in mock interviews with students.

Career exploration is most prevalent among the high school and under-graduate age groups. It is a process of specifying and refining the occupational information acquired. It is a period of choice, where the information produces alternatives and then an ultimate decision for a career. Career exploration can also occur later with career refinement and career changes. Adults responding to a career change or market changes may require them to engage in another round of career exploration. Students may use computer-assisted career guidance programs to provide current job market information. Assessments, job qualifications, and other tools may be available via computer program. The Career Information System and the career information delivery system serve to provide occupational and education information. Students can search multiple databases to gain information about careers, employment outlook, and salary information.

Counselors must observe many things about their client. The counselor is looking for personality cues, appearance, comfort with the interview, and the student's knowledge of self and career. They must make the student comfortable in the interview, and that includes a need for the counselor to be comfortable with self-disclosure. It may help if the counselor describes his own weaknesses, experiences, and feelings. Open-ended questions might be used to solicit explanatory answers, which in turn provide the advisor with the student's level of understanding. The counselor should restate and paraphrase the student's words to provide clarity, confirmation, and mutual understanding. The student may be encouraged to continue or expound on a thought, giving the counselor more knowledge of the student and provide direction for the interview. The conversation should be focused on the student and the needs at hand.

In understanding students, an advisor needs to learn of the student's current condition and family circumstances. This requires the counselor to look for appearance, attitude and behavior of students. The counselor must attempt to match personality and strength characteristics of the student to those required in various occupations, as this may shorten the list of possibilities. He should identify the level of career maturity and job knowledge. He should also look for indicators of self-concept and self-worth. It is important to help the student understand that a career is a combination of life roles. The counselor should remove irrational or incorrect beliefs about career choice or self-perception. He should look for opportunities to build positive reinforcement for the student, aiding in career exploration and planning skills. What may be most important for the counselor is to form a supportive and trusting relationship with the student, teaching self-empowerment to help students assume responsibility for their career.

Advisors must create a mattering climate, where students matter.

This includes a feeling of visibility and importance by the student. This becomes more important when the student/graduate is looking for a job and is being ignored. The counselor may address this by noticing students when they enter the office, providing prompt and courteous assistance, and staying in a counseling relationship with the student over time. The highest levels of mattering exist where the student has a personal and professional relationship with the advisor. Thus, it is important to have a long-term relationship, building bridges and a lasting personal bond..

Everyone needs some supportive advice and direction from a well-placed mentor or counselor, preferably one who has been there and has pertinent knowledge. In the event of unemployment, clients have to normalize reactions to unemployment by identifying their accomplishments and transferable skills. Self-conscious clients may be assisted by allowing a counselor to help them identify and remove self-defeating beliefs. Supportive acts may be limited to encouragement and emotional support.

CAREER OPPORTUNITY TECHNIQUES

Trait-and-factor and person-environment-fit (PEF) have converged gradually. Cognitive and affective processes are now involved. Clinical information and qualitative data are included in the student appraisal. The counselor is no longer expected to direct, but to negotiate and collaborate with students. The basic steps of this new model are: (1) intake interview; (2) identify developmental variables; (3) assessment; (4) identify and solve problems; (5) generate PEF analysis; (6) confirm, explore, and decide; and (7) follow-up.

In the intake interview, the client and counselor form a compatible working relationship.

Discussions and questionnaires can provide biographical background information. The counselor may look for emotional cues, cognitive clarity, and personality characteristics. In identifying developmental variables, a counselor may look for signs regarding perception, personal identity, and self-concept. Environmental variables or contextual interactions that affect a person's life may also be identified. In the assessment stage, the counselor can evaluate the client's cognitive abilities, values, and interests. This information can match client needs to occupations that may be likely to result in satisfaction, self-fulfillment, and achievement. In identifying and solving problems, information is used to identify any affective concerns, self-knowledge, and the client's level of information processing. Clients who have emotional problems, unrealistic beliefs, or faulty perceptions of themselves and the work environment are given other specialized counseling. There are four-steps of information processing: goal setting, plan development and pattern matching, and action. In generating PEF analysis, the counselor and client develop a cognitive schema or conceptual framework. The client's ability patterns are used to predict satisfaction in different occupations. In confirming, exploring, and deciding, the counselor and client review test data and prediction analyses to determine if the client is comfortable with the results. In follow-up sessions, there is a continuation to evaluate the client's progress and any new changes that might be needed.

The developmental model is based on the premise that career development is a lifelong process. It includes the development of goals, learning strategies, and the timing of interventions. Overarching goals are problem identification and the development of intervention strategies to overcome them. It also stresses the importance of discovering each client's uniqueness of development. This model has four stages: (1) establishing client individuality, (2) identifying and selecting strategies, (3) teaching and aiding implementation, and (4) verifying goal achievement.

The cognitive information-processing model is a seven-step sequence for problem solving and decision-making in career services. At the lower levels, a new career entrant develops self-knowledge and occupational knowledge. Then, decision skills and information processing skills are reinforced. At the level of meta-cognition, a person is capable of broad, executive decision-making. The seven steps in this career-counseling model are as follows: initial interview, preliminary assessment, defining the problem and analyzing causes, formulating goals, developing the individual learning plan, executing the individual learning plan, and preparing a summative review and generalization. The cognitive information processing theory allows people to make a career choice, learning improved problem-solving and decision-making skills. Career decisions involve our emotions (affect) and thoughts (cognition). Our knowledge and our thinking affect such decisions.

CAREER COUNSELING ASSESSMENTS

Assessments are formal or informal techniques, instruments, tools, and inventories used to collect data about a client. These are only of predictive value, as life and time bring many changes. They do assess characteristics of the individual and attempt to fill occupations that match. Steps in the relationship of assessment to career planning: (1) become aware of the need to make career decisions, (2) learn about and reevaluate self-concept, (3) identify occupational alternatives, (4) obtain information about identified alternatives, (5) make tentative choices from among available occupations, make educational choices, and (7) implement a vocational choice. Standardized tests and assessments have been common on college campuses for years. They are used for achievement tests, aptitude and vocational tests, and college entrance exams. They are also controversial. In career counseling more emphasis has been placed on skills identification through informal techniques. Just as a person can accrue life experience not found on a resume, so can a student have skills, abilities, and a level of initiative that are not indicated by a standardized test. Some people do not test well, and the results of such vocational tests may provide advice or clues for students, which are in no way compatible with the student. Counselors must be able to assess a student in a subjective and qualitative manner. Assessments in career counseling should look to identify core elements. Assessments should reveal career beliefs, especially if those beliefs may affect career decisions. Assessments must identify skills, proficiencies, and abilities that will be used to predict performance on a given job. They should identify academic achievement, thus a test battery must cover a variety of career fields and then pursue those occupations where the student has the greatest strengths. They should identify and confirm interest levels. They are also useful if they can identify personality variables and what values a student has; yet such personality factor assessments are not widely used. Informal assessments are a conversational counseling technique. Role-playing activities allow individuals to think of and experience some aspects of different jobs. Counselors may encourage a career fantasy where an individual imagines their dream job. Other options included a forced-choice activity, card sort, or a structured interview. The latter attempts to draw out the student's knowledge of careers.

Qualitative assessments are not as concrete or scientific, but is subjective. This kind of assessment is derived from an open-ended conversation. This tool focuses on the multiple influences of career development. Considering the holistic development of the student, more than just limited academic information is obtained. Qualitative methods lend themselves to creativity on the part of the student, though they are not something that can be systematically taught. It comes about through a relationship, and likely varies based on student needs.

MATCHING ACADEMIC AND EXPERIENTIAL LEARNING

Relationships are essential for student success. Student learning is positively correlated with student contact with faculty and staff. Positive relationships with other students contribute to interaction, satisfaction, and the overall learning experience. Students should be self-aware and interpersonally sensitive, thereby stressing the value of relationships and interaction. Fostering relationships and social integration may be key to keeping more students in college. Counselors and staff members can help students in maintaining their educational aspirations through tutoring, advising, encouragement, and in addressing student problems. Following a student-centered approach, staff should form strong personal relationships involving themselves, students, and other stakeholders. They must act with the students, revise strategies, and assist students in their transition into and out of college.

Student affairs professionals have the task of helping students and making the college experience the best time of their lives. Counselors and other professionals begin by helping the student clarify what he wants or desires in college. Counselors and other student affairs professionals must consider intellectual and personal development together. The student activities and secondary involvements cannot take away from the primary focus of educating the student, but those activities should complement academic and career development.

Student-oriented staff members have been surveyed on their opinions of leadership in student affairs, considering the needs, wants, and desires of students. One common thing they mention is the value of one-on-one relationships with students and having a positive attitude in working with students. They consider that a privilege and acknowledge the role of staff in student development. They acknowledge that leadership is a relationship, where leading and following overlap. Such leaders value the worth, dignity, and potential of students, seeing the importance of a constructive, supportive, and positive community environment. These professionals exhibit mutual trust and respect toward student. They believe in the students and identify with student concerns. They are advocates for the students and represent the best interests of students. They want students to be responsible for themselves, and they believe that student leaders are an integral part of the university structure, as full partners. The best advisors and student service professionals seek input and endorsement from students, stressing the importance of a strong faculty-staff relationship. Students prefer close relationships, mentoring, and small class size. Students who are involved with faculty and other students are happy, grow academically, and get the most out of college. Students often report that they do not have time for extracurricular activities, because they have to work to support going to college. There is no clear relationship between involvement and grades, but there is a strong correlation between involvement and satisfaction. A feeling of isolation by a student is of greater concern than grades.

PERSONAL AND COMPREHENSIVE CAREER DEVELOPMENT

Career development programs are commonly designed to produce the greatest benefit to students, on the lowest per-person cost basis. Career services are processes that must be thought out before delivery. Though every student cannot expect an entirely unique program, the program must be able to accommodate students with a variety of circumstances, needs, styles, and backgrounds. In their advocacy role, counselors use their skills and influence to work with all members of the institution to achieve objectives and improve career services for the student. In the coordination role, counselors work with internal constituents and external entities, such as employers and community organizations, to assist with job and internship opportunities. In the participation role, counselors personally deliver the counseling services, through assessments, instruction, discussions, and other support. Since counselors are experienced and trained in their role, they also work to design and develop such services.

Several steps are common to designing and implementing a career development program. Student affairs professionals must understand the target population and the characteristics of those being served. The needs of those students must be identified, even if it is only in general terms. Written and measurable objectives should be established to meet needs.

Counselors and other staff members must determine how to deliver the career planning services.

The content of the program must be determined, based on the objectives. Costs must be determined and a budget prepared that can continuously fund the desired program. When the program is ready, it must be promoted in a way that will make students interested in participating. After meeting with initial clients, the full program must be promoted and delivered. Finally, it should be evaluated for improvements and changes along the way.

A systematic and comprehensive career development program requires counselors to operate from well-designed models of service delivery. As students progress, they need services that focus on specific occupational needs. Students begin by exploring options, then crystallizing, specifying a major, and implementing the selected option. At that point they require specialized course selections and job-related opportunities to help them grow. A model may also allow for continual assessment and feedback, to identify changes in students' needs.

Career counseling must go beyond objective assessment. Careers are very personal decisions. Career choices may be intertwined with personality characteristics, personal strengths, and those innate desires that are unique to one individual. Students often report a value on the relationship dimension of the counseling experience. Counselors should not view the student as a problem and the counselor as the solution. This encounter with a student is an opportunity to empower him to take control of his future, with only assistance from the advisor.

Holistic student development incorporates many things, such as personal and social development. Others may employ community projects or activities to bring people together and to allow students to learn more from those around them. Such programming activities must be pertinent to student needs, rather than merely satisfying a university objective that is not directly related to student development. Students need help with degree plans and career exploration.

Often, students ask about course selection and teacher selection, because they do not want to have to drop the class later. They learn these things from interaction with those around them. Holistic student development goes beyond social skills and academics. Students can always use more help in the game of life.

CONCLUSION AND IMPLICATIONS FOR FUTURE RESEARCH

It is important to start with the correct mindset. Students are the boss and the customer, all at the same time. They pay the tuition that pays the faculty and staff. As such, all college services are designed around their needs, as determined by the students. Students are often very intentional in determining what they want at a campus, but they may find instructors, administration, policies, or other hurdles in their way. In their role as consumer, students want to determine the degree plan, course selection, and policies and programs that serve them. It would be productive to delve further into the needs, wants, and desires of students. Students should be asked to air their grievances and concerns. The comparison should be between students' needs with what is being provided to students.

Students have needs beyond just making an *A*. How can the university assist them with career choices and employment connections? For all the increases in tuition, students have a right to expect more from university services and career counseling services. Another area for study is in the area of relationships between students and staff. What do students need from faculty and staff? How can faculty and staff best serve students? The greatest challenge of long-term relationships is probably the matching of students with the appropriate staff, faculty, mentor, advisor, or industry professionals who will coach them and advise them over a long period of time. Success in staff-student relations and in student services is determined by whether or not the needs, wants, and desires of the student have been met. If a person drops out of college or makes a career change, it is not a failure if that action is in the student's best interest. The focus is on the development of the students and their future.

REFERENCES

Career Information System http://career-info.uoregon.edu

Career and College Quest http://www.petersons.com

Career Visions http://www.ccw.wisc.edu

Choices http://www.careerware.com

Computer-Based Career Planning Systems: Dreams and Realities. *The Career Development Quarterly*, 49.

Career exploration as a precursor to career establishment. *The Career Development Quarterly*, 51.

Effective Leadership in Student Services: Frost, S.H. (1991). Academic Advising for Student Success: A system of shared responsibility.

Focus II http://www.focuscareer.com

"Human Resource Development" by Shashi K. Gupta.

Human Resource And Personnel Management by "K. Aswathappa".

http://www.jobtrak.com

http://www.experience.com

http://www.readyminds.com

http://www.careerplanner.com

The Career Development Quarterly, 51. Clement, L.M. and Rickard, S.T. (1992).

10

Electronic Human Resource Management

MONIKA KHANNA AND AARTI

ABSTRACT

One stated purpose of electronic human resource management is to make the entire HRM function more strategic. E-hrm is relatively a new term for this IT supported HRM, especially through the use of web technology. E-HRM technology is a way of aligning and coping with the organization. The employee can also keep track of his/her achievement without having to go through litigious procedure. It uses internet, intranet and other web technology channels. It stores information regarding payroll, employee personal data, performance management, training, recruitment and strategic orientation. Competitive business environment has compelled business to think speedily to innovate and excel for their survival. With the state of IT, hrm has become more effective through the use of e-hrm technologies. The new system have enabled HR professionals to provide better services to all of their stakeholder such as applicants, managers and employees and it can reduce the administrative burden in the field as it is very cost effective.

The keywords used in this study are: E-HRM, information technology, cost effective, employee satisfaction.

INTRODUCTION

It stores information regarding payroll, employee personal data, performance management, training, recruitment and strategic orientation. Information technology has change the way of handling records and information sharing among HR departments. It reduces the paperwork and allows easy access of data. From this base E-HRM has expanded to embrace the delivery of virtually all HR policies. Employees can also use a system of E-HRM to plan their personal development, apply for promotion and new jobs, and access a range of information on HR policies.

Systems of E-HRM are increasingly supported by dedicated software produced by private suppliers. Computers have simplified the task of analyzing vast amount of data and they can be invaluable aids in HR management, from payroll processing to record retention. With computer hardware, software and databases, organizations can keep records and information better as well as retrieve them with greater ease. E-HRM is the new field of technology that is widely spreading in organizations around the world. It aims at transforming the HR function into one, i.e. paperless, more flexible, and resource efficient.

Traditionally, e-hrm studies have concentrated mainly on Europe, and the USA, perhaps due to relatively high adoption rates of E-HRM application in North America and European organizations. More recently, some empirical research has come from Asean and South American countries and Australia and Newzealand. Now the scope of E-HRM has been also increased in India in all organizations. Interestingly, some companies in India estimate indicates that large firms are using 100% internet and 82% intranet.

A 2007 CIPD survey states that "the initial research indicates that much commented on development such as shared services, outsourcing and E-HRM have had relatively little importance on cost or staff members."

Moreover, the adoption of an E-HRM strategy promises to promote employee empowerment, employee satisfaction, retention rates and employee work life balance due to increased transparency and visibility of HR data.

E-HRM is an umbrella term covering all possible mechanism and interactions between human resource management and information technology (IT), aiming at creating value within and across organizations for targeted employees and management. The use of E-HRM has increased greatly over recent years with most large organizations now using technology to some extent in their management of human resource. E-HRM may improve efficiency and facilitate a shift in HR role to a more strategic level. The words e-recruitment, online recruitment, cyber recruiting or internet recruiting are synonymous. They imply formal sourcing of job online. It is a complete process which includes job advertisements, receiving resumes and building human resource database with candidates and incumbents. It is the use of internet to attract high quality candidate, screening of suitable profile, streamlining the applications and selection process.

In the analysis and design of work, employees in geographically dispersed locations can work together in virtual teams using videos, email, etc. under recruitment function, job openings can be posted online and candidates can apply for job online. On compensation and benefits issues, E-HRM will make it easy for employees to review salary and bonus information and seek information about bonus plan.

RESEARCH METHODOLOGY

Research methodology shows the various means of data collection for the present study. The study is carried out by using secondary data i.e the data which have already been collected and analyzed. The present study is done to define E-HRM and to find out how E-HRM will reduce the cost of organizations. To find answers to such questions descriptive research is done. The data of this study were obtained from the secondary sources such as from various websites, journals, and magazines. I tried my best to take the data from various sources. This research paper may requires additional citations for verification.

OBJECTIVE OF THE STUDY

- To know how E-HRM will reduce the cost of an organization.
- To know employee attitude towards E-HRM.
- To know the advantages of E-HRM

REVIEW OF LITERATURE

The focus of this literature review is to summarize and synthesize the arguments and idea of other researcher about E-HRM. In its inception definition, different types or levels, goals, objectives, functions of E-HRM have been illustrated. Further it consists of various types of electronic human resource management with impact on many organizations. In later stage of literature review it deals with how E-HRM is different and more efficient and effective from traditional HRM.

E-HRM

In an organization the most valuable input is human element. The success or failure of an organization depends to a large extent on the person who manages and run the organization. There was a time when manpower was considered as a cost factor but now it is recognized as an investment. E-HR provides information required to manage HR processes. These may be core employee database and payroll system but can be extended to include such system as recruitment, e-learning, e-performance management and reward.

The evaluation of the E-HRM department is based on 6 driving forces. The following six forces must be addressed by HRM departments that want to continuously increase their value while reducing costs. Six driving forces are:

FORCE 1: Information technology
FORCE 2: Processes re-engineering
FORCE 3: High speed management
FORCE 4: Networked organizations
FORCE 5: Knowledge workers
FORCE 6: Globalization

In nutshell all of the aforementioned forces are designed to get rid of outmoded organizational processes, producers, layers and boundaries that add cost and form barriers between hrm department and the company employees. Moreover, all these forces reflect the enormous impact that information technology has and will continue to have on every process and procedure in hrm departments. Successful information of a virtual hrm department will clearly increase a company competitive advantage.

OBJECTIVES OF E-HRM

E-HRM is designed to achieve the following objectives:

- To offer an adequate, comprehensive and on-going information system about people and jobs at a reasonable cost.
- To offer data security and personal privacy.

- To automate employee related information.
- To enable faster response to employee related services and faster HR related decisions.
- Standardization.
- Ease of administering employee records reduction to cost, time and labour.

SCOPE OF E-HRM

- A more dynamic workflow in the business process, productivity and employee satisfaction.
- Significant reduction of administrative burden.
- Higher speed of retrieval and processing of data.
- More transparency in the system.
- Fast response to answer queries.

E-HRM GOALS

The main goals of E-HRM are as follows:

- Improving the strategic orientation of HRM.
- Cost reduction/efficiency gains.
- Clients service improvements/facilitating management and employees.

TYPES OF E-HRM

Lepak and snell (1998) distinguished three areas of HRM as operational E-HRM, relational E-HRM and transformational E-HRM.

1. **OPERATIONAL E-HRM:** E-HRM is concerned with administrative functions like—payroll, employee personal data etc.
2. **RELATIONAL E-HRM:** E-HRM is concerned with supportive business process by means of training, recruitment, performance management etc.
3. **TRANSFORMATIONAL E-HRM:** E-HRM is concerned with strategic HR activities such as—knowledge management, strategic reorientation, etc.

EMPLOYEE ATTITUDE TOWARDS E-HRM IN ITS ORGANIZATIONS

The employee attitude is a management tool to learn about the views and opinions of their employees on issues pertaining to the company and their role within the organization methodology and process to help management understand the different needs of the organization from the perspective of the employees. Survey is conducted to measure employee attitude towards E-HRM. Stratified random sampling technique was used. Data was collected using questionnaires and analyzed using descriptive statistics such percentage and tables.

Employee attitude regarding	*Highly satisfied*	*Satisfied*	*Unsatisfied*	*Total*
Implementation of E-HRM	69%	22%	09%	100%
Faster recruitment process	72%	25%	03%	100%
Improve admin. efficiency and productivity	54%	27%	19%	100%
Highly secured about database	77%	13%	—	100%
Easier communication among various departments	47%	51%	02%	100%
Save times	69%	17%	14%	100%
User-friendly	71%	11%	18%	100%
High speed of receiving and processing of data	87%	12%	01%	100%
Web-based HRM application	77%	23%	—	100%
Improve client service	83%	13%	04%	100%

Source : Survey report conducted by *Asian Journal of Multidisciplinary Studies,* 1(3) in Pune, India on October, 2013.

The table above shown indicates the employee attitude towards electronic human ressouce management. It is observed that more than 50% employees were highly satisfied with the implementation of E-HRM. Only few employees that is 9% were not satisfied with E-HRM. The reason for their dissatisfaction may be lack of knowledge among employees or the unwillingness of the employees towards learning the new techniques due to fear of job insecurity in them. Most of the employees from entire population said that E-HRM is helpful to improve admin efficiency and productivity. More than 75% employees are highly satisfied with secured about database in E-HRM. Maximum employees, i.e. 51% was satisfied with easier communication Among various departments. more than 50% employees said that it helps to save time. Most of employees, i.e. 71% said that it is user friendly. 87% employees were highly satisfied with higher speed of retrieval and processing of data. Most of the employees were highly satisfied with web-based HRM application and improve the client service, i.e. 87% and 83% respectively.

E-HRM TOOLS

Tool 1: E-employee Profile

The e-employee profile web application provides central points of access to the employee contact information and provides a comprehensive employee database solution, simplifying HR management and team building by providing an employee skills, organization chart and even pictures. E-EMPLOYEE profile consists of certification, honor, competency, membership, past work experience, education, job information, service details, calendar, employee locator, employee exception hours.

Tool 2: E-recruitment

In terms of organizations objectives, the primary goal of recruitment process is to attract potential applicants needed to meet the requirement of organizational roles. Thus, organization FIRST started using computer as a recruiting tool by advertising jobs on a bulletin boards service from which respective applicants would contact employers. Then some companies began to take e-applications.

Today the internet has become a primary means of employers to search for job candidates and for applicants to look for job. As many as 100000 recruiting websites are available to employers and job candidates and which to post jobs and review resumes of various types. But the explosive growth of internet recruiting also means the HR professionals can be overwhelmed by the breadth and scope of internet recruiting.

E-RECRUITMENT methods are:

- Job boards
- Professional/career
- Websites
- Employer websites

In March 1997, an Indian company, naukari.com began its first internet portal operation with basic HTML operation. Naukri earns a majority of its revenue by way of subscription fees paid by job seekers. It has seen a gradual rise in its operating margins over the past seven years- from around 38% at the start of 2007 to around 53% as of February 2014.

Tool 3: E-selection

Most employers seem to be embracing internet recruitment with enthusiasm, the penetration of on-line assessment tools such as personality assessment or ability tests has so far been limited. Employers use various sites to recruit their employees from online job search engines such as—Naukari.com and new selection process are keeping tests online by testing their level of knowledge, behavior, and attitude.

Tool 4: E-learning

E-learning refers to any programmed of learning, training or education where electronic devices, applications and processes are used for knowledge creation, management and transfer. E-learning is a team covering a wide set of applications and processes such as web-based learning, computer based learning, virtual class room, digital collaboration. It includes the delivery of the content via internet, intranet, extranet (LAN/WAN), audio-video tape, satellite broadcast, interactive TV, CD-ROM.

Tool 5: E-training

Most companies start to think of online learning primarily as a more efficient way to distribute training inside the organization, making it available "anywhere" reducing DIRECT COST of instructions, printed material, training facilities and also reduce INDIRECT COST of travel time, lodging and travel expenses, workforce downtimes.

Tool 6: E-performance Management System

A web-based appraisal system can be defined as the system which uses the web (internet/intranet) to effectively evaluate the skills, knowledge and the performance of employees. The softwares are available for e-performance management systems are MANAGE to WIN, Training Partner, ONOR, PeopleGoal, Leadership 360, etc.

Survey Result: as per latest article in "The Economic Times" on Sept. 12, 2014, India is a fast growing market and seeing a faster rate of adoption of technology. There is relatively strong adoption of cloud-based technologies in the country, with nearly 83%of Indian companies planning to consider the use of cloud a rate of adoption much faster than in US; the survey covered 55 organizations in India including Indian companies and global MNCs such as—Aditya Birla group, GE, Microsoft, cognizant among others.

Tool 7: E-compensation

During 1980s and early 1990s spreadsheets had been used to manage compensation information of the employees, i.e. for each manager one spreadsheets including its subordinates data which had been static and time consuming.

In 1990s client-server applications replaced. As organizations have started expanding their boundaries, usage of intranet and internet has become vital.

Tool 8: E-leave

It helps to reduce the cost by defining the work force in advance and to review the past data records of employee leave.

Advantages of E-HRM

The E-HRM models are designed for human resource professionals and executives managers who need support to manage the work force, monitor changes and gather information needed in decision-making. At the same time, it enables all employees to participate in the process and keep track of relevant information.

- Collection and store of information regarding the work force, which will act as the basis for strategic decision-making.
- Integral support for management of human resources and all other basic and support processes within the company.
- Prompt insight into reporting and analysis.
- A more dynamic workflow in the business process and productivity and employee satisfaction.
- A decision step towards a paperless office.
- Makes the work to get over fast.

Disadvantages of E-HRM

- Employees and line managers' mindset need to be changed, they have to realize and accept the usefulness of web-based HR tools.
- They generally feel that lack the time space needed to work quietly and thoughtfully with the web-based HR tools and so, if there is no need, they will not do it.

- Guaranteeing the security and confidentiality of input data is an important issue for employees in order that they should feel employees in order that they should feel 'safe' when using HR based tools.

Thus, E-HRM is a web-based tool to automate and support HR processes. The implementation of E-HRM is an opportunity to delegate the data entry to employee. E-HRM facilitates the usage of HR market place and offer more self-service to the employees. E-HRM is advance business solution which provides a complete online support in the management of all processes, activities, data and information required to manage human resource in the modern company. It is an efficient, reliable and easy to use tool, accessible to broad group of different users. E-HRM is a way of implementing HR strategies, policies and practices in the organization through a conscious and directed support of web technology -based channels. It covers all aspects of human resource management like personnel management, education and training, career development, corporate organization, job descriptions hiring process and annual interviews with employees. Therefore, E-HRM is a way of doing HRM in cost effective manner.

References

Goyal, S. (2008), "e-recruitment a growing arena of job portals". *HRM Review.*
K. Aswathappa, 2013, "Human Resource Management".
http://danialarj.wordpress.com,
www.inderscience.com,
www.ukessays.co.uk,
www.books.google.co.in,
www.articles.economictimes.indiatimes.com,
www.indianjournals.com.
www.ajms.co.in
www.ircjournals.org
www.humanresourcesolution.com
www.123oye.com
www.safalniveshak.com
S. foster, 2010,"Making sense of E-HRM".

11

Assessment of the Performance Appraisal Practice Among the Employees in Reliance Communication Limited

A Case Study of Zonal Office, Chandigarh

PROMILA KANWAR AND ANU JASROTIA

ABSTRACT

Performance appraisal is a formal, structured system of measuring and evaluating an employee job, related behaviour and outcomes to discover how and why the employee is presently perfuming on the job and how the employee can perform more effectively in the future so that the employee, organisation, and society all benefit. It is an ongoing process of obtaining, researching, analyzing and recording information about the worth of an employee in the organisation. The main objective of Performance Appraisal is to assess and improve the performance of employees to increase their future potential and value to the organisation. Besides, it provides feedback to the employees about their performance, also identify their training needs and also link rewards with their achievement. The present study is an effort to evaluate the Performance Appraisal System among the employees of

Reliance Communication Limited working in the Chandigarh Zonal Office.

Organizations are run and steered by employees. It is through employees that goals are set and objectives are realized. The performance of an organization is thus dependent upon the sum total of performance of its employees. The success of an organization will therefore depend on its ability to measure accurately the performance of its members and use it objectively to optimize them as a vital resource1 In the highly competitive environment, organizations have to ensure peak performance of their employees continuously in order to compete and survive at the market place effectively.[2] Performance of an individual can be defined as the record of outcomes produced as specified job functions or activities during a specified time period.[3] The term performance refers to a set of outcome produced during a certain period of their job time and does not refer to the traits, personal characteristics, or competencies of the performer. The evaluation of employee's performance reveals the contribution of an individual in attaining the organization's objectives. Employees do not learn unless they are given feedback on the results of their actions. For corrective actions to take place feedback must be provided regularly and it should register both successes and failures of the employees.[4]

WHAT IS PERFORMANCE APPRAISAL?

Appraisals are judgments of the characteristics, traits and performance of others. On the basis of these judgments we assess the worth or value of others and identify what is good or bad. In industry performance appraisal is a systematic evaluation of employees by supervisors. Employees also wish to know their position in the organization. Appraisals are essential for making many administrative decisions: selection, training, promotion, transfer, wage and salary administration, etc. Besides they aid in personnel research.

Performance Appraisal thus is a systematic and objective way of judging the relative worth of ability of an employee in performing his task. Performance appraisal helps to identify those who are performing their assigned tasks well and those who are not and the reasons for such performance.[5]

DEFINITIONS

Dale S. Beach, "Performance appraisal is systematic evaluation of the individual with respect to his or her performance on the job and his or her potential for development".

Randall S. Schuler, "Performance appraisal is a formal,

structured system of measuring and evaluating an employees' job, related behaviour and outcomes to discover how and why the employee is presently perfuming on the job and how the employee can perform more effectively in the future so that the employee, organisation, and society all benefit".

Dale Yoder, "Performance appraisal includes all formal procedures used to evaluate personalities and contributions and potentials of group members in a working organisation. It is a continuous process to secure information necessary for making correct and objective decisions on employees".

HOW OFTEN SHOULD APPRAISAL TAKE PLACE?

Performance appraisal in any organisation will be done at a specific period, like annually or half yearly or quarterly or maybe regularly. It all depends upon the nature or size of the organisation, and sometimes necessity of the managers decide the period of performance appraisal of their employees. Most of organisations are insisting employee's appraisal should be a continuous process and should not be limited to a formal review once a year. Thus, the frequency of formal appraisals will depend on the nature of the organization and on the objectives of the system. For example, in a high technology organisation objectives may be changing quickly so that formal appraisals may need to be carried out more than once a year. In an environment which is less subject to change, annual appraisals may be sufficient. Most employees receive a formal appraisal annually, although more frequent appraisals are often needed for new employees, for longer serving staff who have moved to new posts or for those who are below acceptable performance standards.[6]

OBJECTIVES OF PERFORMANCE APPRAISAL

The main objective of performance appraisals is to measure and improve the performance of employees and increase their future potential and value to the company. Other objectives include providing feedback, improving communication, understanding training needs, clarifying roles and responsibilities and determining how to allocate rewards.

Providing Feedback. Providing feedback is the most common justification for an organization to have a performance appraisal system. Through its performance appraisal process the individual learns exactly how well he/she did during the previous twelve months and can then use that information to improve his/her performance in the future.

Facilitating Promotion Decisions. Performance appraisal makes it easier for the organization to make good decisions about making sure that the most important positions are filled by the most capable individuals.

Facilitating Layoff or Downsizing Decisions. If promotions are what everybody wants, layoffs are what everybody wishes to avoid. But when economic realities force an organization to downsize, performance appraisal helps make sure that the most talented individuals are retained and to identify poor performers who effects the productivity of the organisation.

Encouraging Performance Improvement. A good performance appraisal points out areas where individuals need to improve their performance.

Motivating Superior Performance. Performance appraisal helps motivate people to deliver superior performance in several ways. First, the appraisal process helps them learn just what it is that the organization considers to be "superior." Second, since most people want to be seen as superior performers, a performance appraisal process provides them with a means to demonstrate that they actually are. Finally, performance appraisal encourages employees to avoid being stigmatized as inferior performers (or, often worse, as merely "average").

Setting and Measuring Goals. The performance appraisal process is commonly used to make sure that every member of the organization sets and achieves effective goals.

Counseling Poor Performers. Not everyone meets the organization's standards. Performance appraisal forces managers to confront those whose performance is not meeting the company's expectations.

Determining Compensation Changes. Performance appraisal provides the mechanism to make sure that those who do better work receive more pay.

Encouraging Coaching and Mentoring. Performance appraisal identities the areas where coaching is necessary and encourages managers to take an active coaching role.

Supporting Manpower Planning. Performance appraisal gives companies the tool they need to make sure they have the intellectual horsepower required for the future.

Validating Hiring Decisions. Only when the performance of newly hired individuals is assessed can the company learn whether it is hiring the right people.

Providing Legal Defensibility for Personnel Decisions. A solid record of performance appraisals greatly facilitates legal defensibility when a complaint about discrimination is made.

Improving Overall Organizational Performance. A performance appraisal procedure allows the organization to communicate performance expectations to every member of the team and assess exactly how well each person is doing.

Training Needed: These appraisals also identify the necessary training and development the employee needs to close the gap between current performance and desired performance.[7]

METHODS OF PERFORMANCE APPRAISAL

Numerous methods have been devised to measure the quantity and quality of performance appraisals. Each of the methods is effective for some purposes for some organizations only. None should be dismissed or accepted as appropriate except as they relate to the particular needs of the organization or an employee.

Broadly all methods of appraisals can be divided into two different categories.

- Past Oriented Methods
- Future Oriented Methods

Past Oriented Methods

1. **Rating Scales:** Rating scales consists of several numerical scales representing job related performance criterions such as dependability, initiative, output, attendance, attitude etc. Each scales ranges from excellent to poor. The total numerical scores are computed and final conclusions are derived. Advantages—Adaptability, easy to use, low cost, every type of job can be evaluated, large number of employees covered, no formal training required. Disadvantages—Rater's biases
2. **Checklist:** Under this method, checklist of statements of traits of employee in the form of Yes or No based questions is prepared. Here the rater only does the reporting or checking and HR department does the actual evaluation. Advantages—economy, ease of administration, limited training required, standardization. Disadvantages—

Raters biases, use of improper weighs by HR, does not allow rater to give relative ratings

3. **Forced Choice Method:** The series of statements arranged in the blocks of two or more are given and the rater indicates which statement is true or false. The rater is forced to make a choice. HR department does actual assessment. Advantages—Absence of personal biases because of forced choice. Disadvantages—Statements may be wrongly framed.
4. **Forced Distribution Method:** Here employees are clustered around a high point on a rating scale. Rater is compelled to distribute the employees on all points on the scale. It is assumed that the performance is conformed to normal distribution. Advantages—Eliminates, Disadvantages—Assumption of normal distribution, unrealistic, errors of central tendency.
5. **Critical Incidents Method:** The approach is focused on certain critical behaviors of employee that makes all the difference in the performance. Supervisors as and when they occur record such incidents. Advantages—Evaluations are based on actual job behaviors, ratings are supported by descriptions, feedback is easy, reduces recency biases, chances of subordinate improvement are high. Disadvantages—Negative incidents can be prioritized, forgetting incidents, overly close supervision; feedback may be too much and may appear to be punishment.
6. **Behaviorally Anchored Rating Scales:** Statements of effective and ineffective behaviors determine the points. They are said to be behaviorally anchored. The rater is supposed to say, which behavior describes the employee performance. Advantages—Helps overcome rating errors. Disadvantages—Suffers from distortions inherent in most rating techniques.
7. **Field Review Method:** This is an appraisal done by someone outside employees' own department usually from corporate or HR department. Advantages—Useful for managerial level promotions, when comparable information is needed. Disadvantages—Outsider is generally not familiar with employees work environment, Observation of actual behaviors not possible.

8. **Performance Tests and Observations:** This is based on the test of knowledge or skills. The tests may be written or an actual presentation of skills. Tests must be reliable and validated to be useful. Advantage—Tests may be apt to measure potential more than actual performance. Disadvantages—Tests may suffer if costs of test development or administration are high.
9. **Confidential Records:** Mostly used by government departments, however its application in industry is not ruled out. Here the report is given in the form of Annual Confidentiality Report (ACR) and may record ratings with respect to following items; attendance, self expression, team work, leadership, initiative, technical ability, reasoning ability, originality and resourcefulness, etc. The system is highly secretive and confidential. Feedback to the assessee is given only in case of an adverse entry. Disadvantage is that it is highly subjective and ratings can be manipulated because the evaluations are linked to HR actions like promotions, etc.
10. **Essay Method:** In this method the rater writes down the employee description in detail within a number of broad categories like, overall impression of performance, promoteability of employee, existing capabilities and qualifications of performing jobs, strengths and weaknesses and training needs of the employee. Advantage—It is extremely useful in filing information gaps about the employees that often occur in a better-structured checklist. Disadvantages—It is highly dependent upon the writing skills of rater and most of them are not good writers. They may get confused success depends on the memory power of raters.
11. **Cost Accounting Method:** Here performance is evaluated from the monetary returns yields to his or her organization. Cost to keep employee, and benefit the organization derives is ascertained. Hence, it is more dependent upon cost and benefit analysis.
12. **Comparative Evaluation Method (Ranking & Paired Comparisons):** These are collection of different methods that compare performance with that of other co-workers. The usual techniques used may be ranking methods and paired comparison method.

- **Ranking Methods:** Superior ranks his worker based on merit, from best to worst. However, how best and why best are not elaborated in this method. It is easy to administer and explanation.
- **Paired Comparison Methods:** In this method each employee is rated with another employee in the form of pairs. The number of comparisons may be calculated with the help of a formula as under.

FUTURE ORIENTED METHODS

1. **Management By Objectives:** It means management by objectives and the performance is rated against the achievement of objectives stated by the management. MBO process goes as under:

- Establish goals and desired outcomes for each subordinate
- Setting performance standards
- Comparison of actual goals with goals attained by the employee
- Establish new goals and new strategies for goals not achieved in previous year.

Advantages—It is more useful for managerial positions.

Disadvantages—Not applicable to all jobs, allocation of merit pay may result in setting short-term goals rather than important and long-term goals, etc.

2. **Psychological Appraisals:** These appraisals are more directed to assess employees potential for future performance rather than the past one. It is done in the form of in-depth interviews, psychological tests, and discussion with supervisors and review of other evaluations. It is more focused on employees emotional, intellectual, and motivational and other personal characteristics affecting his performance. This approach is slow and costly and may be useful for bright young members who may have considerable potential. However, quality of these appraisals largely depend upon the skills of psychologists who perform the evaluation.

3. **Assessment Centers:** This technique was first developed in USA and UK in 1943. An assessment center is a central location where managers may come together to have their participation in job related exercises evaluated by trained observers. It is more focused on observation of behaviors across a series of select exercises or work samples. Assessees are requested to participate in in-basket exercises,

work groups, computer simulations, role playing and other similar activities which require same attributes for successful performance in actual job. The characteristics assessed in assessment center can be assertiveness, persuasive ability, communicating ability, planning and organizational ability, self confidence, resistance to stress, energy level, decision making, sensitivity to feelings, administrative ability, creativity and mental alertness etc. Disadvantages—Costs of employees traveling and lodging, psychologists, ratings strongly influenced by assessee's inter-personal skills. Solid performers may feel suffocated in simulated situations. Those who are not selected for this also may get affected.

Advantages—Well-conducted assessment center can achieve better forecasts of future performance and progress than other methods of appraisals. Also reliability, content validity and predictive ability are said to be high in assessment centers. The tests also make sure that the wrong people are not hired or promoted. Finally, it clearly defines the criteria for selection and promotion.

4. **360-Degree Feedback:** It is a technique which is systematic collection of performance data on an individual group, derived from a number of stakeholders like immediate supervisors, team members, customers, peers and self. In fact anyone who has useful information on how an employee does a job may be one of the appraisers. This technique is highly useful in terms of broader perspective, greater self-development and multi-source feedback is useful. 360-degree appraisals are useful to measure inter-personal skills, customer satisfaction and team building skills. However on the negative side, receiving feedback from multiple sources can be intimidating, threatening, etc. Multiple raters may be less adept at providing balanced and objective feedback.[8]

Objectives

The objective of the study is (a) assess the performance appraisal system of the employees of Reliance Communication Limited working in the Chandigarh Zonal Office.

Research Methodology

The present study relates to the HRD practices followed by the Bharti Airtel. For the purpose of the study both primary and secondary data was used. Out of the total 250 employees from Sales department, a sample of 45 respondents was taken as primary data on the basis of convenience sampling. Secondary data was collected from the records available at Zonal Offices and Head Office, which included Service Manuals, Annual Reports, Policy Guidelines, Books, Magazines, Journals and other Publications of the Company. Therefore, on the basis of the sample, Interview Schedules were prepared for the respondents. The collected data was analyzed and the findings were tabulated and interpreted.

In the background of these aspects of employee appraisal the following queries were put to the employees of Reliance Communication Limited.

Analysis of the Statements

Sl. No.	*Statement*	*Agree*	*Disagree*	*Undecided*
	(1)	*(2)*	*(3)*	*(4)*
1.	Performance Appraisal provides an opportunity to the employees for self review	6 (13%)	39 (87%)	0 (0%)
2.	Appraising your own performance would enhance your awareness of your performance	0 (0%)	45 (100%)	0 (0%)
3.	You think the parameters used to evaluate performance appraisal are relevant	12 (27%)	33 (73%)	0 (0%)
4.	Promotion of the employees is based on his/her performance appraisal report	6 (13%)	39 (87%)	0 (0%)
5.	Performance Appraisal is done impartially in the organization	0 (0%)	38 (84%)	7 (16%)
6.	Performance Appraisal acts as a tool of control in the organization	0 (0%)	31 (69%)	14 (31%)
7.	The performance appraisal process results in better communication between employee and immediate supervisor	0 (0%)	45 (100%)	0 (0%)
8.	Before an employee is asked to perform a job, he is apprised of Key responsibility areas	19 (42%)	26 (58%)	0 (0%)
9.	If you have problem with your performance evaluation you can communicate your concerns openly to your supervisor	6 (13%)	39 (87%)	0 (0%)
10.	You receive regular and timely performance feedback besides the annual performance review	0 (0%)	45 (100%)	0 (0%)

(Contd.)

(Contd.)

	(1)	*(2)*	*(3)*	*(4)*
11.	The Performance feedback you receive is helpful in improving your on the job performance and in attaining your goals	0 (0%)	45 (100%)	0 (0%)
12.	There is clear, direct and compelling linkages between performance and pay package offered	0 (0%)	45 (100%)	0 (0%)
13.	The immediate supervisor take the process of Performance Appraisal seriously	6 (13%)	39 (87%)	0 (0%)
14.	The method of Performance Appraisal in the organization is to your satisfaction	0 (0%)	45 (100%)	0 (0%)
15.	Performance Appraisal system provide you opportunity for professional development	0 (0%)	45 (100%)	0 (0%)

Source : Computed from primary data.

Data Analysis

After analyzing the data, it was found that significant majority (87 per cent) of the respondents stated that Performance Appraisal did not provided an opportunity to them for self review whereas very small proportion of them viewed that performance appraisal provided to them opportunity for self assessment.

Further, it was found that cent per cent of the respondents did not agree that Appraising their own performance would enhance their awareness of their performance as they did not got opportunity to evaluate their strength and weakness.

Further, on asking that the parameters used to evaluate performance appraisal are relevant, it was established that high majority of the respondents (73 per cent) did not agree that the parameters used to evaluate performance appraisal were relevant. However, marginal proportion of the respondents (27 per cent) agreed that the parameters used to evaluate performance appraisal were relevant.

On assessing the aspect that Promotion of the employees is based on his/her performance appraisal report, significant majority of the respondents (87 per cent) did not agree that Promotion of the employees was based on his/her performance appraisal report, whereas small proportion of the respondents (13 per cent) agreed that

Promotion of the employees was based on their performance appraisal report.

On exploring whether the Performance Appraisal was done impartially in the organization, it was found that none of the respondent agreed that performance appraisal was done impartially in the organization reflecting that Performance Appraisal was biased.

On analyzing the responses related to the aspect that Performance Appraisal acted as a tool of control in the organization, it was found that majority (69 per cent) of the respondents did not agree that Performance Appraisal acted as a tool of control in the organization whereas some of the respondents (31 per cent) remained undecided with the statement indicating their reservation.

On assessing the data, it was found that none of the respondent agreed that the performance appraisal process resulted in better communication between employees and the management.

On examing the data, it was found that majority of the respondents (58 per cent) did not agree that key responsibility areas were assigned to them before they were asked to perform any job. However, noticeable proportion of the respondents (42 per cent) were of the view that Key responsibility areas were assigned to them before they were asked to perform any job.

On asking the employees, if they had problem with their performance evaluation they could communicate their concerns openly to their supervisor, the higher proportion (87 per cent) of the respondents did not agree with the statement whereas very few respondents (13 per cent) agreed with the statement.

On assessing the aspect that they received regular and timely performance feedback besides the annual performance review, all the respondents did not agree with the statement.

Further, it was found that all the respondents did not agree that the Performance feedback they received was helpful in improving their on the job performance and in attaining their goals.

All the respondents did not agree that there was a clear, direct and compelling linkage between performance and pay package offered.

On analyzing the issue that the immediate supervisor took the process of Performance Appraisal seriously, it was observed that significant majority of the respondents (87 per cent) did not agree that supervisor took it seriously.

To the poser that the method of Performance Appraisal in the organization was to their satisfaction, it was found that all the respondents were not satisfied with the method of Performance Appraisal of the Company.

On analyzing the responses that Performance Appraisal system provided them opportunity for professional development, it was found that all of the respondents did not agree that Performance Appraisal provided them opportunity for the professional growth.

FINDINGS OF THE STUDY

1. Performance Appraisal did not provided an opportunity to the employee for self review.
2. Performance appraisal did not provided an opportunity to the employees to enhance their awareness about their performance as they could evaluate their own strength and weakness.
3. Majority of the employees did not agree that the parameters used to evaluate performance appraisal were relevant.
4. Majority of the respondent did not agree that Promotion of the employees was based on the performance appraisal report.
5. All the employees disagreed that Performance Appraisal was done impartially in the organization.
6. Majority of the respondent disagreed that Performance Appraisal system acted as a tool of control in the organization.
7. None of the respondent agreed that performance appraisal system resulted in better communication between employee and immediate supervisor.
8. Majority of the respondents disagreed that they were apprised of Key responsibility areas of the job before being asked to perform the job.
9. Majority of the employees did not agree that performance evaluation system helped the employees to communicate their concerns openly to their supervisor.
10. All the respondents disagreed that they received regular and timely performance feedback besides the annual performance review.
11. Majority of the respondents did not receive any performance feedback in improving their on-the-job performance and in attaining their goals.
12. Majority of the respondents disagreed that there was a

clear, direct and compelling linkage between performance and pay package.

13. All the respondents were of the view that the method of Performance Appraisal in the organization was not up to their satisfaction.
14. The performance appraisal system did not provide opportunity for the professional development of the employees.

SUMMARY AND SUGGESTIONS

The performance appraisal practices followed in the Reliance Communicationl Limited have been examined with the help of responses. The employees of the Reliance Communication Limited were assessed for their performance with the help of performance appraisal reports to be filled by the employees or the immediate supervising authority. It has been observed that the organization is not performing well so there were some areas which needed to be looked after. In the light of the discussion, it is suggested that:

1. The practice of Performance Appraisal System should be transparent.
2. Use formal appraisals annually or twice a year, alongside informal appraisals and feedback sessions throughout the year.
3. Involve employees in the process of evaluation.

To conclude, it was found that the employees of the Reliance Zonal office, Chandigarh were not satisfied with the performance appraisal practices followed by the company.

NOTES AND REFERENCES

1. B. Pattanayak, Human Resource Management (PHI Learning Private Limited, 2009).
2. L.M. Prasad, Human Resource Management (Sultan Chand & Sons: Educational Publishers, 2006).
3. H. John Bernardin, Human Resource Management (Tata McGraw-Hill Publishing Company Limited, 2007).
4. B. Pattanayak, Human Resource Management (PHI Learning Private Limited, 2009).
5. L.M. Prasad, Human Resource Management (Sultan Chand & Sons: Educational Publishers, 2006).
6. http://www.whatishumanresource.com/performance-appraisal
7. http://www.whatishumanresource.com/objectives-of-performance-appraisal
8. http://corehr.wordpress.com/performance-management/performance-appraisal methods/

12

Effect of Pay and Promotional Factors on Job Satisfaction of Insurance Personnel

A Study of New India Insurance Company Limited

GAYTRI

ABSTRACT

In the text of human resource the term 'job satisfaction' is very commonly used for individuals' attitude towards the specific aspects of total work situation. Since the time when the occupation of individuals became a socially significant phenomenon, social scientists focused their attention on the problem of job satisfaction. Even from early days social scientists like Blum stressed out the significance of studying job satisfaction of workers in an industrial atmosphere. Job is not the only means of satisfying the employees' needs, but employees' spend nearly half of their life at work. To the society as a whole plus, from an individual employee viewpoint job satisfaction is a desirable outcome. Job satisfaction has been described as an output of a work environment. An attempt is made in this study to identify the levels of employee job satisfaction in NIACL-based on the selected parameters. Around twenty five per cent of the employees in Haryana were selected based on stratified random sampling and the collected data was analyzed using Mean, Standard Deviation, F-tests and t-tests. Among the selected parameters, salary and allowances and promotion and organizational policies emerged as important factors for job satisfaction. Employees are satisfied with the basis of promotion, pay scales and their fairness, openness of organizational structure and organizational policies and employees were found with the favorable attitude for their job and organization.

Keywords : Job, job satisfaction, work environment, promotion, organizational policies.

INTRODUCTION

Today, Organisations that are able to acquire, build-up, motivate and keep outstanding workers, will be both effective and efficient as human assets but probably the most critical and difficult to manage. Human Resources are the only active resources at the disposal of every organisation and the effective use of all other resources directly depends on efficient utilization of these resources. Rensis Likert rightly observes, "all the activities of any enterprises are initiated and determined by the people who make up the institutions, plants, offices, computers, automated equipments and all else that modern firm uses are unproductive except for human efforts and directions. Human beings devise or order the equipment, they modernize the technology employed, they secure the capital needed and decide on the accounting and physical procedures to be used. Every aspect of organisational activities is determined by the competence, motivation and general effectiveness of its human organisation.[1]

Any organisation that wants to be dynamic and growth-oriented or to succeed in fast changing environment needs human resource management. Organisations can become dynamic and grow only through the efforts and expertise of their human resources. Personnel policies can keep the morale and motivation of employees high, but these efforts are not enough to make the organisation dynamic and take it to new directions.[2] Organisation climate and philosophy is not enough to yield the desired results. Planned efforts should be made to develop human skills in managers at all levels helping them to adopt a more balanced approach towards human resource.[3]

Moreover, every large public and private sector enterprise in India is using the techniques of human resource management to develop their employees for the accomplishment of organisational goals with individual satisfaction and growth. Present day workforce is better educated, possesses greater skills, has more sophisticated technology for its use and enjoys higher standards of living than the earlier ones.[4] Thus, it becomes quite clear that the human resource management has acquired the status of an indispensable ingredient of public administration.

JOB SATISFACTION

Concept of Job satisfaction has attracted the concentration of researchers and managers as most well known, frequently measured, and extensively researched work attitude. Job satisfaction means the overall approach of employees towards their jobs. Job satisfaction is a pleasurable or positive emotional state resulting from the appraisal of one's job or job experience.[5] If the attitude of employee towards his/her job is positive, it reflects job satisfaction. Negative attitude reflects dissatisfaction. Job satisfaction often is a collection of attitudes about specific factors of the job. Employees can be satisfied with some elements of the job while simultaneously dissatisfied with others.[6] Lawler has pointed out that drug abuse, alcoholism and mental and physical health results from psychological harmful jobs.[7]

LITERATURE REVIEW

G. Balachandar, Dr. N. Panchanatham and Dr. K. Subramanian (2010) study the impact of job situation factor on the motivation of insurance company officers. For this research work, private, government owned life Insurance and general insurance company officers are the respondents. Motivation results in commitment and dedication on the part of the officers in their duty. It results in the accomplishment of the organizational objectives at the appropriate time.[8]

S.R. Padala (2010) tried to identify the various parameters for employee job satisfaction in Electronics Corporation of India Ltd., (ECIL) Hyderabad, to examine the relationship between employees' socio-economic character and the motivating parameters, and to measure the level of employees' job satisfaction in the ECIL based on the selected parameters. Salary and allowances and promotion emerged as important factors for job satisfaction. The study also revealed that younger workers have greater job satisfaction than older ones.[9]

Ajay Solkhe, Dr. Nirmala Chaudhary (2011) attempts to analyse and determine the relationship, further the impact of HRD

Climate, OCTAPACE Culture on Job Satisfaction as an Organizational Performance measure in the selected public sector enterprise. The study is based on the responses sought from 71 executives from various departments and different hierarchical levels of a public sector undertaking located in North India. The findings indicate that HRD Climate has a definite impact on Job Satisfaction which in turn leads to the increased organizational performance.[10]

INFERENCES DRAWN FROM REVIEW OF LITERATURE

All these related studies provide the notion that job satisfaction affects the overall behavior of the employees at their work place covering the issues related to performance, accidents occurrence, absenteeism, turnover etc. Insurance is a service provider sector absorbing large number of employees. The quality of service provided will largely depend on the fact how satisfied the employees are? Nowadays, Globalization and Liberalization have compelled the organizations to function in a cut-throat competitive business environment. And thus, to survive in such an environment every business needs to possess the best and most productive resources. Job satisfaction in the area of human resource management particularly in Insurance industry remained a neglected area from research point of view. Further it can be seen that with the opening up of insurance industry and globalization of economies of world every sector is growing and to find competitive edge. Insurance industry has to search for its strengths and weakness and concentrate on improving the satisfaction level of Human Resources which are now considered to be an asset for a company and the success of any company depends on strength of its satisfied manpower. The present study will analyse job satisfaction levels prevailing in NIACL.

Objectives

- To evaluate the job satisfaction among the employees of NIACL in relation to pay factor.
- To assess the job satisfaction among the employees of NIACL in relation to promotion factor.

Research Methodology

The present study has been designed to examine the degree of job satisfaction of public sector insurance companies in India. The study is mainly related to NIACL insurance industry. The locale of the study was offices in Haryana State.

Descriptive research design was applied for investigation of the research problem. For the purpose of the study both primary and secondary data were used. Primary data was collected from the 53 employees of NIACL of the RO's of Haryana region. Sample of the 25% of employees of the company at Haryana State level, drawn on the basis of stratified random sampling technique. While drawing the sample, care was taken that all the levels of officers get adequate representation. The primary data was collected by administering an interview schedule which included the different queries relating to the selected parameters of the study. Employees of Divisional and Branch offices were also included in the above samples.

Job satisfaction is one of the important factors, which had drawn attention of the managers in the organization. Various studies related to find out the factors responsible for and effects of Job satisfaction. A satisfied employee may not necessarily lead to increased productivity but a dissatisfied employee may lead to lower productivity. Therefore, managers should take concrete steps to improve the level of satisfaction. These steps may be in the form of job redesigning to make the job more interesting and challenging, improving quality of work life, linking rewards with performance, and improving overall organizational climate. In this perspective the query was made from the employees in NIACL regarding their level of satisfaction and the responses are as follows:

TABLE 1

Both Merit and Seniority Basis are Used for Promotion

Attributes/ Responses	*Ranks*	*Agree*	*Undecided*	*Disagree*	*p*
Class	Class 1	23 (92.0)	0 0.0	2 (8.0)	0.227
	Class 2	39 (86.7)	1 (2.2)	5 (11.1)	
	Class 3	12 (80.0)	2 (13.3)	1 (6.7)	
Age at present	30-40 years	7 (100.0)	0 0.0	0 0.0	0.398
	40-50 years	35 (83.3)	3 (7.1)	4 (9.5)	
	50-60 years	32 (88.9)	0 0.0	4 (11.1)	

Gender	Male	60 (87.0)	3 (4.3)	6 (8.7)	0.639
	Female	14 (87.5)	0 0.0	2 (12.5)	
Educational Qualifications at present	Graduate	48 (88.9)	3 (5.6)	3 (5.6)	0.429
	Post graduate	21 (80.8)	0 0.0	5 (19.2)	
	M.Phil.	4 (100.0)	0 0.0	0 0.0	
	Ph.D.	1 (100.0)	0 0.0	0 0.0	

Source : Computed from primary data. Figures in parentheses are percentages. p value significant at 0.05 level.

Table 1 (a)
Pearson's Correlation between the Variables

		Value	*Asymp. Std. Error(a)*	*Approx. T(b)*	*Approx. Sig.*
Interval by Interval	Pearson's R	0.065	0.101	0.591	0.556(c)
		0.048	0.090	0.434	0.666(c)
		0.021	0.117	0.193	0.847(c)
		0.053	0.090	0.482	0.631(c)

Source : Computed from Primary Data.

Table 1: The data demonstrated in the Table 1 examines the aspect that both merit and seniority basis are used for promotion and on analyzing the data it was established that significant majority of employees provided the assent to the issue.

Class: On segregating the data on the basis of class it was found that significant majority of employees (92 per cent) in class 1 as compared to significant majority of employees (above 80 percent) in class 2 and class 3 agreed with the issue.

Association: Statistically no significant association was found between the variable of class and the query.

Age: On classifying the data on the basis of age it was established that absolute majority of employees (100 per cent) in the age group of 30-40 years in comparison to significant majority of employees (above 83 per cent) in the age group of 40-60 years provided the positive responses to the poser.

Association: Statistically no significant association was found between the variable of age and the query.

Gender: Analyzing the responses on the basis of gender it was ascertained that significant majority of employees (Above 87 per cent) irrespective of their gender favored the issue.

Association: Statistically no significant association was found between the variable of gender and the query.

Educational Qualifications: Categorizing the data on the basis of variable of Educational Qualifications it was found that absolute majority of employees (100 per cent) with M.Phil. and Ph.D. qualification while significant majority of (above 80 per cent) graduate and post graduate employees favored the point of view.

Association: Statistically no significant association was found between the variable of Educational Qualifications and the statement under analysis.

The coefficient of correlation as represented by R is presented in Table 1(a) indicates that the correlation is positive between the variable and the response of the employees and from the value of coefficient it can be seen that the variable of class, age and educational qualifications represented with low relationship with the responses of the employees. The remaining variable gender however, demonstrated the relationship of significant level.

TABLE 2

Pay System of My Organization is Simple and Fair

Attributes/ Responses	*Ranks*	*Agree*	*Undecided*	*Disagree*	*p*
Class	Class 1	21 (84.0)	1 (4.0)	3 (12.0)	0.447
	Class 2	37 (82.2)	2 (4.4)	6 (13.3)	
	Class 3	13 (86.7)	2 (13.3)	0 0.0	
Age at present	30-40 years	7 (100.0)	0 0.0	0 0.0	0.744
	40-50 years	35 (83.3)	3 (7.1)	4 (9.5)	
	50-60 years	29 (80.6)	2 (5.6)	5 (13.9)	
Gender	Male	57 (82.6)	4 (5.8)	8 (11.6)	0.822

	Female		14	1	1
		(87.5)	(6.3)	(6.3)	
Educational Qualifications at present	Graduate	46	4	4	0.335
		(85.2)	(7.4)	(7.4)	
	Post graduate	22	0	4	
		(84.6)	0.0	(15.4)	
	M.Phil.	2	1	1	
		(50.0)	(25.0)	(25.0)	
	Ph.D.	1	0	0	
		(100.0)	0.0	0.0	

Source : Computed from primary data. Figures in parentheses are percentages. p value significant at 0.05 level.

TABLE 2(a)
Pearson's Correlation between the Variables

		Value	*Asymp. Std. Error(a)*	*Approx. T(b)*	*Approx. Sig.*
Interval by Interval	Pearson's R	-0.062	0.089	-0.570	0570(c)
		0.122	0.090	1.124	0.264(c)
		-0.063	0.093	-0.571	0.570(c)
		0.114	0.115	1.050	0.297(c)

Source : Computed from Primary Data.

On analyzing the data highlighted in the Table 2 it was found that significant majority of employees agreed with the view point that Pay system of their organization is simple and fair.

Class: Analyzing the responses on the basis of the class variable it was established that significant majority of employees (above 82.00 per cent) irrespective of their class supported the view point.

Association: Statistically no significant association was found between the variable of class and the statement.

Age: On classifying the data on the basis of age it was inferred that absolute majority of employees (100.00 percent) in the age group of 30-40 years as against the significant majority of employees (above 80.00 percent) in the age group of 40-60 years agreed with the issue.

Association: Statistically no significant association was found between the variable of age and the query.

Gender: Categorizing the data on the basis of gender variable it was inferred that significant majority of female employees (87.50 per cent) in comparison to the significant majority of male employees (82.60 per cent) agreed the aspect.

Association: No significant association was found between the variable of gender and the statement.

Educational Qualifications: On segregating the data on the basis of variable of educational qualifications it was inferred that absolute majority of employees (100.00 per cent) with PhD qualification, significant majority of graduate employees and postgraduate employees (above 84.00 per cent)while near majority of M Phil employees (50.00 per cent) endorsed the point of view.

Association: Statistically no significant association was found between the variable of Educational Qualifications and the statement.

The coefficient of correlation as presented in Table 2(a) indicates that the correlation is positive between the variable and the response of the employees but from deep analysis of the value of coefficient it can be seen that the variable of class and gender had demonstrated moderate relationship, variable of age and educational qualification represented low relationship with the responses of the employees.

TABLE 3

Pay System of my Organization is in Line with my Expectations

Attributes/ Responses	*Ranks*	*Agree*	*Undecided*	*Disagree*	*p*
Class	Class 1	18 (72.0)	0 0.0	7 (28.0)	0.018
	Class 2	32 (71.1)	0 0.0	13 (28.9)	
	Class 3	12 (80.0)	2 (13.3)	1 (6.7)	
Age at present	30-40 years	6 (85.7)	0 0.0	1 (14.3)	0.616
	40-50 years	29 (69.0)	2 (4.8)	11 (26.2)	
	50-60 years	27 (75.0)	0 0.0	9 (25.0)	
Gender	Male	51 (73.9)	2 (2.9)	16 (23.2)	0.653

	Female	11 (68.8)	0 0.0	5 (31.3)	
Educational Qualifications at present	Graduate	42 (77.8)	2 (3.7)	10 (18.5)	0.326
	Post Graduate	18 (69.2)	0 0.0	8 (30.8)	
	M.Phil.	2 (50.0)	0 0.0	2 (50.0)	
	Ph.D.	0 0.0	0 0.0	1 (100.0)	

Source : Computed from primary data. Figures in parentheses are percentages. p value significant at 0.05 level.

TABLE 3(a)
Pearson's Correlation between the Variables

		Value	*Asymp. Std. Error(a)*	*Approx. T(b)*	*Approx. Sig.*
Interval by Interval	Pearson's R	-0.097	0.096	-0.891	0.375(c)
		0.022	0.103	0.197	0.844(c)
		0.060	0.115	0.547	0.586(c)
		0.231	0.116	2.162	0.033(c)

Source : Computed from Primary Data.

Table 3: The data demonstrated in the Table 3 regarding the aspect that and on analyzing the data it was found that fair majority of employees provided the assent to the issue.

Class: On segregating the data on the basis of class it was ascertained that significant majority of employees (80 percent) in class 3 as compared to high majority of employees (above 71 per cent) in class 1 and class 2 agreed to the statement.

Association: Statistically significant association was found between the variable of class and the query.

Age: On classifying the data on the basis of age it was established that significant majority of employees (85.70 per cent) in the age group of 30-40 years, the high majority of employees (75 per cent) in the age group of 50-60 years in comparison to fair majority of employees (69 per cent) in the age group of 40-50 years provided the positive responses to the poser.

Association: Statistically no significant association was found between the variable of age and the query.

Gender: Analyzing the responses on the basis of gender it was ascertained that high majority of male employees (73.90 per cent) and fair majority of female employees (68.80 percent) favoured the issue.

Association: Statistically no significant association was found between the variable of gender and the query.

Educational Qualifications: Categorizing the data on the basis of variable of Educational Qualifications it was found that high majority of (77.80 per cent) graduate employees, fair majority of post-graduate employee (69.20 per cent) and high proportion of employees (50 per cent) with M. Phil. went along with the point of view.

Association: Statistically no significant association was found between the variable of Educational Qualifications and the statement under analysis.

The coefficient of correlation as represented by R is presented in Table 3(a) clearly indicates that the correlation is positive between the variable and the response of the employees and from the value of coefficient it can be seen that the variable of class and Educational Qualifications sustained a low relationship with the responses of the employees. The variable of class demonstrated the relationship of highly significant relationship. However, the variable of age had shown moderate relationship with the responses of the employees.

TABLE 4

Promotion Leads to Considerable Increase in Authority and Responsibility

Attributes/ Responses	*Ranks*	*Agree*	*Undecided*	*Disagree*	*p*
Class	Class 1	20 (80.0)	2 (8.0)	3 (12.0)	0.951
	Class 2	36 (80.0)	3 (6.7)	6 (13.3)	
	Class 3	11 (73.3)	2 (13.3)	2 (13.3)	
Age at present	30-40 years	7 (100.0)	0 0.0	0 0.0	0.306
	40-50 years	35 (83.3)	2 (4.8)	5 (11.9)	

	50-60 years	25 (69.4)	5 (13.9)	6 (16.7)	
Gender	Male	53 (76.8)	5 (7.2)	11 (15.9)	0.205
	Female	14 (87.5)	2 (12.5)	0 0.0	
Educational Qualifications at present	Graduate	43 (79.6)	3 (5.6)	8 (14.8)	0.033
	Post graduate	21 (80.8)	2 (7.7)	3 (11.5)	
	M. Phil.	3 (75.0)	1 (25.0)	0 0.0	
	PhD.	0 0.0	1 (100.0)	0 0.0	

Source : Computed from primary data. Figures in parentheses are percentages. p value significant at 0.05 level.

TABLE 4(a)

Pearson's Correlation between the Variables

		Value	*Asymp. Std. Error(a)*	*Approx. T(b)*	*Approx. Sig.*
Interval by Interval	Pearson's R	0.035	0.108	0.322	0.748(c)
		0.193	0.089	1.788	0.077(c)
		-0.150	0.062	-1.379	0.172(c)
		0.010	0.098	0.091	0.928(c)

Source : Computed from Primary Data.

The data projected in the Table 4 relates to the query that whether promotion leads to considerable increase in authority and responsibility, it was found that high majority of employees agreed with the view point.

Class: Exploring the responses on the basis of the class variable it was established that significant majority of employees (above 80 per cent) in Class 1 and Class 2 as against high majority of employees (73.30 per cent) in class 3 acknowledged the statement.

Association: Statistically no significant association was found between the variable of class and the statement.

Age: On classifying the data on the basis of age it was inferred that absolute majority of employees (100 per cent) in the age group of 30-50 years, significant majority of employees (83.30 percent) in the age group of 40-50 years as against the fair majority of employees (69.40 percent) in the age group of 50-60 year fairly agreed with the issue.

Association: Statistically no significant association was found between the variable of age and the query.

Gender: Categorizing the data on the basis of gender variable it was inferred that significant majority of female employees (87.50 per cent) in comparison to the high majority of male employees (76.80 per cent) endorse the aspect.

Association: No significant association was found between the variable of gender and the statement.

Educational Qualifications: On assessing the data on the basis of variable of Educational Qualifications it was inferred that Significant majority of post graduate employees (80.80 per cent), in contrast to M. Phil. employees and graduate employees (above 75 per cent) gave support to the view. Single employee with Ph.D. remained undecided about the issue.

Association: Statistically significant association was found between the variable of Educational Qualifications and the statement.

The coefficient of correlation as presented in Table 4(a) indicates that the correlation is positive between the variable and the response of the employees but from deep analysis of the value of coefficient it can be seen that the variable of age and gender and educational qualification had demonstrated low relationship with the responses of the employees. The variable of educational qualification had shown significant, the variable of class had shown highly significant relationship with the responses of the employees.

TABLE 5

Promotion in my Organization Leads to Higher Salary, more Freedom and Less Supervision

Attributes/ Responses	*Ranks*	*Agree*	*Undecided*	*Disagree*	*p*
Class	Class 1	17 (68.0)	1 (4.0)	7 (28.0)	0.228
	Class 2	36 (80.0)	1 (2.2)	8 (17.8)	
	Class 3	8 (53.3)	2 (13.3)	5 (33.3)	

Age at present	30-40 years	4 (57.1)	0 0.0	3 (42.9)	0.139
	40-50 years	35 (83.3)	2 (4.8)	5 (11.9)	
	50-60 years	22 (61.1)	2 (5.6)	12 (33.3)	
Gender	Male	50 (72.5)	3 (4.3)	16 (23.2)	0.931
	Female	11 (68.8)	1 (6.3)	4 (25.0)	
Educational Qualifications at present	Graduate	39 (72.2)	2 (3.7)	13 (24.1)	0.826
	Post graduate	17 (65.4)	2 (7.7)	7 (26.9)	
	M Phil	4 (100.0)	0 0.0	0 0.0	
	PhD	1 (100.0)	0 0.0	0 0.0	

Source : Computed from primary data. Figures in parentheses are percentages. p value significant at 0.05 level.

TABLE 5(a)
Pearson's Correlation between the Variables

		Value	*Asymp. Std. Error(a)*	*Approx. T(b)*	*Approx. Sig.*
Interval by Interval	Pearson's R	0.045	0.118	0.407	.685(c)
		0.111	0.123	1.016	0.313(c)
		0.025	0.110	0.232	0.817(c)
		-0.068	0.089	-0.623	0.535(c)

Source : Computed from Primary Data.

Table 5: The data demonstrated in the Table 5 regarding the aspect that promotion in organization leads to higher salary, more freedom and less supervision and on analyzing the data it was found that fair majority of employees provided the assent to the issue.

Class: On segregating the data on the basis of class it was ascertained that significant majority of employees (80.00 percent) in class 2 and fair majority of employees (68.00 per cent) in class 1 as against near majority of employees (53.30 percent) agreed with the issue.

Association: Statistically no significant association was found between the variable of class and the query.

Age: On classifying the data on the basis of age it was established that significant majority of employees (83.30 per cent) in the age group of 40-50 years, fair majority of employees (61.10 per cent) in the age group of 50-60 years and near majority of employees (57.10 per cent) in the age group of 30-40 years provided the positive responses to the poser.

Association: Statistically no significant association was found between the variable of age and the query.

Gender: Observing the responses on the basis of gender it was ascertained that fair majority of female employees (68.80 per cent) and high majority of male employees (72.50 per cent) supported the issue.

Association: Statistically no significant association was found between the variable of gender and the query.

Educational Qualifications: Categorizing the data on the basis of variable of Educational Qualifications it was found that absolute majority of employees with M Phil and PhD degree (100 per cent), high majority of (72.20 per cent) graduate and fair majority of employees with post graduate degree (65.40 per cent) favored the point of view.

Association: Statistically no significant association was found between the variable of Educational Qualifications and the statement under analysis.

The coefficient of correlation as represented by R is presented in Table 5(a) clearly indicates that the correlation is positive between the variable and the response of the employees and from the value of coefficient it can be seen that the variable of class and Educational Qualifications sustained a moderate relationship, with the responses of the employees. The variable of age had shown relationship of low intensity with the responses of the employees. The variable of gender had provided relationship of significant level.

Notes and References

1. Rensis Likert, *Human Organisation,* McGraw-Hill, New York, 1967, p. 1.
2. Udai Pareek, and T.V. Rao, *Designing and Managing Human Resource System,* Oxford and IBH Publishing Company, New Delhi, 1991, p. 11.
3. P.P. Arya, and B.B. Tandon, *Human Resource Development*, Deep and Deep Publications, New Delhi, 1985, p. 37.

4. R. Jayagopal, *Human Resource Development*, Sterling Publishers, New Delhi, 1990, p. 12.
5. Locke, Edwin A. (1976), "The Nature and Causes of Job Satisfaction." In M.D. Dunnette, ed., *Handbook of Industrial and Organizational Psychology*. Chicago: Rand McNally.
6. Steven L Mc Shane and Mary Ann Von Glinow, *Organisational Behaviour*, TMH, 2000, p. 204.
7. E.E. Lawler, Measuring the psychology quality of working life, Free Press, New York, 1975, p. 84.
8. G.Balachandar, Dr. N. Panchanatham and Dr. K. Subramanian, "Impact of Job Situation on the Motivation of Insurance Companies Officers: A Developmental Perspective." *International Journal of Trade, Economics and Finance,* Vol. 1, No. 4, December, 2010.
9. S.R. Padala, "Employees job Satisfaction in Electronics Corporation of India Ltd. Hydrabad." *Prerana,* September 2010, Volume 2, Issue 2, pp. 1-14.
10. Ajay Solkhe, Dr. N. Chaudhary, "HRD Climate And Job Satisfaction: An Empirical Investigation." *International Journal of Computing and Business Research,* ISSN (Online) : 2229-6166, Volume 2, Issue 2, May 2011.

13

Interpersonal Relationship in School Education

An Empirical Study based on Students' Perspective

NEELAM KUMARI

Student-Teacher-Relationship has been the most venerated and successful vehicle of human transformation. In Indian history and culture, the Guru-Shishya relations had remained a strong factor in transmitting teachings and knowledge to next generation. In earlier times, when reading and writing materials was unknown commodity the main means to convey the knowledge was through teacher (guru) disciple (Shishya) relationship where guru passed on the acquired knowledge to his disciples who further passed it on to the coming generations. In the early oral traditions of the Upanishads, the *guru-shishya* relationship had evolved into a fundamental component of Hinduism.[1] The term Upanishad" derives from the Sanskrit words *"upa"* (near), *"ni"* (down) and *"ad"* (to sit) which means to sit down near a spiritual teacher to receive instructions.

In the Ancient times, the history holds several of such age old examples such as the Krishna and Arjuna in the Bhagavad Gita and between Rama and Hanuman in the Ramayana. The mention of Lord Buddha going to his two teachers to attain spiritual knowledge is of immense relevance. However, the relationship of teachers and students became focus of inquiry in the society for more than 200-years, since Plato, Socrates and Confucius established much of the philosophical guidelines for teaching. Each of the scholar has emphasized on the importance of teacher- student relationship.

THE IMPORTANCE OF STUDENT–TEACHER RELATIONSHIPS

A sizable literature provides evidence that strong and supportive relationships between teachers and students are fundamental to the healthy development of all students in schools (Birch & Ladd[2], 1998; Hamre & Pianta, 2001; Pianta, 1999)[3]. Positive student-teacher relationships serve as a resource for students at risk of school failure, whereas conflict or disconnection between students and adults may compound that risk (Ladd & Burgess, 2001)[4]. Although the nature of these relationships changes as students' mature, the need for connection between students and adults in the school setting remains strong from preschool to 12th grade (Crosnoe, Johnson, & Elder, 2004)[5]. Furthermore, even as schools place increasing attention on accountability and standardized testing, the social quality of student-teacher relationships contributes to both academic and social-emotional development (Gregory[6] & Weinstein, 2004; Hamre & Pianta, 2001)[7]. As such, student-teacher relationships provide a unique entry point for educators and others working to improve the social and learning environments of schools and classrooms. These relationships may be a direct focus of intervention or may be viewed as one important feature of successful implementation of many of the other interventions which have been described.

One of the study on the importance of the teacher-students relationship suggested following as the factors responsible to make the relation cordial between the two.[8]

i. Caring
ii. Respect
iii. Going the extra mile
iv. Patience and perseverance
v. Belief in the ability of each other

It is an established fact that learning is a social event and many of the cognitive theorists and studies have supported and proven that both teachers and students have to pay heavy price if teachers neglect to form emotionally warm, supportive relationship with and among their students. An American psychologist Robert Pianta in the famous writing on 'Enhancing Relationship between the Children and Teachers (1999) has highlighted open communication, emotional and academic support as the factors responsible for positive students-teachers relationships.

The students believed that it is important that teacher should treat them respectfully and value their efforts to make the students-teacher realtionships all the more meaning.[9]

Objectives

The major objective of this paper is:

1. To assess and examine the Students-Teachers Relationships from students point of view in the select government schools imparting Secondary Education.

Research Methodology

Both primary and secondary data has been used.

Universe: The present paper attempts to assess and examine the relationship from (student's point of view) between the students and the school teachers in the select District S.A.S. Nagar, Punjab. For the purpose of this study, 36 schools, imparting secondary education in the District (99), have been selected considering the fair representation to each education block (8).

Sample: A sample of 800 students, both Boys (400) and Girls (400) has been selected randomly from class 9th (380) and 10th (420) from all the 36 select schools.

Discussion and Analysis

The respondents were put across certain posers/statements to reach the findings. The data has been crossed tabulated and statistically tested on Chi Square Technique to find out the significant level (p-value).

On analysing the responses presented in the Table 1 illustrated that statistically **significant association** was found between the classification of school variable and the statement however **non-significant association** was found in case of other variables such as gender, class and the statement. Further, it was found that students from rural schools than the urban schools more strongly viewed that they were treated respectfully by their teachers.

TABLE 1
You are Treated Respectfully by Your Teacher

Variables	*Groups*	*Agree*	*Undecided*	*Disagree*	*Total*	*Pearson Chi Square*	*p-value*
Gender	Boys	361 90.2%	2 .5%	37 9.2%	400 100.0%	2.842	.241ns
	Girls	370 92.5%	0 .0%	30 7.5%	400 100.0%		
Class	9TH	353 92.9%	0 .0%	27 7.1%	380 100.0%	3.386	.184ns
	10TH	378 90.0%	2 .5%	40 9.5%	420 100.0%		
Classification of School	Urban	183 89.7%	2 1.0%	19 9.3%	204 100.0%	6.215	.045*
	Rural	548 91.9%	0 .0%	48 8.1%	596 100.0%		
Total		731 91.4%	2 .2%	67 8.4%	800 100.0%		

Source : Computed from Primary Data p-value ≤ 0.05 is significant denote.
* p-value ≤ 0.01 is significant denote.
** p-value >.05 is non-significant denote ns.

Overall analysis of the responses suggested that 91.4 per cent of the respondents **agreed** with the statement whereas negligible proportion 8.4 percent of respondents **disagreed** with the statement indicating that possibly some of the teachers did not treat the students with all fairness as a result the students nurtured the grudge.

Irrespective of all the variables, it was found that highly significant proportion of the respondents agreed that they were treated respectfully by their teachers.

Observation: It was observed by the researcher that the students were treated politely by the teachers but exceptions were always there. In the recent directions of the court (Supreme Court, 2000) and the administration banned the Corporal Punishment (RTE Act under section 35) in India. Ever since the punishment of children has become offence the teachers have become conscious about their beheviour with the students.

TABLE 2
Your Teacher Encourages Class Discussion

Variables	*Groups*	*Agree*	*Undecided*	*Disagree*	*Total*	*Pearson Chi Square*	*p-value*
Gender	Boys	53 13.2%	3 .8%	344 86.0%	400 100.0%	1.917	.383ns
	Girls	62 15.5%	6 1.5%	332 83.0%	400 100.0%		
Class	9TH	62 16.3%	4 1.1%	314 82.6%	380 100.0%	2.229	.328ns
	10TH	53 12.6%	5 1.2%	362 86.2%	420 100.0%		
Classification of school	Urban	49 24.0%	8 3.9%	147 72.1%	204 100.0%	41.770	.000**
	Rural	66 11.1%	1 .2%	529 88.8%	596 100.0%		
	Total	115 14.4%	9 1.1%	676 84.5%	800 100.0%		

Source : Computed from Primary Data p-value ≤ 0.05 is significant denote.
* p-value ≤ 0.01 is significant denote
** p-value >.05 is non-significant denote ns.

The data presented in the Table 2 highlighted that statistically **highly significant association** was found between the classification of school variable and the statement however **non-significant association** was found in case of other variables like class, gender and the statement. Further, it was found that more of the respondents of rural schools more convincingly stated that teachers did not encourage class discussion than their opposite groups.

Overall analysis of the responses indicated that 14.4 per cent of respondents **agreed** with statement whereas 84.5 per cent of the respondents **disagreed** with statement. The possible reason for the disagreed responses could be that teachers did not wish to waste time on discussions rather they wished to finish the syllabi.

Irrespective of any variable, significant proportion of the respondents expressed that teachers did not encourage class discussions.

Observation: It was observed on the basis of interaction with the students and the teachers that often classrooms discussions were not encouraged. The students were asked to raise their queries after the lecture. Some of the teachers were of the opinion that classroom discussions led to indiscipline and wastage of time.

TABLE 3

Your Teacher is Easy to Talk to

Variables	*Groups*	*Agree*	*Undecided*	*Disagree*	*Total*	*Pearson Chi-Square*	*p-value*
Gender	Boys	302 75.5%	8 2.0%	90 22.5%	400 100.0%	.704	.703ns
	Girls	304 76.0%	5 1.2%	91 22.8%	400 100.0%		
Class	9TH	286 75.3%	8 2.1%	86 22.6%	380 100.0%	1.050	.592ns
	10TH	320 76.2%	5 1.2%	95 22.6%	420 100.0%		
Classification of School	Urban	153 75.0%	3 1.5%	48 23.5%	204 100.0%	.160	.923ns
	Rural	453 76.0%	10 1.7%	133 22.3%	596 100.0%		
	Total	606 75.8%	13 1.6%	181 22.6%	800 100.0%		

Source : Computed from Primary Data p-value ≤ 0.05 is significant denote.
* p-value ≤ 0.01 is significant denote.
** p-value >.05 is non-significant denote ns.

On analysing the responses presented in the Table 3, it was found that statistically **non-significant association** was found between all variables and the statement.

Overall analysis of the responses suggested that 75.8 per cent of the respondents **agreed** with the statement whereas 22.6 percent of respondents who **disagreed** with statement and possible reason for the disagreement could be the shy nature of the students or the attitude of the teachers.

Irrespective of all the variables, high proportion of the respondents opined that the teachers were easy to talk to.

Observation: It was observed by the researcher that the

students were more confident while talking or communicating with the lady teachers. They were shy or scared of talking to male teachers. The senior male students were more comfortable in interacting with male teachers even.

TABLE 4

The Teacher Assesses the Students Fairly

Variables	*Groups*	*Agree*	*Undecided*	*Disagree*	*Total*	*Pearson Chi Square*	*p-value*
Gender	Boys	323 80.8%	23 5.8%	54 13.5%	400 100.0%	1.033	.596ns
	Girls	334 83.5%	20 5.0%	46 11.5%	400 100.0%		
Class	9TH	315 82.9%	22 5.8%	43 11.3%	380 100.0%	1.096	.578ns
	10TH	342 81.4%	21 5.0%	57 13.6%	420 100.0%		
Classification of school	Urban	156 76.5%	14 6.9%	34 16.7%	204 100.0%	5.997	.050*
	Rural	501 84.1%	29 4.9%	66 11.1%	596 100.0%		
	Total	657 82.1%	43 5.4%	100 12.5%	800 100.0%		

Source : Computed from Primary Data p-value ≤ 0.05 is significant denote.
* p-value ≤ 0.01 is significant denote.
** p-value >.05 is non-significant denote ns.

The responses presented in the Table 4 illustrated that statistically **significant association** was found between the classification of school variable and the statement. However, **non-significant association** was found between the other variables and the statement. Further, it was noticed that more of the respondents of rural schools than the urban schools strongly stated that the teachers assessed them fairly.

Overall responses revealed that 82.1 per cent of the respondents **agreed** with the statement whereas 12.5 percent of respondents **disagreed** with the statement that the teachers did not assess them fairly and no specific reason could be assigned to this.

Irrespective of the variables, it was found that significant proportion of the respondents agreed that the teachers assessed them fairly.

Observation: Based on informal interaction with the students and teachers, it was observed that teachers treated all the students alike, without any bias. Therefore, the students were assessed fairly by the teachers without any partiality.

TABLE 5

You Receive Sufficient Feedback from Your Teacher

Variables	*Groups*	*Agree*	*Undecided*	*Disagree*	*Total*	*Pearson Chi Square*	*p-value*
Gender	Boys	96	25 24.0%	279 6.2%	400 69.8%	1.989 100.0%	.370ns
	Girls	85 21.2%	19 4.8%	296 74.0%	400 100.0%		
Class	9TH	96 25.3%	20 5.3%	264 69.5%	380 100.0%	2.881	.237ns
	10TH	85 20.2%	24 5.7%	311 74.0%	420 100.0%		
Classification of School	Urban	68 33.3%	12 5.9%	124 60.8%	204 100.0%	18.637	.000**
	Rural	113 19.0%	32 5.4%	451 75.7%	596 100.0%		
	Total	181 22.6%	44 5.5%	575 71.9%	800 100.0%		

Source : Computed from Primary Data p-value ≤ 0.05 is significant denote.
* p-value ≤ 0.01 is significant denote.
** p-value >.05 is non-significant denote ns.

On analysing the responses projected in the Table 5 it was found that statistically **highly significant association** was found between the classification of school variable and the statement whereas **non-significant association** was found between the other variables. Further, it was seen that more of the students of rural schools strongly stated that they received sufficient feedback from the teachers as against the students of urban schools.

Overall analysis of the responses reflected that 22.6 percent of respondents **agreed** with the statement whereas 71.9 per cent of the respondents **disagreed** with the statement. The possible reason for the high proportion of disagreed responses could be that there was no such formal or informal practice of providing feedback to the students in the schools.

Irrespective of any variable, high proportion of respondents disagreed that they received sufficient feedback from their teachers.

Observation: On the basis of interaction with the students and the teachers, it became evident that due to the gap between the teachers and the students especially in the rural schools, the students were not given sufficient feedback by the respective teachers regarding their studies.

TABLE 6

The Background of the Student was taken into Account while Imparting Instructions

Variables	*Groups*	*Agree*	*Undecided*	*Disagree*	*Total*	*Pearson Chi Square*	*p-value*
Gender	Boys	66 16.5%	6 1.5%	328 82.0%	400 100.0%	2.036	.361ns
	Girls	68 17.0%	2 .5%	330 82.5%	400 100.0%		
Class	9TH	68 17.9%	4 1.1%	308 81.1%	380 100.0%	.712	.700ns
	10TH	66 15.7%	4 1.0%	350 83.3%	420 100.0%		
Classification of Schools	Urban	48 23.5%	3 1.5%	153 75.0%	204 100.0%	9.870	.007**
	Rural	86 14.4%	5 .8%	505 84.7%	596 100.0%		
	Total	134 16.8%	8 1.0%	658 82.2%	800 100.0%		

Source : Computed from Primary Data p-value ≤ 0.05 is significant denote.
* p-value ≤ 0.01 is significant denote.
** p-value >.05 is non-significant denote ns.

The analysis of Table 6 reflected that statistically **highly significant association** was found between the classification of school variable and the statement whereas **non-significant association** was found between the other variables and the statement. Further, it was seen that more of the students from rural schools strongly expressed that the students background was not taken into account while imparting instructions than the students from urban schools.

Overall analysis of the responses established that 16.8 percent of respondents **agreed** with the statement whereas 82.2 per cent of the respondents **disagreed** with the statement. The significant proportion of disagreed responses could possibly due to the reason that there was no formal mechanism to know the backgrounds of the students. Thus, teachers imparted the instructions the way they wished.

Irrespective of the any variable, it was found that significant proportion of the respondents disagreed that the students with different background were given consideration while imparting instructions.

Table 7
Teacher's Professional Skills are up to date

Variables	*Groups*	*Agree*	*Undecided*	*Disagree*	*Total*	*Pearson Chi-Square*	*p-value*
Gender	Boys	373 93.2%	6 1.5%	21 5.2%	400 100.0%	.709	.702ns
	Girls	378 94.5%	6 1.5%	16 4.0%	400 100.0%		
Class	9TH	353 92.9%	6 1.6%	21 5.5%	380 100.0%	1.376	.503ns
	10TH	398 94.8%	6 1.4%	16 3.8%	420 100.0%		
Classification of School	Urban	181 88.7%	4 2.0%	19 9.3%	204 100.0%	14.177	.001**
	Rural	570 95.6%	8 1.3%	18 3.0%	596 100.0%		
	Total	751 93.9%	12 1.5%	37 4.6%	800 100.0%		

Source : Computed from Primary Data p-value ≤ 0.05 is significant denote.
* p-value ≤ 0.01 is significant denote.
** p-value >.05 is non-significant denote ns.

Observation: The irony of the government schools has been that no such efforts were made to consider the background of the students while imparting instructions. All the students were treated alike without considering their IQ in view. Thus, at times the IQ level of the students demanded something different than what was imparted to them.

The data projected in the Table 7 indicated that statistically **highly significant association** was found between the classification of school variable and the statement whereas **non-significant association** was found between the other variables and the statement. Further, it was found that more of students from rural schools than urban schools strongly opined that teacher's professional skills were up to date.

Overall responses revealed that 93.9 per cent of the respondents **agreed** with the statement whereas a very negligible proportion of 4.6 percent of respondents **disagreed** with the statement.

Irrespective of the variables, it was found that highly significant proportion of the respondents agreed with the statement that teacher's professional skills were up to date.

TABLE 8

There is Good Rapport between Faculty and Students

Variables	*Groups*	*Agree*	*Undecided*	*Disagree*	*Total*	*Pearson Chi Square*	*p-value*
Gender	Boys	310 77.5%	9 2.2%	81 20.2%	400 100.0%	2.040	.361ns
	Girls	295 73.8%	14 3.5%	91 22.8%	400 100.0%		
Class	9TH	284 74.7%	8 2.1%	88 23.2%	380 100.0%	2.492	.288ns
	10TH	321 76.4%	15 3.6%	84 20.0%	420 100.0%		
Classification of Schools	Urban	141 69.1%	8 3.9%	55 27.0%	204 100.0%	6.374	.041*
	Rural	464 77.9%	15 2.5%	117 19.6%	596 100.0%		
	Total	605 75.6%	23 2.9%	172 21.5%	800 100.0%		

Source : Computed from Primary Data p-value ≤ 0.05 is significant denote.
* p-value ≤ 0.01 is significant denote.
** p-value >.05 is non-significant denote ns.

Observation: The students expressed their satisfaction with the professional skills of their teachers. The students of the urban schools were little apprehensive about the professional skills of their teachers as these students were more exposed to the new trends of teaching and learning.

On analysing the responses presented in the Table 8, it was found that statistically **significant association** was found between the classification of school variable and the statement however **non-significant association** was found between the other variables such as gender, class and the statement. Further, it was seen that students from rural schools than urban schools convincingly stated that there was good rapport between faculty and the students.

Overall analysis of the responses reflected that 75.6 per cent of the respondents **agreed** with the statement whereas 21.5 percent of the respondents **disagreed** with the statement indicating that no good rapport was found between the two and possibly this could be attributed to their attitude.

Irrespective of any variable, it was found that high proportion of the respondents agreed that there was good rapport between faculty and the students.

Observation: Generally the staff and the students enjoyed good rapport with due respect for each other but there were certain students who were shy and had some complexes and for the same reason they had unfriendly relations with their teachers.

FINDINGS OF THE STUDY

1. Highly significant proportion of the respondents (91.4 per cent) **expressed** that they were treated respectfully by their teachers.
2. Significant proportion of the respondents (84.5 per cent) was in **disagreement** that those teachers encouraged the class discussion.
3. High proportion of the respondents (75.8 per cent) **opined** that teachers were easy to talk to them.
4. Significant proportion of the respondents (82.1 per cent) **supported** the statement that the teachers assessed the students fairly.
5. High proportion of the respondents (71.9 per cent) **disagreed** that they received sufficient feedback from their teacher regarding their studies.
6. Significant proportion of the respondents (82.2 per cent) **disagreed** that the background of the students was not taken into account while imparting instructions.

7. Highly significant proportion of the respondents (93.9 per cent) **favoured** the statement that the teachers' professional skills were up to date.
8. High proportion of the respondents (75.6 per cent) was in **agreement** that there was good rapport between faculty and the students.

SUMMARY

The study revealed that students were treated respectfully by their teachers and it was easy to talk to them. Further, students opined that they were fairly assessed by the teachers and they enjoyed good rapport with faculty. The students expressed convincingly that professional skills of their teachers were up to date.

However, most of the students were of the view that their teachers did not encourage the classroom discussion and they were not given the sufficient feedback regarding their studies. Ironically the background of the students was not taken into account while imparting instructions.

SUGGESTIONS

On the basis of above given findings it is suggested that teachers should encourage classroom discussions which will go long way to develop the personality of the students and also facilitate the learning process. The teachers must keep in mind the IQ level and background of the class students so that comfortable level with the learning teaching process be achieved.

Students are likely to be emotionally and intellectually invested in the classes in which they have positive relationship with their teachers.[10] The gap between the relationships of the two can prove drastic for the students having difficulties in their academic behaviours. The teachers must exhibit positive, lenient and liberal approach towards students without attaching any importance to their social, economic and political status.

NOTES AND REFERENCES

1. *http://en.wikipedia.org/wiki/Guru-shishya_tradition*
2. Birch, S.H. and Ladd, G.W. (1998). Children's interpersonal behaviors and the teacher–child relationship. *Developmental Psychology,* 34, 934-946.
3. Pianta, R.C. "Enhancing relationships between children and teachers", Washington, DC: American Psychological Association, (1999).

4. Ladd, G.W. and Burgess, K.B. (2001). Do relational risks and protective factors moderate the linkages between childhood aggression and early psychological and school adjustment? *Child Development,* 72, 1579-1601.
5. Crosnoe, R., Johnson, M.K. and Elder, G.H. (2004). Intergenerational bonding in school: the behavioral and contextual correlates of student–teacher relationships. *Sociology of Education,* 77, 60-81.
6. Gregory, A. and Weinstein, R.S. (2004). Connection and regulation at home and in school: Predicting growth in achievement for adolescents. *Journal of Adolescent Research,* 19, 405-27.
7. Hamre, B. and Pianta, R. (2001). Early teacher–child relationships and the trajectory of children's school outcomes through eighth grade. *Child Development,* 72, 625–38.
8. http://www.educationgroup.co.nz/uploads/Publications/The%20 importance%20of%20the%20teacher-student%20relationship.pdf
9. Phelan, Patrica, Ann Davidson, Hanh Locke and Cao Thanh, "Speaking Up : Students' Prospectives on School" (1992), pp. 695-704.
10. *Ibid.*

14

Pertinence of Human Resource Development Strategies

The Importance and Gingery Areas of Hassels in Service Sector Companies in India

Aakashdeep Sharma and Rupender Aulakh

ABSTRACT

The springing forces of competitive environment, technological advancement and commencing new trends in the municipal as well as foreign economies has fostered cognizance that productive utilization of human resource is key to steer towards organizational success. Human resource being the active factor of production is widely reckoned as nexus of strategic advantage which pool the gaps between the dynamic demands and supply as continuously changing forces of service sector. Only trained, skilled, up-to-date and pliable human resource is capable of withstanding and vanquishing all the challenges and give fruitful rendition with graft. Hence, investment in development of human resource is must to attain competitive success. The organisation must have well developed and timely updated strategies for the development of manpower to synchronize the exigency of changing scenario and the response of the organisation being goal-oriented. Only well-oriented and skilled human resource can bridge the gap between them. Human resource development strategies are the foundation stone for strengthening the manpower and in turn the edifice of service sector set-up.

Keywords: Soft Skills, Service Sector Companies, Competitive Advantage, Competence development.

INTRODUCTION

The development of our human resource is an area in which we need to do well as it is decisive in determining the success of our diversification programme.[1]

Services sector in India being an umbrella term embodies the activities such as transportation, logistics, financial, BPO services, healthcare, trading, hospitality, mass media, consultancies, telecommunications, community and professional services including accounting, legal services and management counselling. The services sector with an around 57% contribution to GDP has made pronto strides in last few years and has emerged as the largest and fastest growing sector of the economy.[2] It has also added to the foreign investment flows, exports and employment. As per the Department of Industrial Policy and Promotion, Indian services sector has attracted the highest amount of FDI equity inflows in the period April 2000-December 2014, amounting to about US$ 41,755 million which is about 18% of the total foreign inflows.[2] Today's service sector calls for soft skills rather operational skills to meet the needs and requirement of awarded end users including well educated, skilled, flexible employees having transparent image for their clients.[3] The primary focus of service sector is integration of human with capital and technological resources as well as business strategies.

The most important need in this sector absolutely and prominently is Human resource development.[4] Human Resource Development is pivotal to the success of contemporary service sector organisation as the substantial source of competitive advantage.[5] Human resource being the core to the functioning of these service sector companies; different methods and strategies are concocted and applied to fulfil the aspect.

The buzzword human resource development gained wide acceptability in India since the early 1980s with forces of globalisation, liberalisation, advancement in information and communication. With the growing passage of time, new and emerging service sector companies are in vogue and have given new dimension to the business and investment in human resource development venture. They provide employment opportunities to a large number of human resources. Organisation wants commitment and integrity; a successful combination of committed people and a well framed venture of organisation is the key to meet the competitive environment.[6]

CONCEPTUALISATION OF HUMAN RESOURCE DEVELOPMENT

The concept of human resource development is multidimensional i.e. in individual, organisation human resource development covers three aspects such as : (a) human aspects, (b) resource aspects, and (c) development aspect. Human resource development is the process by which the employees are supported in a crafted, continuous and precise way to:

a) orient abilities essential to perform different functions associated to their required roles,
b) gain the capabilities and turf to explore and utilize their expertise for the purpose of own as well as organisation development,
c) Prepare a culture of supervisor-subordinate relationship, collective work, communication; system of feedback, collaboration contributes towards professional well-being, motivation and productivity of employees.

In the words of Tanvir Kayani, human resource development has been considered as one of the most important area of research. The aim of human resource development policy is based on the development of human resource.[7]Human resource development includes any effort that provides learning and training opportunities to team and individuals within organisations in order to improve their performance.[8]

Walton says that the area of human resource development has gone beyond training and employee development to the building of strong corporate strategy, individual learning, team learning, career development, internal consultancy, organisational learning and knowledge management.[9] Fredrick Charles considered it as the first step towards modernisation.[10]

Sriyen advocates human resource development as a method of enhancing knowledge, skills and capacity of human resource in the society. As per economic point of view, it can be recognised as an accretion of human resource and its sustainable investment for the development of economy.[11]

It basically develops the human resources enabling them to adjust to their jobs, the environment of organisation, to involve in the frame of teamwork by enhancing cooperative and comprehensive abilities of human resource. It is the key to introduce human resource to the values of humanity as well as organisation in a systematic manner to promote intellectual, moral, social ,cultural, psychological development pro-actively.it is now recognised as the systematic application of methods, process, developing and using a person's abilities to a large extent for individual well being and organisational growth.

In other words, human resource development comprises both training concepts and competence development (lifelong learning process) with workplace learning, optimistic leadership skills and by interlinking the staff.[12] Proper human resource development policies and techniques are essential to be followed by the organisation from time to time which directly has it impact on the productivity and growth of the organisation. A combination of proper man power planning, recruitment process, selection, crafting the training and development strategies, teamwork, performance appraisal, feedback process, provision for rewards is the core for making successful human resource development programmes.[13]

Strategies of human resource development in the service sector: Crafting the well suited Strategies which the help of which human resources are enabled to imbibe knowledge, expertise, potential and sustainability are cornerstone for the continuous functioning of service sector companies. The strategies are core and form the entire edifice of the organisational and resource set-up. There is abundance of strategies prevalent in the modern era where experts are there to programme them keeping in view the requirements of the human resource and need of the changing circumstances which enable the personnel as well as organisation to carry out their activities for the realisation of short-term as well as long-terms objectives such as:

a) **Brain storming and brain writing pool**: Brain storming is a group creativity technique to generate ideas on a particular topic in search of few ideas. The members facilitate various ideas as possible as remedial measures to a certain problem without criticizing the ideas. All are welcomed to quip and later on the ideas are discussed and analysed in order to carry out appropriate solution. Worthy implement able suggestions are substantially circulated for necessary action. Whereas brain writing pool is a highly productive process where members of a particular team feel difficult to get together at the same time so sheets are circulated to unable to gather ideas by way of computer networking systems. The records are maintained regarding the outcome of the processes.

b) **Career counselling and development workshops**: This technique aims at developing career of a human resource by matching his aspirations, exigencies and opportunities available are precisely taken into account and further steps are identified and planned for further career development. The development workshops generate a criteria with the help of which the employees and their supervisors share their views on the areas of mismatches. These re entry and later workshops which are helpful in retaining the human resource the service sector and prepare them for further even after retirement.

c) **Quality and study circles**: Study circle aims at generating the self-potential and self-development of employee by emancipating the desire to acquire and update knowledge, information and learning advantages to make him competitive. Experts are invited to impart and share their expertise on gleaming issues through power point presentation, guest lectures and group discussions. Quality circle as the name suggests aims at enhancing the proficiency, team spirit, work environment, commitment, communication and active participation of human resources in the organisational framework.

d) **Delphi technique**: It is not important to have face to face interaction among the members. Certain matters are sorted out by identification of problems and solutions are received via questionnaire. In this consensus decision making technique, the process is repeated along with the feedback procedure unless and until the satisfaction of sorting the problem with an adequate solution is compiles. It also promotes creating and sharing of ideas among the human resources and their sill formation and wider outlook.

e) **Quotidian and electronic meeting (staff meeting, managerial discussion, group interactions and active participation)**: Staff meetings aim at group synergy, team building, creation a work culture, family feeling and talent recognition which directly and indirectly benefit the organisation. The goals and targets are usually discussed at all levels to bring harmonious functioning of the different administrative units through greater involvement and collective contribution of all the members. The electronic meeting is a widely used phenomenon in the yester years as decision making in groups. Members sit around with the series of terminals. They are presented different issues and they give their responses to the issues on screen. The members of group comments and the solutions and their perspectives are depicted on the projection screen. It brings honesty, speed and quick responsiveness.

f) **Individualised training and development**: Training helps the job holders to increase skills and knowledge for doing a particular job whereas development enable them to prepare for present as well as future jobs.[14] It reduces turnover, brings efficiency, innovation etc. Training programmes play an important role in the welfare and growth aspect of human resource with improvement in work capability. This kind of training is individual specific and includes practice of specific skills, superior-subordinate unison on certain methods to promote and simulate work situations. In this method not only the competency is tested but motivation skills are also exposed.

g) **Job description and job enrichment:** The complete description regarding the job content, job environment, conditions of work. A common form of description includes job title, duties associated to job, the authority and responsibility of the job holder. His is a way to make job clear and more meaningful as the job holder comes to know the expectations from the job and how he/she has to perform his/her role in the organisation. Job enrichment gives job holder more responsibility, skills, knowledge and autonomy regarding planning, controlling and directing his own performance. It helps in filtering down the decision-making power and rights to each individual regarding the areas which affect his job performance. Moreover, job rotation is a tool to enhance the potential and capability of the employees by turning them from specialist to generalists. They become jack of all trades and his helps in avoiding monotony and bring creativity.

h) **Sabbatical**: The sabbatical is an extension in the leave of absence away from the work. It is a way to enable the human resource to attend conferences, executive development, continuous reading. It is considered useful for better career development without distracting from the continuous and smooth operational and efficient concentration.

i) **Seminars and syndicates**: They provide opportunity to exchange with participatory measure to exchange ideas, information, views and experiences. It is a natural and practical process of learning. They wider the way of thinking help in growth and development of career and competencies of human resources. This acts as an exercise of mind through reading, preparing material for discussion and participation in the general discussion.

j) **Gripe boxes**: Feedback system is base to this technique as it is very important and the employees are facilitated to express their thoughts freely without hassle. The employees drop their suggestions, complaints, opinions into these boxes freely and this is an indirect way of participation in the organisational setting by way of sharing. The employees mention their names along with the suggestions and they are awarded for the better suggestions which are essentially worthy for the organisation. They HRD department seriously peep into the boxes and initiate changes on their basis.

BENEFITS OF HUMAN RESOURCE DEVELOPMENT STRATEGIES

These strategies are very helpful as per the human resource and organisational growth perspectives. It brings with it a wide range of benefits which in turn help in building the edifice of long term benefits to the organisation by enabling it to develop competitive ability to withstand the challenges and help in updating the spectrums from time to time.

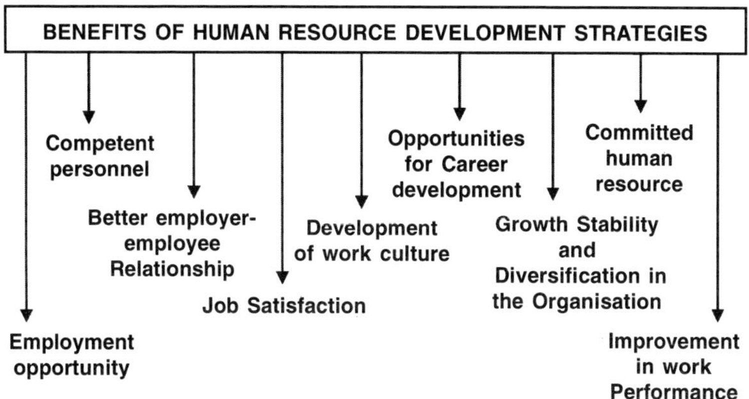

These strategies help in building a cooperative and workaholic culture in the workplace. They help in increasing job satisfaction, productivity, adapt capacity for new technologies and methods. The human resource feel gratified with the effervescence and the process being cynosure help in attaining all the goals and pursuits. These strategies are fruitful only if they are well build catering to the need of the needs of human resources and organisational setup as a whole.

The gingery areas of hassles regarding the effective implication of human resource development strategies:

> Apart from the various benefits of these strategies, there are various backwashes which give birth to certain spectrums of hassles within the organisation structure regarding the human resources and other conditional ties. These are the boulders for the smooth and continuous functioning of the organisation. Manpower strategies have to face various challenges in the present time which they have to tackle out with expertise and provide aid to them. The various hassles are:

a) **Human resource retention problem**: It is the biggest area of challenge for the organisation to keep and train the best employees having specialised potential, skills and attitude to their job. The service sector enterprises differentiate themselves with regard to their white collar expert employees. It is essential to stick them to their job so as to reduce the threat of leakages of secrecy from the organization as continuous shift of employees leads to replication and pose a threat to the existence of the organisation in the competitive world.

b) **Elimination of skill gap**: The time is changing; there is skilled workforce in abundance in the economy. The need of the job keeps on changing everyday with the change in the international as well as municipal market. So there is the intense need to invest in the human resource in such a manner so as to keep the employees up to date with the changing work environment and the demands they have to fulfil. The gap between the skills retains by them and the need of the changing circumstances is essential to cover up. It also bells for highly technically trained staff and efficient ways of responding to the environment.

c) **Competitive global environment**: The environment is highly competitive and it is very essential to respond to the changing demands of business culture in order to survive in the market. The HRD strategies also need to be crafted and maintained at regular intervals of time so as to retain the best employees in the organisation so that they all could prove to the asses. It needs huge financial investment and time devotion as without experts it is difficult to implement these strategies in the dynamic environment.

d) **Monotonous, routine and repetitive tasks**: Besides the various strategies, there is still the problem related to the overlapping functions in the organisation. The job holders feel jam packed with the burden to perform well and diverse as well as the repetitive jobs put the snarl ups on their development ways so it rather hampers their capabilities. The strategies must focus on making the job interesting rather clearing the duties and responsibilities associated towards their jobs.

e) **Lack of educational advancement**: Most of the men are not given sabbatical to upgrade their educational qualification. This put a barrier for the human resource development and the employees have to leave their job in order to upgrade the educational qualification to get promoted and to acquire higher status in the society.[15]

f) **Lack of fund for human resource development**: Now-a-days it has been observed that the companies are reducing their budget day-by-day for the human resource development and they are spending more on capital investment and management, asset management, fund management, research and development and market research.[16]

g) **The influence of public sector:** There are certain rigidities which have become the part of developing the human resource development strategies in the service sector enterprises as these are considered as the retired civil servants and higher level police personnel as the employer in these service sector enterprises. So the influence of their authority and way of working is seen in the strategies, programmes and plans for uplifting the human resource and the organisational growth as well.

These pose a severe challenge before setting up and updating the human resource development strategies in the dynamic environment under the impact of various changing pattern of services.

CONCLUSION

An organisation can be dynamic, growth-oriented and succeed only with its efficacious manpower. There is need of lifelong learning process and a proper organised learning system. Human resource development serves as foundation for the development of various perspectives of employees in service sector companies. Human resource development is the need of hour and has good impact on industrial relation, productivity and can remove hurdles in the organisational set up which are hidden. If human resources are well specialised and expert in the field and satisfied in their working environment this would add to the output and goodwill of the respective organisation. HRD department has to empower, engage and energise the employees to create effectiveness and efficiency through various motivation organisation structures, procedures and systems. There is need to focus on this aspect with great attention. The service sector companies would be able to render better services upto the mark. The service sector has to mark the feasibility of proper incentive structure, need to collaborate with the higher and professional institutions to link up with the patterns of pre job training in the form of education. Moreover, the global patterns of practices are essential to be taken in the consideration as the horizons of the service sector are expanding and it calls for the well trained, industrious and assiduous human resource.

Notes and References

1. www.quotes.lifehack.org
2. www.ibef.org
3. *Ibid.*
4. Dr. Reinard Klose, "Supporting Sustainable Economic Development through Labour Market-Oriented Technical and Vocational Education [TVET] and Corporate Human Resource Development", in *Final Report of International Conference Corporate HRD and Skills Development for Employment: Scope and Strategies*, 24-26 November, 2008.
5. unevoc.unesco.org.
6. *Ibid.*
7. Tanvir Kayani, "Challenges of Human Resource Development to pace with Globalisation, National University of Modern Language, Islamabad, 2008.
8. Abhishek Singal and Vijayshri Tiwari, "Challenges Faced by the Indian Organisation for Human Resource Development", in *International Journal of Marketing and Human Resource Management (IJMHRM)*, Volume 3, Issue 1, January-December, 2012.
9. J.S. Walton, The Provision of Learning Support for Non-employees, in: J. Stewart and J. McGoldrick (Eds.) *Human Resource Development: Perspectives, Strategies and Practice,* Pitman, London, 1996.
10. H. Fredrick. and A. Charles, Education, Manpower and Economic Growth: Strategies of Human Resource Development, McGraw hill, USA, 1964.
11. D.S. Sriyen, Human Resource Development for Competiveness: A Priority for Employers ILO Workshop on Employers' Organisation in Asia Pacific in the Twenty-first Centaury Turin, Italy, 1997.
12. Workers, Oxford, UK, Oxfam Publishers, 2003.
13. J.K. Sharma and Raaz Maheshwari, "Human Resource Development and its Technique", in *International Journal of Educational Research and Technology*, Volume 4[2], June 2013.
14. Parampal Singh, Ramneek Kaur and Harpreet Singh, Principal and Practice of Management, Kalyani Publishers, Ludhiana, 2008.
15. Abhishek Singal and Vijayshri Tiwari, "Challenges Faced by the Indian Organisation for Human Resource Development", in *International Journal of Marketing and Human Resource Management (IJMHRM)*, Volume 3, Issue 1, January-December, 2012.
16. *Ibid.*

Part III
FINANCIAL MANAGEMENT

15

Performance Evaluation of Central Cooperative Bank Panchkula

A Study

MANISHA

ABSTRACT

Co-operative banks are socio-economical financial institutions because they fulfil the social and economical objectives of their members. These banks provide a wide range of financial and banking services to their members. Co-operative banks have their own rules, values and principles which make it differ from others. The present paper attempts to examine the growth of Central Co-operative Bank (DCCB) Panchkula through selective indicators, it analysis the credits and C/D ratios. This paper also studies the investments, capitals, income, expenditures and profits of the DCCB in Panchkula. To achieve the objectives of the paper, data has been collected from secondary sources. This data has analysed by various statistical techniques.

INTRODUCTION

Co-operative bank are the financial institutions which takes deposits then lending it to their members. Co-operatives are democratic institutions of the members, by the members and for the members. Co-operative as a formal association came to set up in India at 1904 mainly as credit societies. These banks are controlled and supervised by the banking authorities. Each member has a voting right in decision making. Indian economy is a rural economy because a high proportion of the economy living in rural areas. Co-operative organisations help the farmer's interest by eliminating middlemen between them. Co-operatives banks play very important role in terms of coverage and total supply of agriculture including credit. It helps the farmer in warehousing and storage of agriculture goods. It also help the farmer's to sell their products at favourable prices.

Co-operative banks mainly created to meet the requirement of small traders, weavers and farmers. These banks provide a number of services to their customers. Co-operatives banks are a lot of branches all over the world. Co-operative banking structure is a three tier federal one as follow:

1) State level central Co-operative banks,
2) District central Co-operative banks,
3) Primary Co-operative credit societies works at village level.

The Central Co-operative bank Panchkula has some branches. These branches are:

Panchkula	Pinjore
Kalka	Morni Hills
Barwala	Raipur Rani
Mouli	Ramgarh
Sector-12 Panchkula	Ganouli
Manak Tabra	Kakkar Majra

1. REVIEW OF LITERATURE

The literature involves an overview of researches that have already been existing in the field over a period of time.

Dr. Jai Kishan Chandel has made a study on "Financial performance of DCCBs in Haryana—a comparative study." He reveals that all the DCCBs performed poorly on profitability, liquidity, solvency and efficiency parameters but little comfortable on risk parameter. The DCCBS Jhajjar and Karnal was the best performer in their respective divisions. The DCCBs Panchkula and Jind were found the worst performers in their respective divisions. The reasons behind this week performance were financial mismanagement, improper capital structure and improper investment.

Thirupathi kanchu has attempt a study on "Performance evaluation of DCCBs in INDIA" taking some selective indicators into account namely capital, deposits, investment and C/D ratios. He concluded that the growth of number of DCCBs and their branches have negative trend up to certain period, later there is negligible positive trend and the membership in Co-operatives has been increased. The capital, reserves and borrowings increased almost double during the study period.

Gupta and Jain stated that the financial performance of urban Co-operative banks with in the Rural Co-operative sectors improved in 2010-2011 through some concerns with regard to some UCBs reporting negative CRAR. In rural Co-operative sectors state Co-operative bank and district Co-operative bank reported profits.

Dr. E Gnanasekaran, Dr. M. Anbalgan and N. Abdul nazar has make a study on "A study on the Urban Co-operative bank success and growth in Vellore district-statistical analysis." The study shows that the overall financial performance of UCBs in all fronts namely membership, share capital, deposits, advance, profits and loans are showing a significantly and undistrubing trends. The USBs are the road of progress. This also clears that the USBs enjoying a predominant position in the banking industry.

Prof. Amparo Melian —Navarro has conduct a study on "The Role of Co-operative banking system in the European Union-27 an analysis of the Spanish case." they explain the role of Co-operatives in European countries. The European Co-operative groups are linked to the financial groups UNICO, the top exponent of the European Co-operative banking system.

A study on "Putting Co-operative Learning to the Test" is made by Laurel Shaper Walters. There's some evidence that even poorly organised co-operative learning is probably improving things like race relations and attitude towards mainstreamed kids. They are just missing out on a lot of the potential.

2. OBJECTIVES

Following are the main objectives of the study :

1) To examine the study of performance of DCCB Panchkula by selective indicators.
2) To analysis the capital, deposits, borrowings and reserves of DCCB Panchkula.

3) To study the growth of investments of DCCB Panchkula.
4) To evaluate the income, expenditure and profits of DCCB Panchkula.
5) To analysis the credits and C/D ratios of DCCB Panchkula.
6) To understand the financial position of DCCB Panchkula.

3. DATA COLLECTION

The present paper is based on secondary data which is collected from secondary sources drawn from annual reports of DCCB panchkula, paper, websites, and journals relating to Co-operating banking sectors. This data is analysed by various statistical techniques like mean, S.D., C.V. and trend analysis. Only 5 year data is collected for present study.

4. ANALYSIS OF THE DATA

The financial position of the DCCB panchkula can be well assessed by the analysis of the balance sheet of the banks. Balance sheet provides an actual picture of the financial position of the bank. Certain items have been taken to analysis the financial position of DCCB panchkula from the year 2009-10 to 2013-14.

TABLE 1

Position of Capital, Reserves and Borrowings

(*Rs. in Lakhs*)

Year	*Capital*	*Trend%*	*Reserves*	*Trend%*	*Borrowings*	*Trend%*
2009-10	648.85	100	1421.70	100	5654.85	100
2010-11	721.57	111.21	1425.04	100.23	6700.00	118.48
2011-12	796.01	122.68	1428.47	100.48	8950.00	158.27
2012-13	800.56	123.38	1873.47	131.78	10100.00	178.61
2013-14	1086.86	167.51	1892.11	133.09	11300.00	199.83
Mean.	810.77	124.96	1608.16	113.12	8540.97	151.04
S D	148.81	22.94	224.32	15.78	2094.23	37.04
C V	18.35	18.35	13.95	13.95	24.52	24.52

Base Year: 2009-10.

Source : Annual Reports of Central Co-operative Bank Panchkula.

Graph 1 : Trend % of Capital, Reserves and Borrowings

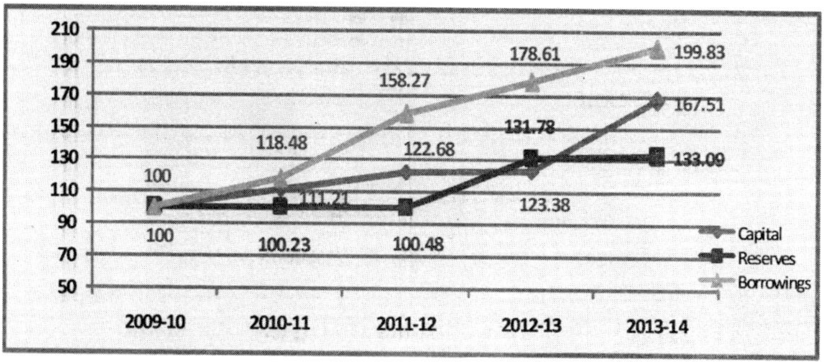

Interpretation

Table 1 depicts the funds of DCCBs and their trends in the forms of capitals, reserves and borrowings. The capital is 648.85 Lakhs in 2009-10 and it has been increased and reached 1086.86 Lakhs in 2013-14 with a growth of 67.51%. In 2009-10, the reserves are 1421.70 lakhs and in 2013-14 these reserves are increased up to 1892.11 with a percentage of 33.09%. The borrowings are 5654.85 lakhs during 2009-10 and in 2013-14 they are recorded 11300 lakhs with a percentage of (199.83-100) 99.83%. The banks are collected borrowings because of their medium and short term needs. The average of capital, reserves and borrowings is 810.77, 1608.16, 8540. 97 lakhs.

TABLE 2
Growth of Investments

(Rs. in Lakhs)

Year	*Investments*	*Trend %*
2009-10	504.81	100
2010-11	516.31	102.28
2011-12	621.01	123.02
2012-13	685.16	135.73
2013-14	676.38	133.99
Mean	600.73	119.00
S D	76.93	15.24
C V	12.81	12.81

Base Year: 2009-10.
Source : Annual Reports of Central Co-operative Bank Panchkula.

Graph 2 : Investments Growth %

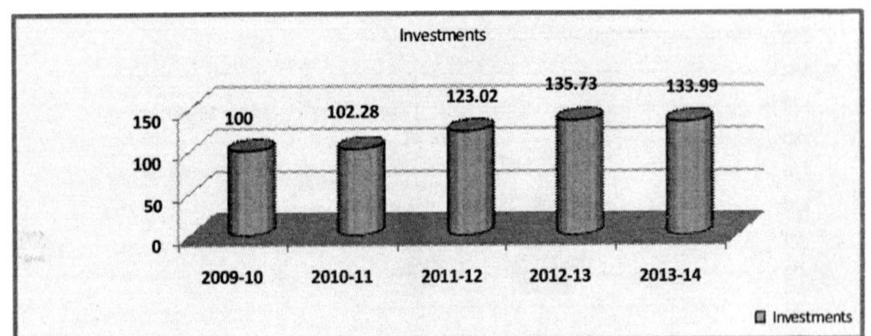

Interpretation

Table 2 depicts the investment by DCCBs and their growth patterns. During the year 2009-10, the investments are 504.81 lakhs and it has been increased gradually and reached 676.38 lakhs with a growth of 33.99%. The average of investments of the bank is 600.73 lakhs during the study period. The S D of the bank is 76.93 lakhs and C.V is 12.81.

TABLE 3

Deposits, Credits and CD Ratios

(Rs. in Lakhs)

Year	*Deposits*	*Trend %*	*Advances*	*Trend %*	*C/D ratio*
2009-10	11727.73	100	14165.02	100	120.78
2010-11	14805.58	126.24	16790.56	118.54	113.41
2011-12	13857.25	118.16	17998.01	127.06	129.88
2012-13	13855.07	118.14	19610.44	138.44	141.54
2013-14	14219.58	121.25	21828.34	154.10	153.51
Mean.	13693.04	116.76	18078.47	127.63	132.03
S D	1042.18	8.89	2584.13	18.24	247.95
C V	7.61	7.61	14.29	14.29	187.78

Base Year : 2009-10.
Source : Annual Reports of Central Co-operative Bank Panchkula.

Interpretation

The above Table 3 has been show that the deposits are 11727.73 lakhs during the year 2009-10. Later it has been increased to Rs

Graph 3 : C/D Ratio of DCCB Panchkula

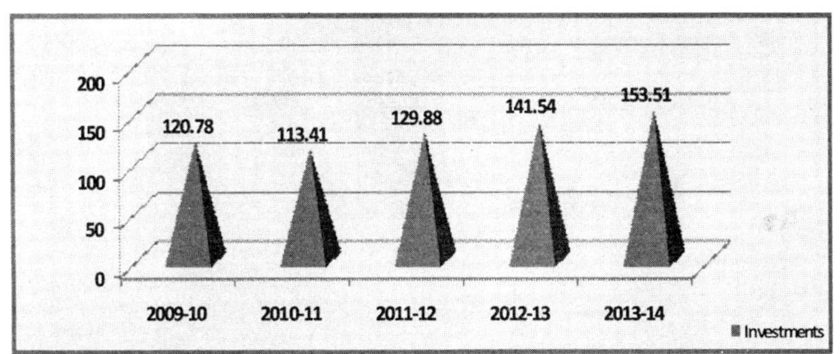

14219.58 lakhs with a trend of 21.25%. Whereas the capital deployment is 14165.02 lakhs and they are increased to Rs. 21828.34 lakhs with a percentage of 54.10%. The average of deposits and advances are 13693.04 and 18078.47.

The proportion of the capital deployed to the deposits mobilised is known as C/D ratio. C/D ratio is the best parameter to measure the performance of a bank. In 2010-11, the C/D ratio is 113.41, it is the lowest ratio during the study period. The C/D is increased year by year and reached 153.51% in 2013-14. It indicates that level at the investors can invest in credit. The average C/D ratio is 132.03%.

Table 4
Position of Incomes and Expenditures

(Rs. In Lakhs)

Year	*Incomes*	*Trend %*	*Expenditures*	*Trend %*
2009-10	1175.51	100	1531.49	100
2010-11	1436.03	122.16	1372.59	89.62
2011-12	1679.88	142.91	1638.62	107.00
2012-13	1892.89	161.03	2271.25	148.30
2013-14	2064.39	175.62	2021.25	131.98
Mean	1649.74	140.34	1767.04	115.38
S D	317.03	26.97	330.58	21.59
C V	19.22	19.22	18.71	18.71

Base Year : 2009-10.

Source : Annual Reports of Central Co-operative Bank Panchkula.

Graph 4 : Trend % of Incomes and Expenditures

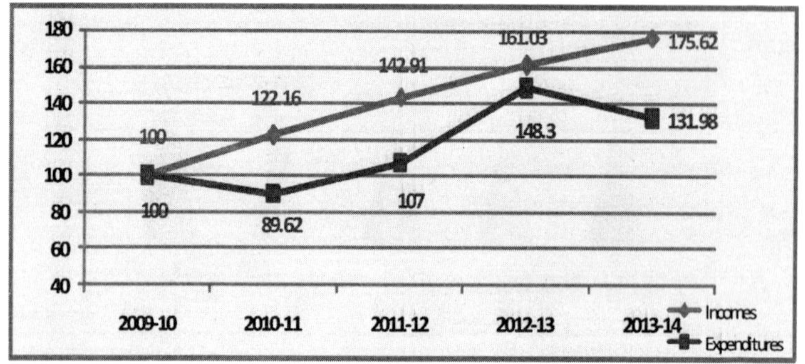

Interpretation

Table 4 analysed the income and expenditure of a bank. The table shows that the expenditure is 1531.49 lakhs in 2009-10 and increase during the year and reached 2021.25 lakh in 2013-14. In 2009-10, the income was1175.51 lakhs. It increase year by year and in 2013-14, income of the bank was 2064.39 lakhs with a percentage of 75.62 %. The S.D and C.V of income and expenditure are 317.03, 19.22% and 330.58, 18.71%.

TABLE 5
Position of Profits

(*Rs. In Lakhs*)

Year	*Profits*	*Trend*
2009-10	-355.98	100
2010-11	63.44	-17.82
2011-12	41.26	-11.59
2012-13	-378.36	106.29
2013-14	43.14	-12.12
Mean	-117.3	32.95
S D	204.29	57.39
C V	-174.16	174.16

Base Year: 2009-10.
Source : Annual Reports of Central Co-operative Bank Panchkula.

Graph 5 : Trend % of Profits

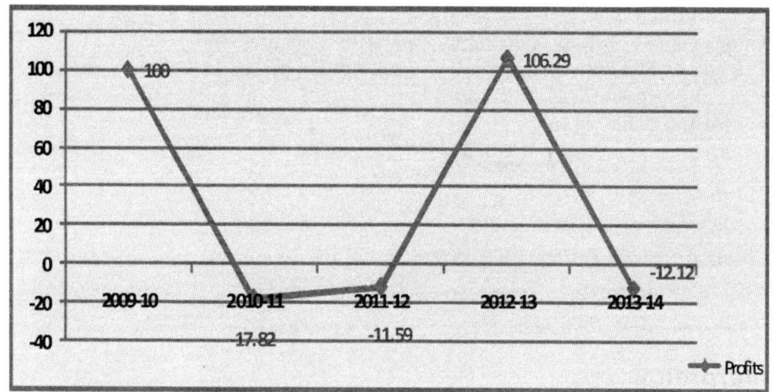

Interpretation

Table 5 depict the profit of a DCCB Panchkula. Profit is a important element to measure the performance of a bank. Profit shows the financial position of a bank. In the above tablet there is a loss of 355.98 lakhs to a bank in 2009-10. The bank earn profits in next two years and gain loss in next year. In 2013-14, the banks have profits of 43.14 lakhs with a growth trend of -12.12%. The average profits are -117.3 lakhs. Profits are the difference between income and expenditures.

CONCLUSION

We used different statistical techniques to measures the performance of DCCB Punchkula. From the above analysis, it is concluded that the performance of this bank is average because in the profits there is negative trend in the starting period later there is negligible positive trend. The capital, reserves and borrowings are increasing with positive trends. Investment is also increasing with positive trends. Deposits are also increasing with increasing positive growth and maintain C.V is 7.61%. The capital deployed have a increasing growth trend and maintain 14.29% C.V.

References

Annual Reports of District Central Co-operative Bank Panchkula.

Prof. Amparo Melian-Navarro: The role of Co-operative Banking System in the European Union-27: An Analysis of the SPANISH case.

Dr. Jai Kishan Chandel: A Study on Financial Performance of DCCBs in Haryana—A Comparative Study.

Dr. E. Gnanasekaran, Dr. M. Anbaigan and N. Abdul Nazar: A Study on the Urban Co-operative Bank Success and Growth in Vellore District—Statistical Analysis.
Laurel Shaper Walters, Putting Co-operative Learning to the Test.
Trirupathi Kanchu, Performance Evaluation of DCCBs in India—A Study.
www.rbi .org. in
www.harcobank.nic.in

16

An Analysis of Service Tax in India

HARVINDER SINGH AND PARVEEN KUMAR

CONCEPT

Service tax is a form of indirect tax imposed on specified services called "taxable services". Service tax can be levied on certain services provided by certain categories of persons including companies, associations, firms, body of individuals, etc. Service sector contribute about 64% to the GDP. Services constitute a very heterogeneous spectrum of economic activities. Today, services cover wide range of activities such as management, banking, insurance, hospitality consultancy, communication, administration, entertainment, research and development activities world over. Service sector is now occupying the centre stage of the Indian economy. In the contemporary world, development of services sector has become synonymous with the advancement of the economy.

SHARES OF SERVICES IN ECONOMY

Service sector has become the main contributors to the GDP not only in developed economies like USA (72.8%) and UK (75%) but also in developing economies like China (42.6%), Pakistan (54.8%) and Brazil (68.5%). Services constitute 54.9% of our GDP.

Economists hold the view that there is no distinction between the consumptions of good and consumption of services as both satisfy human needs. Collection of revenue through direct taxes is a problem in developing nations. With individual income disparities and narrow base there is a persisting attitude to evade the direct tax in India. On the other hand indirect taxes are hidden in the cost of goods and services and it is more convenient the collect indirect taxes the cost of the collecting is also very minimal.

Currently Indian economy is the second fastest growing economy in the World, next only to China. In terms of US dollar exchange rates, it is the 12th largest economy in the World. The GDP has crossed a trillion dollar mark in 2007. Indian is considered to have best macroeconomic stability in the World. The sector of IT, high and services like hospitality and knowledge proven services have received tremendous growth in the past five years.

Through India has the second highest growth rate in the World, its rank in terms of human development index (which is broadly used has a measure of file expectancy, adult literacy and standard of living) has gone down to 128 among 177 countries in 2007 compared to 126 in year 2006.

The contribution of various sectors in the Indian GDP were as followers:

Sector	*Year 1990-91*	*Year 2005-06*	*Year 2006-07*
Agriculture	32%	20%	17%
Industry	27%	26%	29%
Service	41%	54%	54%

Source : Economic Survey, 2006-07.

It is an achievement news that today the service sector is contributing more than half of the Indian GDP. It takes India one step closer to the developed economics of the world. Earlier it was agriculture which mainly contributed to the Indian GDP. The Indian government is still looking up to improve the GDP of the country and so several steps have been taken to boost the economy. Policies of FDI, SEZ's and NRI Investment have been framed to give a past to the economy and enhance the GDP.

HISTORY OF SERVICES TAX IN INDIA

Dr. Man Mohan Singh, the Union Finance Minister introduced

the concept of service tax in the year 1994-95 stating that there is no sound reason for exemption services in India from Taxation but it's a new era to expand the horizon of revenue generating effort.

Service Tax was first brought into force with effect from 1 July 1994. All services providers in India, except the state of Jammu and Kashmir are required to pay service tax in India. Initially only three services were brought under the net of service tax and the tax rate was 5%. Gradually more services came under the service tax. The rate of tax was increased from 5% to 8% w.e.f. 14 May 2003 from 10 September 2004 the rate of service tax was enhanced to 10% to 8%. Besides this 2% education cess on the amount of service tax was also introduces in the Union Budget 2006-07 Service Tax was increased from 10% to 12%. On Feb. 24, 2009 in order to relief the industry. The rate of service tax was reduced from 10% to 9%.

In latest, Union budget which are announced by Finance Minister Mr. Arun Jately on 28th Feb. 2015, the service tax was increased from 12.36 to 14%.

Legal Base of Service Tax

Article 265 of the constitution lays down that no tax shall be levied or collected except by the authority of law. Schedule VII divided this subject into three categories:

1) Union List (only central government has power of legislation)
2) State List (only state government has power of legislation)
3) Concurrent List (both central and state government can pass legislation)

Administration of Service Tax

Service Tax in India is regulated and administered by the Central Excise Commissioner who work directly under the department of revenue, ministry of finance, central board of excise and customs and the Government of India. The interesting thing about service tax in India is that the government of depends heavenly on the voluntary compliance of the service providers.

For collecting service tax in India, this is expected to faster and sustain faith in Indian citizens regarding the Government's tax initiatives.

Justification of the Study

In the late seventees the Govt. of India initiated an exercise to find out alternative services of revenue generation. Government's primary services of revenue are direct and indirect taxes. Central excise duty as the goods manufactured/produced in India and custom duty on imported goods constitute the major secrecy of indirect taxes in India. But revenue receipts from customers and excise duty are declined due to WTO commitments and rationalisation of commodity duties. It is also a well known and an established fact that services constitute a larger proportion of the consumption of the rich rather than the poor as the demand for servicing in income is elastic. Depending in the socio-economic compulsion, each country evolved a taxation system on services adopting either a comprehensive approach or a selecting approach unless they are specifically excluded, whereas under the selective approach only specified services are taxable. India has adopted the system of selective approach.

Objectives

The study has the following objectives :

1) To analyze the concept of Service Tax in India.
2) To study of services tax revenue collection from various sectors.
3) To identify the various activity of services. No. of assesses which comes under preview of service tax.

Hypothesis of the Study

i) H_0 : There is no significant difference between tax revenue from service tax collection and number of Assesses.

H_1 : There is significant difference between tax revenue from service tax and number of assesses.

Research Methodology

The data of Service tax used in this study, have been taken from secondary services, i.e. published report from 2000 to 2013-14 editing, classification and tabulation of revenue data has been done as per the requirement of the study.

For assessing the service tax revenue collection no. of services under tax net, and number of assesses have been analyzed. For assessing the behavior of data, statistical technique have also been used, e.g. coefficient of correlation and student t-test of analysing the significant of data.

Analysis of Service Tax in India

When the concept of service tax was introduced in 1994-95, only three services came under the preview of the tax. Since, then, the several phases and instalments, the government has brought more than 100 categories under the service tax including :

- Telephone
- General Insurance
- Air Travel Agents
- Market Research Agencies
- Broadcasting
- Fashion Designing
- Internet Cafes
- Intellectual Property Services
- Packaging Services

Table 1

Statement of Revenue Collection and No. of Assesses of Indian Service Tax since 1997-98

Financial Year	*Revenue (Rs. Crore)*	*% growth over previous year*	*No. of Services under tax net*	*No. of assesses*	*% growth over P. Years*
2001-02	3305	Base Year	—	—	—
2002-03	4125	25	41	187577	Base Year
2003-04	7890	91	52	232048	23.71
2004-05	14196	80	62	403856	74.04
2005-06	23053	62	75	774988	91.89
2006-07	37482	63	84	846155	9.18
2007-08	51133	36	99	940641	11.17
2008-09	60702	19	100	1073075	14.08
2009-10	58336	-3.87	106	1204570	8.78
2010-11	71016	22	117	1307286	8.53
2011-12	97509	37	119	1409335	7.80
2012-13	132697	36	All (except pew)	1506220	6.87
2013-14	180141	36	All (except pew)	1603205	6.43

Table 1 shows that annual growth rate of service tax revenue collection and no. of assesses, during the study period may found that highest growth rate of service tax revenue was in the year of 2003-04, 2004-05, 2005-06, 2006-07, which was 91%, 80%, 63% and 62% and lowest growth rate was in the year 2009-10, which is -3.89%.

Testing of Hypothesis

There is no significant difference between service tax revenue collection from various services and number of assesses. This hypothesis is tested by student 't' – test at the level of 5%.

Value of co-efficient of correlation is

$$t = \frac{t\ 0.398}{\sqrt{1-r^2}} \times \sqrt{n-2}$$

$$T = \frac{0.398}{1\ -\ (0.398)2} \times \sqrt{13-2}$$

$t\ =\ \angle 4394$

d.f. = n–2, = 13-2, t.005 = 2.201

Calculated Value < table value

1.4394 < 2.201

Decision

So, in this case H_0 accepted, and so therefore, there is no significant difference between the tax revenue collection and no. of assesses. That tax revenue collection is having a positive relationship with the number of assesses.

CONCLUSION

On the basis of this study we can say that the main purpose of imposing various taxes like service tax on various services which are taxable under the service tax act to generate revenue and increases revenue collection for the economic development of the country. The reason behind that the assesses is not only generate revenue but also to eliminate disparity between the rich and the poor. But service taxes do not fulfill this objective because some services are used by both rich and poor and they have to bear the service tax irrespective of their economic condition on 28 Feb. 2015. Finance Minister Mr. Arun Jatley was to increased the service tax from 12.36% to 14% in the union budget. This situation is not favourable in the case of weaker section because they cannot afford such taxes so this is a injustice towards economically weaker section.

References

Charted secretary, Dec. 2009.
Indirect tax manual 2009-10.
The economic times, June 2009.
The economic survey, 2009-10.
The economic survey, 2010-11.
Union Budget General 2009-10.
Union Budget General 2010-11.
Union Budget General 2011-12.
Union Budget General 2012-13.
Union Budget General 2013-14.

17

Banking Sector Reforms

E-banking

RICHA LOMAS AND PRABJOT KAUR

ABSTRACT

India's banking sector is constantly growing since the turn of the century, there has been a noticeable upsurge in transactions through ATM's, internet and mobile banking. In the 21st century, banking has also became innovative. The IT Act 1999 has given new dimensions to Indian banking industry. The new evolution is E-banking that is electronic banking through telephone, cellphone and internet. E-banking aids in effective payment and accounting system which ultimately enhances speed of delivery of banking services and leads to fast customer service and results in customer satisfaction. Internet banking quality is important factor that influence adoption of internet banking and customers' loyalty. Following the passing of Banking laws (amendments) bill by Indian parliament in 2012, banking industry observed major modifications. This bill allows RBI (reserve bank of India) to make final guidelines on issuing new licences, which will result in bigger number of banks in the country. No doubt E-banking has considerably improved efficiency and convenience but there are several challenges for regulators and supervisors. This paper focuses on issues, challenges before the banks regarding E-banking and measures to face them and at the end, paper suggests how banks can convert the emerging challenges into fruitful opportunities.

Keywords: E-Banking, RBI, Internet Banking, Customer Service.

INTRODUCTION

Electronic banking is the wave of future. It is also popular as "Virtual banking". It is the outcome of growing expectations of bank's customers. Online banking has become an accepted norm of monetary transaction for millions of people in the world. The ease with which a customer can check his account, make online payments and transfer money between accounts has made this mode of banking popular among those who have shortage of time to visit the bank physically. According to Ram Sangapura, General Manager, Central Bank of India, facilities like online banking, mobile banking have drastically cut down the cost of providing a service. This saving is passed on to customers who are willing to go beyond the traditional banking channel. According to Industry experts a bank spends an average of Rs. 40 for each transaction conducted at a branch. If a customer uses the ATM facility, the cost drops to Rs. 18.20 per transaction but it is still much higher than the cost involved in E-Banking. According to Ozuru *et al.* (2010)". The importance of electronic payment system in any country can never be over emphasized, due to the dramatic transformation in technological advancement that is being experienced by the global financial industry.

REVIEW OF LITERATURE

Internet banking, however, is now used as the term for new age banking system (Singhal and Padhmanbhan, 2008). Internet banking is defined as the use of the Internet to deliver banking activities such as funds transfer, paying bills, viewing current and savings account balance, paying mortgages and purchasing financial instruments and certificates of deposits (Singhal and Padhmanbhan, 2008; Ahasanul *et al.*, 2009). Internet banking is also called Online banking, e-payment and e-banking (Ozuru *et al.*, 2010; Singhal and Padhmanbhan, 2008; Beer, 2006; Jun and Cai, 2001; IAMAI, 2006). E–payment is described as a means whereby banking businesses are transacted through automated processes and electronic devices such as personal computers, telephones, and fax machines, Internet card payments and other electronic channels (Turban *et al.*, 2006; Ozuru *et al.*, 2010). The electronic communications used in Internet banking includes: Internet, e-mail, e-books, data base and mobile phones (Chaffey *et al.*, 2006). Cell phone banking apart from Internet banking is considered the way of the future (Fisher–French, 2007;

Masocha *et al.*, 2011). In the recent time, the development in technology has affected business organizations in several ways, most especially in terms of management and control; marketing and research; operations and decision-making. It is therefore, the vogue that every organization wants to tap the benefits accrue from technology development. In other word, most organizations find means of enjoying the advantages encapsulated in the new technologies (Larpsiri and Speece, 2004; Durkin and Howcroft, 2003; Masocha *et al.*, 2011).

Objectives

1. The primary objective of this paper is to get full acquaintance of E-Banking and its benefits.
2. To know the challenges in E-banking.

Research Methodology

The primary source of the information in this research study is the secondary data.The available information on internet regarding the E-Banking has been extensively used to complete the research paper. All the available Journals, Articles, papers provided necessary information to the group to finalize the research paper.

INTERNET BANKING HISTORY OF THE WORLD

According Ongkasuwan (2002) UK internet banking has encountered a rise in demand of cross-border payment transaction including small amount. UK banks keep on developing and introducing new internet banking service to satisfy their consumers. By June 1999 the UK and eight of the European countries namely France, Portugal, Germany, Spain, Switzerland, Luxembourg, Holland and Scandinavia has become the leading nation in providing internet banking. Swedish and Finnish market leads the world in internet banking penetration and the quality of their online service. Standinaviska Easkilda Banken (SEB) was the first bank in Sweden to go online in December 1996. Almost all of 150 banks in Norway have established 'net bank'.

Bank of China has given the green light to introduce internet banking in 1996 and in 1997 China Merchant Bank was the first to start internet banking and telephone banking service. The new internet banking provides 24 hours access to financial transaction. In 2004 the number of consumers using internet banking was about 10 million. Internet banking developed quickly to such extent in 2007 it represent about 245.5 trillion RMB of the transaction in China.

South Africa bank starts operating on the internet in 1996. It has been a slow start but consumers are responding because it is convenient, secure and cheap. Amalgamated Bank of South Africa (ABSA) was the first bank to implement internet banking and was followed by Ned Bank. Karin (2000) suggest that 672,000 consumers are banking online or have banked online. ABSA provide it own free internet in order to encourage more consumer to use internet banking. However, consumer acceptance and ease of use are less compare to other country such as UK where internet has reached about 3.5 million of users.

INTERNET BANKING IN INDIA

Finland was the first country in the world to have taken a lead in E-banking. In India, it was ICICI Bank which initiated E-banking as early as 1997 under the brand name Infinity. Several initiatives taken by the Government of India as well as the Reserve Bank of India (RBI) have facilitated the development of E-banking in India. The Government of India enacted the IT Act, 2000 with effect from October 17, 2000, which provides legal recognition to electronic transactions and other means of electronic commerce. A study on the Internet users, conducted by Internet and Mobile Association of India (IAMAI), found that about 23% of the online users prefer IB as the banking channel in India, second to ATM which is preferred by 53%. Out of the 6,365 Internet users sampled, 35% use online banking channels in India.

This shows that a significant number of online users do not use IB, and hence there is a need to understand the reasons for not using it. Until the advent of ATMs, people were unaware were not directly affected by the technological revolutions happening in the banking sector. ATMs became the major revelation for customers, since it offered the facility to avoid long queues in front of the cashiers in banks. It also provided them the flexibility of withdrawing money—anytime, anywhere. In the study by IAMAI, it was found that the people are not doing financial transactions on the banks' Internet sites in India because of reasons such as security concerns (43%), preference for face-to-face transactions (39%), lack of knowledge about transferring online (22%), lack of user friendliness (10%), or lack of the facility in the current bank (2%).

The popular services covered under E-Banking include:

Automated Teller Machine (ATM)—Banks have now installed their own Automated Teller Machine (ATM) throughout the country at convenient locations. By using this, customers can deposits or withdrew money from their own account any time.

Debit Cards—Banks are now providing Debit Cards to their customers can use this cards for purchasing goods and services at different places in lieu of cash. The amount paid through debit card is automatically debited from the customer's account.

Credit Cards—Credit Cards are issued by the bank to persons who may or may not have an account in the bank. Just like Debit Cards. Credit Cards are used to make payment for purchase, so that the person does not have to carry cash. Banks allow certain credit period to the credit cardholders to make payment of credit cards. Interest is charged if the cardholders are not able to pay back the credit extended to him within a stipulated period. This interest rate is generally quite high.

Phone Banking—The person having an account can get information of his account; make banking transaction like fixed deposits, money transfer, demand drafts, collection and payment of bills, etc. by using telephone. In mobile phone a customer can receive and send messages (SMS) from and to the bank in addition to all the function possible through phone banking.

Smart Cards—Smart Cards usually contains an embedded 8-bit micro-processor. The microprocessor is under a contact pad on one side of the card. The microprocessor can replace the usual magnetic strips present on a credit card or debit card. The chips in the cards are capable of many kinds of transaction.

E-cheques—An E-cheque is the electronic version of paper cheque. The information and legal framework on the E-cheque is the same as that of the paper cheque, it can now be used in place of paper cheques to do any and all remote transaction. An E-cheque works in the same way a paper cheque does.

Plastic Money—At the end of 20th century another form of money emerged which is called plastic money. The emergence of this money started from the introduction of credit cards. At the beginning economist classified credit cards also as credit money but introduction of Debit Cards and ATM cards compelled economist to admit that another form of currency has evolved that is plastic money. A PIN code is used perform transaction with plastic money.

Internet Banking—Transaction at the convince of customers, saving times and cost through computers is popularly known as Online Banking. It is also known as Net Banking. It is also done through a computer with internet facilities. Customers can monitor and control their funds through Internet Banking. They can check account balance view their account, get summary statement, make bill payments, etc.

BENEFITS OF E-BANKING

The main advantages of e-banking for corporate customers are as follows (BankAway! 2001; Gurău, 2002).

1. Cost Savings

According to Burnham (1998) it required less than US$25000 to establish an internet site and less than $25000 to maintain it one year compared to the $1 to 2 million required to set-up traditional branch and about $350,000 needed to operate it. Robinson (2000) argued that the cost is less when transaction is done online as compare in branch. Marketing campaigns and other advertisements are available on the internet 24 hours a day without any additional fees being charged. Internet banking is a paperless transaction which makes financing communication quicker it results in a save of time since everything is done electronically.

2. Attract New Customer

Sheshunoff (2000) admit that the bank introduced internet banking with an attempt to reach new customers and to make exist difficult. As consumer is the most important asset of an organization financial institutions provide personalized banking service to cater their needs. Internet banking is attractive because consumers are more satisfied with all the facilities it offer and it is also said to create positive word of mouth.

3. Geographic Reach

With the widespread use of the internet banking is no longer bound to time and geographic factors. Through internet banking consumers can have easy access to their account wherever they are. The introduction of e-banking has brought the concept of "Anytime Anywhere Banking". For example, if a client is out of country and has a problem of money, the client is able to access his or her account from anywhere given that there is internet access.

4. Improved Image

Internet banking is considered as a norm for almost all banks since it is and may be a useful competition tool for bank to attract new customer and retained existing one. The bank makes use of the internet as means to increase business status for innovation (Yakhlef, 2001). It is easier for bank to introduce new products and services thereby attracting new customers.

5. Consumer Acceptance of Internet Banking

On searching literature review we found different factor that encourages consumer to use and accept internet banking channel. Li *et al.* (1999) argued that understanding of the internet channel, convenience, perceived accessibility, familiarity and utility are key factors that influenced the adoption of electronic banking by consumer.

6. Convenience

Generally all research shows that the more evident, straightforward and easy a new technology is the more advantage it provides the more likely it will be adopted by consumers. Survey done by Pew (2005) show that 73% of the American used the internet because it is convenient. They can have access to it on a 24 hours basis. Accessibility which can be associated to convenience is another factor that influence consumer to use e-banking.

7. Computer Skill and Past Consumption

Karjaluoto *et al.* (2002) argues that consumer readiness to adopt new technologies depend on his or her prior experience and past interaction such as internet, email, e-payment and ATM was a major factor for attitude towards online banking practice. Even thought they think that internet banking might be a necessary tool for doing transaction they might be less confident and comfortable for using it.

8. Demographic Factor

Studies proved that demographic factor such age, education level might affect the adoption of e-banking. Wang *et al.* (2001) found that age affect the use of internet banking. Recent survey confirm the difficulties to attract people aged 65 and more to use e-banking (Ilett 2005; Perumal and Shanmugam, 2005). On the other hand, there are more young adults that are interested in new technologies such as internet to carry out activities.

9. Education Level

Education also plays an important role on consumer preference to use e-banking. People with higher education such university graduates are more comfortable and have knowledge in using these new technology this is because education is correlated with individual computer literacy. Therefore we can say that internet banking is not met for everyone.

10. Social Pressure

Cheung *et al.* (2000) stated that social pressure plays an important part in explaining internet usage. Social pressure can come from any social group such as parent or friend. A survey conducted in HongKong by Cheung (2001) state that classmate and friend may have potential influence on internet users. Social factor are prevailing forces that not only influence consumer to adopt internet banking but also persuade them to continue internet banking.

CHALLENGES IN E-BANKING

This changing financial landscape brings with it new challenges for bank management and regulatory and supervisory authorities. The major ones stem from increased cross-border transactions resulting from drastically lower transaction costs and the greater ease of banking activities, and from the reliance on technology to provide banking services with the necessary security.

Regulatory Risk: Because the Internet allows services to be provided from anywhere in the world, there is a danger that banks will try to avoid regulation and supervision. What can regulators do? They can require even banks that provide their services from a remote location through the Internet to be licensed. Licensing would be particularly appropriate where supervision is weak and cooperation between a virtual bank and the home supervisor is not adequate. Licensing is the norm, for example, in the United States and most of the countries of the European Union. A virtual bank licensed outside these jurisdictions that wishes to offer electronic banking services and take deposits in these countries must first establish a licensed branch.

Legal Risk: Banks might not be fully versed in a jurisdiction's local laws and regulations before they begin to offer services there, either with a license or without a license if one is not required. When a license is not required, a virtual bank—lacking contact with its host country supervisor—may find it even more difficult to stay abreast of regulatory changes. As a consequence, virtual banks could unknowingly violate customer protection laws, including on data collection and privacy, and regulations on soliciting.

Operational Risk: The reliance on new technology to provide services makes security and system availability the central operational risk of electronic banking. Security threats can come from inside or outside the system, so banking regulators and supervisors must ensure that banks have appropriate practices in place to guarantee the confidentiality of data, as well as the integrity of the system and the data. Banks' security practices should be regularly tested and reviewed by outside experts to analyze network vulnerabilities and recovery preparedness. Managing heightened operational risks needs to become an integral part of banks' overall management of risk, and supervisors need to include operational risks in their safety and soundness evaluations.

Reputational Risk: Breaches of security and disruptions to the system's availability can damage a bank's reputation. The more a bank relies on electronic delivery channels, the greater the potential for reputational risks. Reputational risks also stem from customer misuse of security precautions or ignorance about the need for such precautions. Security risks can be amplified and may result in a loss of confidence in electronic delivery channels.

LOOKING FORWARD

An old Chinese saying goes: ***If you don't know where you are going—you will never get there.*** Globally, the financial sector is metamorphosing under the impact of competitive, regulatory and technological forces. The banking sector is currently in a transition phase with re-alignment, mergers and entry of new players from different industry is becoming common. Many countries including are de-regulating their banking sector and government policies no longer form an entry barrier to banks competitors. Technology has leveled the playing field: the bargaining power of consumers is increasing, switching costs are becoming lower and consumer loyalties are harder to retain. Primary goal of the banking sector including every Bank is mainly to make profit, which in turn is ploughed back to increase business and reach, and pay dividends or share profits to the stakeholders. This is perfectly correct, yet generic goal. More over the product (schemes) differentiation is very difficult for banks as most of the products sold are constrained by legal or industry regulations. Now, if you are already thinking about Technology as a tool in Banking you could probably set some of these goals:

- Selling financial products and services
- Cutting operational costs
- Branding and Market recognition
- Keeping profitable customers

CONCLUSION

From all of this, we have learnt that information technology has empowered customers and businesses with information needed to make better investment decisions. At the same time, technology is allowing banks to offer new products, operate more efficiently, raise productivity, expand geographically and compete globally. A more efficient, productive banking industry is providing services of greater quality and value. E-banking has become a necessary survival weapon and is fundamentally changing the banking industry worldwide. Today, the click of the mouse offers customers banking services at a much lower cost and also empowers them with unprecedented freedom in choosing vendors for their financial service needs. No country today has a choice whether to implement E-banking or not given the global and competitive nature of the economy. The invasion of banking by technology has created an information age and commoditization of banking services. Banks have come to realize that survival in the new e-economy depends on delivering some or all of their banking services on the Internet while continuing to support their traditional infrastructure. The rise of E-banking is redefining business relationships and the most successful banks will be those that can truly strengthen their relationship with their customers. Without any doubt, the international scope of E-banking provides new growth perspectives and Internet business is a catalyst for new technologies and new business processes. With rapid advances in telecommunication systems and digital technology, E-banking has become a strategic weapon for banks to remain profitable. It has been transformed beyond what anyone could have foreseen 25 years ago. Two years ago, E-banking was a strategic advantage, nowadays; it is a business reality, if not a necessity.

References

Obaid, Magda (2007). E-BANKING. Amman, Dar Safa to Post.

Rousan, Farouk (2003). Introduction to the E-BANKING, Oman, House thought of printing and publishing.

El, Amal (2002). Society and the ways of the E-BANKING. Cairo, Dar Al-Arab Thought.

Marina, Kamal (1999). Reference in the E-BANKING, Cairo, the publisher of the universities.

18

The Impact on Financial Position of Indian Companies after Adoption and Convergence to IFRS

KAPIL AGGARWAL AND KARAMVIR SHEOKAND

ABSTRACT

The globalization has brought a lot of changes in doing business across the world. The use of different accounting frameworks in different countries creates confusion for users of financial statements resulting into inefficiency in capital markets across the world. The increasing complexity of business transactions and globalization of capital markets call the regulators, multinational companies, auditing firm and investors to see the need for common standards in all areas of financial reporting. Thus, the case for a single set of globally accepted accounting standards has prompted many countries to pursue convergence of national accounting standards with IFRS. International Financial Reporting System (IFRS) is the new language of financial reporting and communication to investors and other stakeholders. More than 120 countries have adopted the process of convergence with IFRS. India has committed itself at the G-20 to make the companies IFRS compliant from April 1st, 2011 in a phased manner. The goal of IFRS is to create comparable, reliable and transparent financial statement that will facilitate greater cross-border capital raising, trade and better corporate governance practice. The paper attempts to show the impact of convergence to IFRS on financial position of the company. The secondary data is studied to know the impact of convergence to IFRS on financial position with the help of case study of WIPRO limited. It also discusses the challenges faced by firms in the process of adoption of IFRS in India. The paper concludes the ways through which these challenges can be addressed.

Keywords: IFRS, Indian GAAP, Accounting Standards, IASB,

INTRODUCTION

IFRS are set of accounting standards developed by International Accounting Standard Board (IASB). IFRS were adopted legally first time in 2005 by European Union. Other countries with developed capital markets have adopted or in the process of adopting IFRS in for reporting purpose.

In India, Accounting standards are formulated by council of Institute of Chartered Accounts of India (ICAI). In 2007, India has decided to converge with IFRS in 2007. ICAI started the process of developing a complete set of accounting standard that are "converged with" IFRS—which will be known as Indian AS . There is a difference between adoption and convergence to IFRS. Adoption means using IFRS as issued by IASB. Convergence means that the Indian Accounting Standard Board and IASB would continue working together to develop high quality, compatible accounting standard over time.

India announced that it will converge to IFRS in phased manner.

Phase I (Opening Balance Sheet as at 1 April, 2011):

- Companies which are part of BSE-Sensex 30 and NSE-Nifty 50;
- Companies whose shares or other securities are listed outside India;
- Companies whether listed or not, having net worth of more than Rs. 1,000 crores.

Phase II (Opening Balance Sheet as at 1 April, 2013)*:

- Companies not covered in Phase 1 and having net worth exceeding Rs. 500 crores.

Phase III (Opening Balance Sheet as at 1 April, 2014)*:

- Listed companies not covered in earlier phases.

If the financial year of a company commences at a date other than 1 April, the nut shall prepare its opening balance sheet at the commencement of immediately following financial year.

Separate Road Map would be prepared for banking and insurance companies.

The issue of convergence with IFRS has gained significant momentum in India recently.

Road Map Revised for Implementation of Indian Accounting Standards for Companies Other Than Banking Companies, Insurance Companies and NBFCs; Notification to Follow Soon

In pursuance of the Budget statement, the Ministry of Corporate Affairs, Government of India after wide consultations with various stakeholders and regulators, has drawn-up a revised Road Map for companies other than Banking Companies, Insurance Companies and Non-Banking Finance Companies (NBFC's) for implementation of Indian Accounting Standards (Ind AS) converged with the International Financial Reporting Standards (IFRS).

The Indian Accounting Standards (Ind AS) shall be applicable to the companies as follows:

A. On voluntary basis for financial statements for accounting periods beginning on or after April 1, 2015, with the comparatives for the periods ending 31st March, 2015 or thereafter;

B. On mandatory basis for the accounting periods beginning on or after April 1, 2016, with comparatives for the periods ending 31st March, 2016, or thereafter, for the companies specified below:

   i. Companies whose equity and/or debt securities are listed or are in the process of listing on any stock exchange in India or outside India and having net worth of Rs. 500 Crore or more.

   ii. Companies other than those covered in (ii) (a) above, having net worth of Rs. 500 Crore or more.

   iii. Holding, subsidiary, joint venture or associate companies of companies covered under (ii) (a) and (ii) (b) above.

C. On mandatory basis for the accounting periods beginning on or after April 1, 2017, with comparatives for the periods ending 31st March, 2017, or thereafter, for the companies specified below:

i. Companies whose equity and/or debt securities are listed or are in the process of being listed on any stock exchange in India or outside India and having net worth of less than rupees 500 Crore.
ii. Companies other than those covered in paragraph (ii) and paragraph (iii)(a) above that is unlisted companies having net worth of rupees 250 crore or more but less than rupees 500 Crore.
iii. Holding, subsidiary, joint venture or associate companies of companies covered under paragraph (iii) (a) and (iii) (b) above.

However, Companies whose securities are listed or in the process of listing on SME exchanges shall not be required to apply Ind AS. Such companies shall continue to comply with the existing Accounting Standards unless they choose otherwise.

D. Once a company opts to follow the Indian Accounting Standards (Ind AS), it shall be required to follow the Ind AS for all the subsequent financial statements.

E. Companies not covered by the above roadmap shall continue to apply existing Accounting Standards prescribed in Annexure to the Companies (Accounting Standards) Rules, 2006.

A notification on the above lines shall be shortly issued by Indian Government.

BENEFITS OF ADOPTING INTERNATIONAL FINANCIAL REPORTING STANDARDS (IFRS)

- It would benefit the economy by increasing growth of international business.
- It would encourage international investing and thereby lead to more foreign capital inflows into the country.
- Investors want the information that is more relevant, reliable, timely and comparable across the jurisdictions.
- IFRS would enhance the comparability between financial statements of various companies across the globe.
- Better understanding of financial statements would benefit investors who wish to invest outside their own country.

- The industry would be able to raise capital from foreign markets at lower cost if it can create confidence in the minds of foreign investors that their financial statements comply with globally accepted accounting standards.
- It would provide professional opportunities to serve international clients.
- It would increase their mobility to work in different parts of the world either in industry or practice.
- It would reduce different accounting requirements prevailing in various countries thereby enabling enterprises to reduce cost of compliances.

INTERNATIONAL FINANCIAL REPORTING STANDARDS (IFRS) CHALLENGES

- Increase in cost initially due to dual reporting requirement which entity might have to meet till full convergence is achieved.
- Unlike several other countries, the accounting framework in India is deeply affected by laws and regulations. Changes may be required to various regulatory requirements under The Companies Act, 1956, Income Tax Act, 1961, SEBI, RBI, etc. so that IFRS financial statements are accepted generally.
- If IFRS has to be uniformly understood and consistently applied, all stakeholders, employees, auditors, regulators, tax authorities, etc. would need to be trained.
- Entity would need to incur additional cost for modifying their IT systems and procedures to enable it to collate data necessary for meeting the new disclosures and reporting requirements.
- Differences between Indian GAAP and IFRS may impact business decision/financial performance of an entity.
- Limited pool of trained resource and persons having expert knowledge on IFRSs.

LITERATURE REVIEW

- El-Gazzar *et al.* (1999) when they examine whether the company attributes—percentage of foreign sales to total sales of company, the number of foreign stock exchanges where the company is listed, the debt-to-equity ratio of the company, and membership of the European Union –

are associated with voluntary compliance with the IFRS. The findings indicate that companies desire to comply with the IFRS in order to enhance their exposure to foreign markets, to improve customer recognition, to secure foreign capital and reduce the political costs of doing business abroad.

- Tower *et al.* (1999) examine the degree of compliance with the IFRS by listed companies on the stock exchanges in six countries in the Asia-Pacific region: Australia, Hong Kong, Malaysia, the Philippines, Singapore and Thailand, and a range of the IFRS compliance determinants. The results suggest that country of location is highly significant, and "days to issuing report" was moderately significant.
- Street and Bryant (2000) examine factors linked with the overall level of disclosure and the level of compliance. The findings show the overall level of disclosure to be greater for companies with US listings, the manner in which accounting policy footnotes referred to the IFRS and the audit opinion references to International Standards of Auditing (ISA). Conversely, the results also reveal a significant extent of non-compliance with IFRS disclosure requirements.
- Joshi and Al-Mudhahki (2001) examined the compliance with IAS-1 by stock exchange listed companies in Bahrain, and the compliance practices of 37 large and medium size companies for ten disclosure items. The results reveal a high level of compliance withIAS-1 requirements.
- Street and Gray (2002) undertook a study to examine the financial statements and footnotes of a worldwide sample of companies referring to the use of the IFRS, and to assess the degree of compliance and provide evidence of the factors linked with compliance. Their findings show a significant positive relationship between the extent of compliance with the IFRS and having a US listing/filing or a non-regional listing, being in the commerce and transportation industries, referring exclusively to the use of the IFRS in the accounting policy note, being audited by a big 5þ2 firm and being domiciled in China or Switzerland. A significant negative relationship was found

between being domiciled in France, Germany, in other Western European countries and the degree of compliance with the IFRS.

- Glaum and Street (2003) examined compliance with both the IFRS and US GAAP by companies listed on Germany's New Market, in their year-2000 financial statements for a sample of 100 companies that applied the IFRS and 100 that had applied US GAAP.
- The findings indicated a substantial degree of non-compliance; that compliance is related positively with the type of auditor, listing status; and with references to the use of ISA or US GAAP in the audit opinion.
- In a recent study, Al-Shammari *et al.* (2008) examine the level of compliance with IFRS by companies in the Gulf Co-Operation Council (GCC) countries, namely: Bahrain, Oman, Kuwait, Qatar, Saudi Arabia and the United Arab Emirates, over the period1996-2002. The findings reveal that there is significant variation in compliance levels among GCC countries and between companies. The average level of compliance for all GCC companies during the study period was 75 percent and there was increase incompliance over time–from 68 percent in 1996 to 82 percent in 2002.
- In more recent studies, Chen and Zhang (2010) show that merely adopting IFRS does not necessarily lead to IFRS-type accounting practices and associated benefit, unless effective regulatory enforcement is on place. Similarly, Mihai *et al.* (2012) identify several benefits associated with adopting IFRS. They provide evidence that IFRS increase transparency, diminish information asymmetry and risk and as a result reduce the cost of capital. However, Mihai *et al.* (2012) emphasize the importance of full compliance. Madawaki (2012) acknowledges challenges face companies in complying with IFRS and recommend strengthening education and training, establishment of an independent body to monitor and enforce IFRS compliance.
- Similarly, Verriest (2011) examines the effect of audit quality on the properties of financial reporting and suggest that audit quality serves as a vital governance mechanism in ensuring compliance with accounting standards.

- Lantto & Sahlstrom (2009) also undertook a study of key financial ratios of companies of Finland and later found that the adoption of IFRS changes the magnitude of the key accounting ratios and also showed that the adoption of Fair Value Accounting rules and stricter requirements on certain Accounting issues are the reasons for the changes observed in Accounting Figures and financial ratios.
- Shobana Swamynathan(2011) studied the impact of IFRS on financial statements. It was found that there is significant change in the Total Equity and total liability position on convergence to IFRS but not prominent changes in the Total Asset Position. It was concluded that IFRS is fair value oriented and Balance Sheet oriented accounting where there are more transparent disclosures and Indian GAAP is conservative approach.
- Capkun *et al.* (2008) analyzed the impact of mandatory change in financial reporting standards in European Union and found that the transition from local GAAP to IFRS had a small but statistically significant impact on total assets, equity, total liabilities and among assets the most pronounced impact on intangible assets and property plant and equipment.
- S. Yadav (2012) studied the impact of adoption of IFRS, challenges that will come up and its adoption procedure in India. And found that transition from Indian GAAP to IFRS will face many difficulties but at the same time looking at the advantages that this adoption will confer, the convergence with IFRS is strongly recommended. This transition is not without difficulties as to the proper implementation process which would require a complete change in formats of accounts, accounting policies and more extensive disclosure requirements.

OBJECTIVES OF THE STUDY

- To examine the impact of adoption and convergence to IFRS on financial position of the company—A case study of Wipro Company.
- To study the problems and challenges faced by Indian companies in the process of convergence to IFRS.

RESEARCH METHODOLOGY

The validity of any research depends on the systematic method of collecting the data, and analyzing the same in appropriate order. The study is primarily qualitative in nature. It has been conducted mainly on the basis of literature survey and secondary Information. Various journals, newspapers and magazines articles have been referred to in writing this paper.

IMPACT OF CONVERGENCE TO IFRS ON FINANCIAL POSITION OF THE COMPANY

Wipro limited is a global leader in providing IT services; outsource R & D, infrastructure service, Business process services and business consulting. In this paper, annual report of Wipro prepared for the year ended 31-3-2014 using IFRS and Indian GAAP is considered.

TABLE 1

Comparison of IFRS and Indian GAAP Statement Balance Sheet pf Wipro as of 31st March, 2014

(Rs. in Millions)

Particulars	*Amount as per GAAP*	*Amount as per IFRS*	*Difference*	*% Change*
(1)	*(2)*	*(3)*	*(4)*	*(5)*
Assets				
Goodwill	58,416	63,422	5,006	8.57
Intangible Assets	404	1,936	1,532	379.21
Property, Plant and Equipment	47,671	51,449	3,778	7.93
Deferred Tax Assets	1553	3362	1,809	116.48
Other Non-Current Assets	42387	27449	-14,938	-35.24
Total Non-Current Assets	150431	147618	-2,813	-1.87
Current Assets				
Inventories	2293	2293	0	0.00
Trade Receivables	85467	85392	-75	-0.09
Other Current Assets	110985	113466	2,481	2.24
Unbilled Revenues	33505	39334	5,829	17.40

(Contd.)

TABLE 1 (*Contd.*)

(1)	*(2)*	*(3)*	*(4)*	*(5)*
Cash and Cash Equivalents	114201	114201	0	0.00
Total Current Assets	346451	354686	8,235	2.38
Total Assets	496882	502304	5,422	1.09
Equity				
Total Equity	321287	344886	23,599	7.35
Liabilities				
Total Non-Current Liabilities	19311	20692	1,381	7.15
Trade Payables and Accrued Expenses	52102	52256	154	0.30
Other Current Liabilities	67087	68436	1,349	2.01
Provisions	37095	1370	-35,725	-96.31
Total Current Liabilities	156284	136456	-19,828	-12.69
Total Liabilities	175595	157148	-18,447	-10.51
Total Equity And Liabilities	496882	502304	5,422	1.09

INTERPRETATION

The total assets and liabilities under IFRS is more than the Indian accounting standards by 1.09%. The most probable reasons are its fair value measurement, difference in the basis of interest capitalization, deferred tax asset recognition and difference in accounting for foreign currency forward contracts. The equity under IFRS has increased by 7.35% when compared to Indian accounting standard and Property, Plant and Equipment has also increased by 7.93% under IFRS.

MAJOR CHALLENGES IN THE PROCESS OF ADOPTION OF IFRS IN INDIA

IFRS is a set of international accounting and reporting standards which will help to harmonize company financial information, improve the transparency of accounting, and ensure that investors receive more accurate and consistent reports. Despite several benefits as may be looked out by the different people, there will be several challenges that will be faced on the way of IFRS convergence.

1. Difference in GAAP and IFRS

Adoption of IFRS means that the entire set of financial statements will be required to go through a severe change. There are ample of differences. It is the challenge to generate awareness of IFRS and to identify its impact among the users of financial statements.

2. Training and Education

Lack of training amenities and academic courses on IFRS will also pose challenge in India. There is a need to be educated on IFRS and its application.

3. Legal and Regulatory Considerations

Presently the reporting requirements are governed by various regulators in India and their provisions override other laws. IFRS does not recognize such overriding laws. The regulatory and legal requirements in India will act as a challenge unless the same laws have addressed by respective regulatory.

4. Taxation Aspect

IFRS convergence would affect the majority of the items in the financial statements and consequently the tax liabilities would also experience a change. Thus the taxation laws should address the dealing with tax liabilities arising on convergence from Indian GAAP to IFRS.

5. Measurement Using Fair Value

Fair value approach is used by IFRS as a measurement base for valuing the majority of the items of financial statements. The application of fair value accounting can bring a lot of volatility and subjectivity to the financial statements. It also involves a lot of hard work in finding the fair value and experts valuation have to be used.

6. Reporting Systems

Companies would have to make sure that the existing business reporting model is amended to go well with the reporting requirements of IFRS. The information systems should be planned to capture new requirements related to fixed assets, segment disclosures, related party transactions, etc.

MEASURES THAT SHOULD BE TAKEN BY COMPANIES TO ADDRESS THE CHALLENGES

The companies should follow the recommendations given by

Accounting Standard board for changes required in rules and regulations of various regulatory bodies.

The companies should use the interpretations of accounting standards issued by ICAI, with a view to resolve various complicated interpretational issues arising in the implementation of new accounting standards.

Companies should take benefit of the guidance notes, background materials on newly issued accounting standards issued by ICAI.

For the purpose of supporting its members, the ICAI council has created an expert advisory committee to answer queries from its members. Companies can ask to the experts for resolving the critical issues.

CONCLUSION

The study investigates the impact of convergence to IFRS on financial position of the company with the help of a case study of Wipro and challenges to be faced by companies in such convergence. It is observed that there are differences in the Total liability and Equity position which is mainly because of reclassification between Equity and Total liability. The Fair value measurement of Available for sale investment in IFRS is higher. From all these observations it can be concluded that IFRS is fair value oriented and Balance Sheet oriented accounting where there are more transparent disclosures and Indian GAAP is conservative approach. It is observed that this transition is not without difficulties. It would require an entire change in formats of accounts, accounting policies and more extensive disclosure requirements. Indian Corporate World which has been preparing its Financial Statements on Historical Cost Basis will have tough time while shifting to Fair Value Accounting. But it is not impossible for Indian companies to converge with IFRS as many helps from ICAI is given such as guidance notes, expert services as well as ICAI have also issued the interpretation notes for complicated issues.

REFERENCES

Alanezi, F.S., Alfaraih, M.M., Alrashaid, E.A. and Albolushi, S.S. (2012), "Dual/joint auditors and the level of compliance with international financial reporting standards (IFRS-required disclosure) the case of financial institutions in Kuwait", *Journal of Economic and Administrative Sciences,* Vol. 28, No. 2, pp. 109-129.

Annual Report Wipro limited for the year 2013-14.

Aggarwal, K., Sheokand, K., (2014) "IFRS in Indian Banking Industry: Adoption process and Challenges ahead", *Zenith International Journal of Business Economics and Management Research* (ZIJBEMR), Vol. 4, Issue 3, March 2014, pp. 59-73.

Al-Shammari, B., Brown, P. and Tarca, A. (2008), "An investigation of compliance with International Accounting Standards by listed companies in the Gulf Co-Operation Council member states", *The International Journal of Accounting,* Vol. 43, No. 4, pp. 425-47.

Chauhan, A. (2013) "To Study the Impact of Convergence to IFRS on Financial Position of a company and challenges faced by the company: A case study in India", Global Research Analysis, Volume: 2, Issue: 10, Oct., pp. 57-58

Csebfalvi, G. (May 2012). The Effects of International Accounting Standardization on Business Performance: Evidence from Hungary. *International Journal of Business and Management.*

Chen, J.J. and Zhang, H. (2010), "The impact of regulatory enforcement and audit upon IFRS compliance—evidence from China", *European Accounting Review,* Vol. 19, No. 4, pp. 665-92.

El-Gazzar, S.M., Finn, P.M. and Jacob, R. (1999), "An empirical investigation of multinational firms' compliance with International Accounting Standards", *International Journal of Accounting,* Vol. 34, No. 2, pp. 239-48.

Glaum, M. and Street, D.L. (2003), "Compliance with the disclosure requirements of Germany's new market: IAS versus US GAAP", *Journal of International Financial Management and Accounting,* Vol. 14, No. 1, pp. 64-100.

Horton, J. (2013), Does Mandatory IFRS adoption improve the information Environment?

Jain, P. (n.d.). IFRS implementation in India: Opportunities and Challenges.

Joshi, L. and Al-Mudhahki, J. (2001), "Empirical study of compliance with International Accounting Standards (IAS 1) by stock exchange listed companies in Bahrain", *Journal of Financial Management and Analysis,* Vol. 14, No. 2, pp. 43-54.

Lantto, H.J.M. (n.d.), Information Content of IFRS *versus* Domestic Accounting Standards: Evidence from Finland.

Mihai, S., Ionascu, M. and Ionascu, I. (2012), "Economic benefits of International Financial Reporting Standards (IFRS) adoption in Romania: Has the cost of equity capital decreased?", *African Journal of Business Management,* Vol. 6, No. 1, pp. 2005.

Madawaki, A. (2012), "Adoption of International Financial Reporting Standards in developing countries: The case of Nigeria", *International Journal of Business and Management,* Vol. 7, No. 3, pp. 152-61.

S. Yadav, D.S. (2012). Convergence to IFRS: What needs to be done by Indian corporate to meet the Emerging Challenges? *International Journal of Computer Engineering & Management.*

Street, D.L. and Bryant, S.M. (2000), "Disclosure level and compliance with IASs: a comparison of compliance with and without US listings and filings", *International Journal of Accounting,* Vol. 35, No. 3, pp. 305-29.

Sahlstrom, L. (2009), Impact of International Financial Reporting Standard Adoption on Key Financial Ratios, *Accounting and Finance.*

Swamynathan, S. (2011), Financial Statement Effects on convergence to IFRS—A case study in India, *International Journal of multidisciplinary Research.*

Tower, G., Hancock, P. and Taplin, R. (1999), "A regional study of listed companies' compliance with International Accounting Standards", *Accounting Forum,* Vol. 23, No. 3, pp. 293-305.

Verriest, A. (2011), "The effect of institutions and Big 4 audits on properties of analyst forecasts", SSRN eLibrary.

http://www.ifrs.com/pdf/IFRSUpdate_V8.pdf

http://www.caalley.com/art/Presentation-IFRS.pdf

http://jbnagarca.org/wp-content/uploads/2012/07/IFRS-in-India-Its-Status-Overview-of-Concepts-and-Impact-in-India-23-January-2011.pdf

http://www.ifrs.org/Use-around-the-world/Documents/Jurisdiction-profiles/India-IFRS Profile.pdf

http://www.ijcem.org/papers112012/ijcem_112012_06.pdf

http://www.wbiconpro. com/106-Pawan.pdf

http://www.ifrs.com/updates/aicpa/ifrs_faq.html

http://www.iica.in/images/1stPPTGargi%20Ray.pdf

http://www.ssmrae.com/review/admin/images/90f788f5b93d523625d96a2551accff9.pdf

http://www.icai.org/resource_file/12436announ1186.pdf

http://www.wipro.com/Documents/IFRS_Press_Release_ Q4_FY_14.pdf

http://www.iasplus.com/en/binary/asia/1009intrackingifrs2.pdf

http://lta.hse.fi/2012/2/lta_2012_02_a1.pdf

http://www.ajbmr.com/articlepdf/ajbmr_v01n01_04.pdf

19

Role of Information Technology in Banking Sector

RIZWAN UL ZAMAN DAR

ABSTRACT

This paper develops the tests to examine the effect of information technology in banking sector. Information technology refers to the processing, storage, disseminations and acquisition of all types of information using computer and telecommunication. An attempt has been made in this paper to examine the innovative instruments that have been introduced by banks in recent time. IT is used to reach maximum customers at lower cost and in highest efficient manner. Use of the IT products have changed the face of Indian banking.

INTRODUCTION

The Information technology referring to computers and peripheral equipment has seen tremendous growth in service industries in the recent past. The most obvious example in perhaps has banking industry, where through the introduction of IT-related products in internet banking, electronic payment, security investment, information exchanges, banks now can provide more diverse services to customers with less manpower. Information technology has become a necessary and important tool in today's organization. Information technology is one of the most important facilitators for the transformation of the Indian banking industry in terms of its transactions as well as other internal system and processes. Technology has brought a complete archetype shift in the functioning of banks and delivery of bank services. For a country like India which is one of the most promising emerging markets, information technology has a great importance. The technological evolution of the Indian banking industry has been largely directed by the various committees set up by the RBI and the government of India to review the implementation of technological change. In the 70's and 80's banks were marketing to a generation raised on old style banking: personal interaction on at a banking office. That generation was disdainful of "impersonal" services and afraid of computers. Long queues in banks, large number of files and waist of time were the main cause to move towards computerization in banking sector.

Impact of IT on banking system: IT has been of great essence in banking system. The banking system slowly shifting from the traditional banking towards relationship banking. IT saves the time of the consumers and the employees conspicuously; IT cut down the expenses and IT facilities the network transactions.

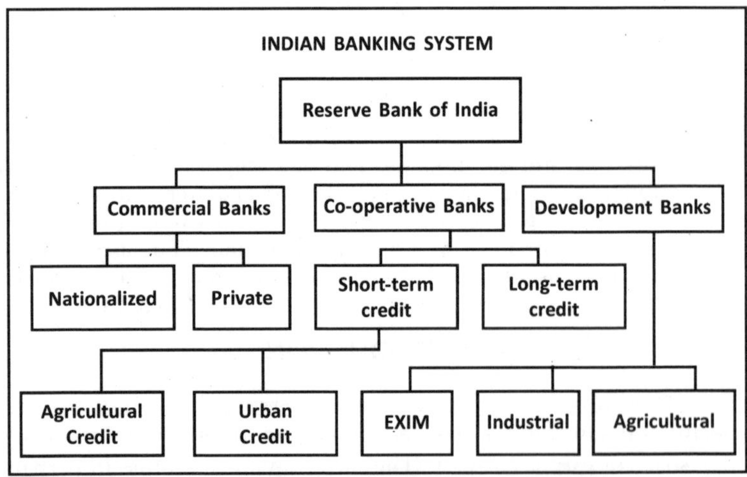

Customers are now demanding new, more convenient, delivery system and services such as internet banking have a dual role to the customer. To do these banks have to create account information layers, which can be accessed both by the bank staff as well as by the customers themselves.

Technological development in banks: Technology has change the face Indian banking sector through the computerizations. These changes are followings:

1. Introduction of Electronic Payment Services—E Cheques
2. Real Time Gross Settlement (RTGS)
3. Introduction of Electronic Fund Transfer (EDI)
4. Introduction of Electronic Clearing Service (ECS)
5. Introduction of Biometrics
6. Introduction of Cheque Truncation System
7. Introduction of Tab Banking
8. Arrival of card-based payment—Debit/Credit/Smart card

EMERGING TRENDS IN BANK TECHNOLOGY

1. Cheque Truncation System (CTS)
2. Financial Inclusion
3. E-Banking
4. Satellite Banking
5. Internet Banking
6. Mobile Banking
7. E-Cash
8. E-Cheques
9. Electronic Fund Transfer
10. Electronic Clearing Service
11. Card based Clearing Service
12. Managing IT Risk

Cheque Truncation System (CTS)

Truncation is the process of stopping the flow of the physical cheque issued by a drawer at some point by the presenting bank en-route to the drawee bank branch. In its place an electronic image of the cheque is transmitted to the drawee branch through the clearing house, along with relevant information like data on the MICR band, date of presentation, presenting bank, etc. Cheque truncation thus obviates the need to move the physical instruments across branches, other than in exceptional circumstances for clearing purposes. This effectively eliminates the associated cost of movement of the physical cheques, reduces the time required for their collection and brings elegance to the entire activity of cheque processing.

Financial Inclusion

Financial inclusion is delivery of banking services at an

affordable cost ('no frills' accounts,) to the vast sections of disadvantaged and low income group. Unrestrained access to public goods and services is the *sine qua non* of an open and efficient society. As banking services are in the nature of public good, it is essential that availability of banking and payment services to the entire population without discrimination is the prime objective of the public policy. Through technology it becomes easier and possible.

E-Banking

E-Banking in India, begins in the last decades of the 18th century.

E-Bank is the electronic bank that provides the financial service to the individual client by the internet. E-Banking includes the various banking activities which made from home, business, on the road, instead of at a physical bank location. The benefits of E-Banking are account information, fund transfer, bill payment, etc.

Satellite Banking

Satellite Banking is also an upcoming technology innovation in the Indian banking industry. Under the proposal made by RBI it would be bearing a part of the leased rentals for satellite connectivity. The use of satellite will help banks to reach rural and hilly areas in a better way.

Internet Banking

Internet banking enables a customer to do banking transaction through the bank's website on the internet. It is more or less bringing the bank to your computer. Now one can operate all type of transaction like withdraw cash, deposit a cheque, etc. on his computer through website of bank. This is also called virtual banking.

Mobile Banking

Mobile banking is an extension of internet banking. The bank is in association with the cellular services providers offer this service. For this service mobile phone should either be SMS or WAP enabled. These services are available to even those customers with only credit card accounts with the bank.

E-Cash

E-Cash was conceived by David Chaum as an anonymous electronic money or electronic cash system in 1983. It was realized through his corporation digicash and used as small payments system on the internet. When you pay online via e-cash, the amount is directly transferred from your account to merchant's account.

E-Cheques

A form of payment made via the internet that is designed to perform the same function as a conventional paper check. Because the check is in an electronic format, it can be processed in fewer steps and has more security features than a standard paper check. Security features provided by electronic checks include authentication, public key cryptography, digital signatures and encryption, among others. Also refers to e-cheques.

Electronic Fund Transfer (EFT)

EFT is the electronic exchange, transfer of money from one account to another, either within single financial institutions or across multiple institutions, through computer-based systems.

The term covers a number of different concepts:

- Cardholder-initiated transactions, using a payment card such as a credit card or a debit card.
- Direct deposit payment initiated by the payer.
- Direct debit payments, sometimes called *electronic checks*, for which a business debits the consumer's bank account for payment for goods or services.
- Wire transfer via an international banking network such as swift.

- Electronic bill payment in online banking, which may be delivered by EFT or paper check.
- Transactions involving *stored value of electronic money*, possibly in a private currency.

Electronic Clearing Service

ECS is an electronic mode of funds transfer from one bank account to another. It can be used by institutions for making payments such as distribution of dividend interest, salary, and pension, among others. It can also be used to pay bills and other charges such as telephone, electricity, water or for making equated monthly installments payments on loans as well as SIP investments. ECS can be used for both credit and debit purposes.

CONCLUSION

This paper is concerned with the impact of information technology on the banking industry, as banks are the intensive user. Computers are getting more sophisticated. They have given bank a potential and have given bank customers high expectations. The banks gain a vital competitive advantage by having a direct marketing and good accountable service environment for their customers and new efficient business process. Mobile banking and internet banking are going to make Indoor in the banking sector in the near future. IT has been of great essence in banking system. The banking system slowly shifting from the traditional banking towards relationship banking. IT saves the time of the consumers and the employees conspicuously; IT cut down the expenses and IT facilities the network transactions. IT course do promise to change the face of banking in the next few years. All the trends in IT sector are discussed to see their relevance and importance to the status of Indian banks. Modern high throughput technologies are providing a vast amount of sequences, experiences, expressions and functional data for genes.

REFERENCES

Elements of Mercantile Law by N.D. Kapoor, Sultan Chand & Sons, New Delhi, 2006.

Reddy, Y.V. (1998), "Financial Sector Reforms: Review and Prospects". *RBI Bulletin,* December.

www.google.com

www.wikepedia.com

http//rbi.org.in

Part IV
CONTEMPORARY ISSUES IN MANAGEMENT

20

Development and Future of Copyright in India

SILVIE AGGARWAL AND SANJANA WALIA

ABSTRACT

Copyright is an established form of Intellectual Property Right. Every creator/author has a right to protect this intellectual property in a civilized society. The protection of copyright is basic necessity for rewarding creativity and to motivate others to create. India, a leading developing country has effective system and laws for protection of copyright.

At the time of independence India was governed by the Copyright Act of 1914. The act was basically an extension of British Copyright Act, 1911. The present Copyright Act, 1957, came into force from January, 1958. The act has been amended six times since then.

The Act gives the creators of literary, dramatic, musical and artistic work, cinematograph films and sound recording exclusive rights to reproduce, perform, translate and communicate their work to the public, in different forms, commonly known as *"economic rights"*. The Act also provides the authors certain *"moral rights"* like right to claim authorship and to restrain or to claim damages for any distortion, mutilation, etc. in respect of their work. The administration of Copyright is with Registrar of Copyright. Act also provides for Copyright Board, a quasi-judicial body. To effectively enforce the copyright several measures have been taken such as setting up of the

Copyright Enforcement Advisory Council and Creation of separate cells in state police headquarters.

The Indian Copyright Act today is compliant with most International conventions and treaties in the field of copyrights. India is a signatory to the 'Universal Copyright Convention' and the 'Berne Copyright Convention'.

India is the largest producer of cinematograph films in terms of volume. With growing software industry and growing entertainment industry, it provides big opportunities to major corporates to invest in India. The protection of copyrights at par with other developed countries can foster economic growth, provide incentives for innovation and attract investment, which will create new job opportunities for India.

To make India a biggest knowledgebase economy, the war against terrorism and the war against piracy has to be fought equally.

Copyright is an established form of Intellectual Property Right. Every creator/author has a right to protect his intellectual property in a civilized society. It is a right given by the law to creators of

- Original literary, dramatic, music and artistic work,
- Cinematograph films and
- Sound records.

The protection of copyright is basic necessity for rewarding creativity and motivating others to create. Economic progress and social development of a country is dependent on creativity. India, a leading developing country has effective system and laws for protection of copyrights. The copyright does not seek to protect ideas. It protects only the unique expression of ideas.

To prove copyright infringement where no direct evidence of copying is available can be difficult, as the courts generally emphasis on the test of substantial reproduction.

The effective copyright laws can help save loss of crores of rupees to government revenue and employment opportunities. With the creation of awareness and adoption of strict anti-piracy policies people can get the true fruits for their labour, they really deserve.

Copyright is sometimes called a negative right, i.e. it is a right to stop others from exploiting the work without the permission of copyright holders.

The importance of protecting Intellectual Property Rights was first recoganised in 1886, in the Paris Convention for Protection of intellectual property.

At the time of independence India was governed by the Copyright Act of 1914. The act was basically an extension of British Copyright Act, 1911. The present Copyright Act, 1957, came into force from January, 1958 and extends to whole of India, including the state of J&K. The Copyright Act, 1957 was also borrowed extensively from the Copyright Act of the United Kingdom of 1956. The act has been amended five times since then, in 1983, 1984, 1992, 1994, 1999 and last in the year 2012.

Subject to certain conditions, a fair deal for research, private study, criticism or review and news reporting, etc. is permitted without specific permission of the copyright owners.

The copyright is not a single right but a bundle of rights, which includes "*economic rights*" and "*moral rights*". The *economic rights* of copyright owner are :

- Reproduction of work,
- Performing the work in public/communicating to public,
- Adaptation,
- Translation of work, and
- Make copies of the work.

The owner of a copyright may allow any one or more of the economic right for a monetary consideration or otherwise for a limited period or full period, with or without some conditions. Even after transfer of economic rights, unless transferred specifically in writing, there are certain moral rights, which remains with the author even after transfer of copyright. The moral rights are :

- The right to decide whether or not to publish the work,
- The right to claim authorship of a published or exhibited work,
- The right to prevent alteration and other actions that may damage the author's honour or reputation.

In the case of a published literary, dramatic, musical or artistic work the copyright subsist during the author's lifetime and 60 years after his death.

The administration under Copyright Act is as under :

Copyright office is situated at New Delhi, and is under the administrative control of the Department of Secondary and Higher Education. The Registrar of Copyrights heads the copyright office. The Registrar holds certain powers of civil courts in handling cases relating to copyright. The main function of Copyright office is to undertake registration of copyright. The copyright office provides the following facilities to the general public :

- information regarding works of copyright,
- inspection of register, taking of extracts thereof.

On an average more than 1000 works are registered in a month in the copyright office.

Copyright Board, a quasi-judicial body, constituted in September,1958, is entrusted with the task of adjudication of disputes pertaining to copyright registration, assignment of copyright, grant of licenses and other matters instituted before it under the Copyright Act, 1957. The copyright board is headed by a Chairman with not less than two and not more than 14 other members. Registrar of the copyrights also acts as Secretary of the copyright Board. The meeting of board is held in different zones of the country.

To effectively enforce the copyright the government has taken several measures, which are :

- setting up of the Copyright Enforcement Advisory Council,
- organizing seminars/workshops to create greater awareness about copyright among the enforcement personnel and general public,
- setting up of collective administration societies, and
- creation of separate cells in almost all state police headquarters.

The Copyright Enforcement Advisory Council was set-up in November 1991 to periodically review the progress of enforcement of copyright and to advise the government regarding measures for the improvement of enforcement of the Act. The term of Copyright Enforcement Advisory Council is 3 years and it is reconstituted after expiry of the term.

To make the Copyright Act more useful, comprehensive and effective, the department of secondary and higher education has a system of inviting views and suggestions from interested members of public, industries, stakeholders and any other interested person.

During Tenth Five Year Plan period three plan schemes were merged to effectively promote the cause of promotion of awareness on copyright/IPR. Under the scheme, financial assistance is provided to UGC recognized universities, institutions affiliated to these universities, educational institutions, copyright societies and registered voluntary organizations for creating general awareness by organizing seminars and workshops on copyright matters.

In 1994, by an amendment in the act, setting up of separate copyright societies for different categories was provided. This is a concept of collective administration of copyright, where management and protection of copyright in works are undertaken by a society of owners for their class of work. The different copyright societies registered are :

- Society for Copyright Regulation of Indian Producers of film and television (SCRIPT) for cinematograph films,
- Indian Performing Right Society Ltd. (IPRS) for Musical works and
- Phonographic Performance Ltd. (PPL) for sound recordings.

These societies have been actively participating in general awareness and frequently interact with Department of Secondary and Higher Education.

To facilitate proper coordination between the industry and the enforcement agencies for enforcement of copyright laws, the ministry had requested the state governments to designate nodal officers. The many states have designated the nodal officer and have created separate cells at state police headquarters. The designation of nodal officers and creation of separate cells has shown steep decline in film and music piracy in the country.

The Copyright Act provides various types of remedies such as civil, criminal and administrative remedies to copyright holders against infringement of copyright. Act provides a minimum punishment of six months and a fine of Rs. 50000 and a maximum punishment of three years and a fine of Rs. two lacs, in cases where infringement is for commercial purpose or for profit. In case the infringement is not made for gain or in the course of trade or business Act provides for punishment for a term less than six months or a fine of less than Rs. 50000. In case of second and subsequent conviction the act provides for higher punishments.

The copyright laws in various nations are governed by their respective laws, which are generally in accordance with the treaties and trade rules of major international conventions. The Indian

Copyright Act today is compliant with most International conventions and treaties in the field of copyrights. India is a signatory to :

- The Berne Convention for the Protection of Literary and Artistic Works—popularly known as 'Berne Copyright Convention' and
- The agreement on trade related aspects of intellectual property rights—popularly known as 'TRIPs', which also incorporates the Berne Convention.

Other copyright-related treaties are WIPO Copyright Treaty (WCT) and the WIPO Performances and Phonograms Treaty (WPPT), which bind signatory countries to additional changes to their copyright laws.

India is only bound to the terms of the Berne Copyright Convention and TRIPs agreement and not by WCT or WPPT.

Before agreeing to some of the proposed amendments to the Act, to introduce the provisions related to WCT and WPPT we need to be extremely careful as some of the proposals such as Digital Rights Management (DRM) may be detrimental to public interest, particularly, in case of India, being a developing country.

India, has effective system and laws for protection of copyright. It is not that there are weaknesses in the Indian Copyright Act. The law is TRIPs compliant. India is a signatory to the Universal Copyright Convention and Berne Copyright Convention and its laws are generally in accordance with the laws of other member countries. The copyright registered in India is protected in the member countries and *vice versa.*

India is the largest producer of cinematograph films in terms of volume and in terms of revenue it occupies the second position in the world, next only to USA. With growing software industry and growing entertainment industry, it provides big opportunities to major corporates to invest in India. The protection of copyrights at par with other developed countries can foster economic growth, provide incentives for innovation and attract investment, which will create new job opportunities for India. With big pool of knowledge workers, India is waiting to become a global superpower.

To make India a big knowledgebase economy and to make it global superpower, the war against terrorism and the war against piracy has to be fought equally.

References

Copyright Act, 1957 amended till date.

Copyright Rules, 1958.

Copyright Handbook.

International Copyright Order, 1999 published in the Gazette of India dated 6th April 1999.

Study on Copyright Piracy in India, Sponsored by Ministry of Human Resource Development.

Uruguay Round Agreement on Trade Related Intellectual Property Rights (TRIPs).

UN Agency World Intellectual Property Organization report on World Intellectual Property Indicators, December 2012.

21

Spirituality at Work Place

HARVANDNA

ABSTRACT

"Lack of spirituality more than religiosity is the root cause of corruption and scams. Nobody is corrupt with their own family. Corruption is happening because there is no sense of belonging. Spirituality enhances the sense of belongingness among people, so that there is natural tendency to be honest and to take care for each others. Corruption, manipulation, dishonesty, hatred, etc. becomes impossible in these cases."—Sri Sri Ravishankar, founder of Art of Living. The recent reports on various scams and corruption rate in India have puzzled all Indians.

Whatever may be the reason for such violence at workplace, corruption, scams etc., various social and economic changes and shift in demographics of the workforce raise the necessity of practicing spirituality at workplace. The contributing factors for such necessity include layoffs, mergers and amalgamation, technological advancements, unethical corporate behaviour, more dependence on contract labour, workplace violence, threats of terrorism, decline in job satisfaction, job insecurity, stress and burnout, etc. In these turbulent times, it is only natural that workers turn to spirituality for remedies, security and inner peace. Therefore, in this paper an attempt has been made to introduce the concept of spirituality at workplace, define it and see how it is relevant for increasing the productivity of employees. In addition an attempt has been made to discuss a model how an individual interacts with the spiritual organisation.

INTRODUCTION

Everybody aims to live a happy, fulfilling and contended life and people work hard to fulfill their dreams. In the view of the industrial development, man has made material progress, but as a result of this progress there have been rise in environmental destruction and exhaustion of natural resources. The advancement of science and technology has also led to the production of nuclear weapons for mass destruction which has deteriorated humanity's spiritual life to a large extent. The modern industrial world has also been affected by these social, environmental and economic problems that have resulted in increase in human greed and lack of love and compassion. These conditions have led humans to search for harmony and peace and this is possible only through a spiritual journey. That is, for bringing about change in external world, internal transformation of people who are willing to act as leaders to bring about these changes, is required.

It is believed that human beings have four types of energies; 1. Physical: our ability to take good care of our bodies and physical well being, 2. Mental: our ability to think clearly, learn and make good decisions, 3. Emotional: our ability to create positive relationships and to handle difficult situations, 4. Spiritual: our ability to connect to something greater than ourselves and to be of service to the world. One's spirituality is the essence of who he or she is. It defines the inner self separately from the body, but including the physical and inner self. It is the state of intimate relationship with the inner self of higher values and morality. It is recognition of the truth of the inner nature of people.

Objectives

The following are the objectives of this research paper:

1. To define spirituality at workplace in organisations.
2. To study the relevance of spirituality to workplace.
3. To examine whether spirituality has any effect on the well being of the employees of the organisation.
4. To draw a model of the process of interaction between the organisation and a spiritual person.

SPIRITUALITY AT WORKPLACE

People have always had spiritual centre, but the trend towards establishing and maintaining a spiritual culture in organisation is relatively new. By uniting employees with a common purpose, workplace spirituality provides organisational members with a way to offset the demanding and stressful workplace environment that is a routine today. A spiritual workplace is also considered beneficial for the companies that provide them. It is seen that companies with spiritual workplace experience improved productivity and reduced turnover from their employees.

Spirituality at workplace is about people seeing their work as a spiritual path, as an opportunity to grow personally and to contribute to society in a meaningful way. It is about integrity, being true to oneself and telling the truth to others. The aspect of workplace spirituality that is required by the organisational members can be categorised into three areas: the quest of meaning and purpose of their work, the desire to connect to other people and the desire to be part of community.

Organisations that provide a culture that embraces workplace spirituality realize that their employees want to feel like a valued member of their community. Spiritual organisations provide ways for their members to make positive contributions to the places they work and live. Spiritual organisations also realize the importance of providing their members with an environment that promotes positive relationships with their co-workers. In the course of performing their jobs, they have opportunities to work with other organisational members and feel they are part of a team that is working towards same goal.

RELEVANCE OF SPIRITUALITY TO WORKPLACE

Organisations that cultivate spirituality look to nurture workers and the needs they bring to the organisation. Spiritual organisations often take reciprocal benefits in their own right. There is a need for organisations to realise that people have spiritual needs, need within the individual that are not necessarily religious, but are based on the inner needs for purpose of work. Through this, organisations can tap the inner resources of individuals. Since individuals spend a considerable time of their lives in work environment, nourishing the individual needs of individuals, helping them find meaning through work, is critical in the organisations that nurture the organisation spirituality.

Another important need that fosters the growth of individual in spiritual organisation environment is enhancing their sense of security, but here again the need is reciprocal. Human beings need to feel secure and that includes the feeling of security in their work environment. Workplace spirituality helps reducing the worker management conflict, turnover, enhances the care, morale and general well being felt about the environment. Spiritual organisations do not just provide inner levels of personal growth on a psychological level of workers but they also derive the benefits from their worker's personal growth as well.

An important key to human development is establishing a sense of purpose and meaning of the work we do and this is possible only through spiritual organisation. At times, work is very difficult and emotionally draining. Therefore, spiritual organisations recognize the need of worker's feeling of purpose and help guard against those destructive forces that may lead to burnout or stagnation of human growth.

Organisations that infuse their culture with the beliefs in spiritual workplace come to find that the benefits they sow ultimately lead to greater team cohesion, less turnover, higher levels of morale, less tension between different work groups, a more enjoyable work environment and workers with greater ethics towards work. It would lead to work environment that is more productive and workers are more satisfied.

SPIRITUALITY AND WORKER'S WELL-BEING

The well being of the employees is in the best interest of communities and organisations. A major portion of individual's life is spent at workplace and it is affected by his well-being and the well-being of community. Thus, well being is looked from social construct, reduction in stress, burnout and work holism and increased worker's morale, commitment to the organisation and subsequent increase in productivity of the workers.

It has been rightly said that organisations are places where people spent most of their lives, develop friendships, create value, and make their most meaningful contributions to society. Work has become central to most people and this is associated with problems like stress, burnout and work holism. Stress induced work holism leads to loss of spiritualism, chronic illness, pain, fatigue, fear, while higher absenteeism, lower productivity and increase in company's expenditure in form of health compensation claims increases due to stress at workplace. Many employees feel unappreciated, unconnected, lost and insecure in their jobs. Encouragement of spirituality in workplace can lead to benefits in the areas of creativity, honesty, personal fulfilment and commitment which ultimately lead to increased organisational performance. These problems can be solved through spirituality with beneficial consequences for the well being of the employees. It is said there is correlation between spirituality and mental health as life satisfaction, happiness, self esteem, hope and optimism and meaning in life. Furthermore, work spirituality programme have positive effects on employees in form of increased job satisfaction and commitment, reduction in employees absenteeism, turnover and increased productivity, improvement in employee attitudes, work satisfaction and job involvement and positive effect on personal well-being and job performance.

INTRODUCING SPIRITUALITY IN ORGANISATIONS

As discussed in the earlier, both employees and organisations benefit from spirituality at workplace. Therefore, the organisations should strive at introducing workplace spirituality with full strength and zest to make their organisations success. Spirituality at work place involves:

- Working towards the realisation of highest potential in each individual.
- Seeking to embody values like love, acceptance, compassion, forgiveness, integrity, honesty in all that we do and also in all our relationships.
- Emphasis should be laid down on sustainable growth, i.e., development that includes long term impacts of the actions of individuals and organisations.
- Spiritual organisations value contributions made by individuals for the betterment to the world.
- These organisations prize creativity.
- These cultivate inclusion and collaborative mindset, thus decreasing or eliminating unhealthy competition.
- These organisations encourage employees to reach out to others to make effective teams and to help others.
- It works on the saying that 'do right things because it is the right thing to do.'

Researchers have identified 19 themes that apply for workplace spirituality. These are:

> Ethics, truth, believe in God or All Mighty, respect, understanding, openness, trust, kindness (bonding and compassion), team orientation, few organisation barriers, a sense of peace and harmony, aesthetically pleasing workplace, acceptance, encouraging creativity, encouraging diversity, being self motivated, interconnectedness and honesty.

These themes are all components a human being brings to the workplace and, when given the proper nurturing environment by management, allowing these traits to flourish has a positive impact on the profitability of the successful organisation. The following model discusses the process of the interaction of the spiritual person with the organisation:

Flow Chart on the Process of Organisation and Spiritual Person.

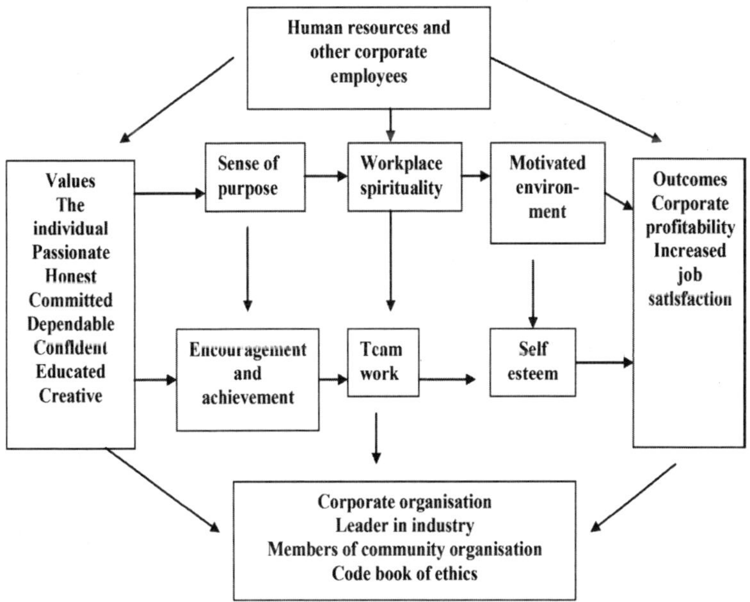

CONCLUSION

Today, we live in the transition period between the old definition of work as survival and the new definition of work as livelihood. New management techniques and new organisation structures are needed to handle this emerging context. Here we can say that next phase of evolution has begun. Spirituality is becoming more openly recognised as an integral part of work for the organisations to encourage ethics in working of the organisations. Therefore, it is high time organisations should realize that they should transform themselves into spiritual organisations if they want to succeed in this changing world. In addition, as we know human resource is the biggest asset of the organisations, so the organisations should take care of the well being of these human resources and one of the best ways is introduction of spiritual organisations.

References

Arias, J.C. (2008). Meditation Effects on Executives' Performance in Business Organisations. *Business Intelligence Journal,* Vol. 1, No. 1, pp. 35-66. Cavanagh, F.G. (1999).

A spiritual perspective on learning in the workplace, *Journal of Managerial Psychology,* Vol. 17, No. 3, pp. 230-42. Retrieved August 21, 2006 from University of Phoenix Library, Emerald database. Kale, H.S. and Shrivastava, S. (2003).

Defining spirit at work: finding common ground, *Journal of Orgnaizational Change Management,* Vol. 17, No. 1, pp. 26-42. Retrieved August 18, 2006 from University of Phoenix, Emerald database. Kouzes, M.J. and Posner, Z.B., (2002).

Fusion Leadership, San Francisco, CA: Berrett Koshler Publisher, Evans, R. (1996). "The Authentic Leader" in the human side of school change. Excerpted in Educational leadership by Fullan, M. (2000). San Francisco, CA: John Wiley & Son, Fairbrother, K. & Warn, J. (2002).

Journal of Organizational Change Management, Vol. 17, No. 1, pp. 62-82. Howard, S. (2002).

Leadership governance from the inside out. Hoboken, NJ: John Wiley & Sons. Garcia-Zamor, C.J. (2003).

Perspectives in business ethics (3rd ed.) New York, NY: McGraw-Hill. Heaton D.P., Schmidt-Wilk J. and Travis F. Constructs, methods, and measures for researching spirituality in organizations (2004).

Spiritual leadership: fulfilling whole-self needs at work, 2009, 155, Bosch, L.— The Inevitable Role of Spirituality in the Workplace Luidolf Bosch Leadership & Organization Development Journal, pp. 11-17. Retrieved August 21, 2006 from University of Phoenix Library, Emerald database. Fry, L.W. (2003).

Spirituality for managers: context and critique, *Journal of Organizational Change Management,* Vol. 12, No. 3, pp. 186-199. Retrieved August 21, 2006 from University of Phoenix Library, Emerald database. Daft, L.R. & Lengel, H.R., (1998).

Servant Leadership, New York, NY: Paulist Press, Hartman, P.L. (2005).

Toward a theory of spiritual leadership Leadership Quarterly, Vol. 14, pp. 693-727, Gandossy, R. and Sonnenfeld, J., (2004).

The ennegram system for enhancing workplace spirituality, *Journal of Management Development,* Vol. 22, No. 4, pp. 308-28. Retrieved August 21, 2006 from University of Phoenix Library, Emerald database. Kinjerski, M.V. and Skrypnek, J.B. (2004).

The leadership challenge, San Francisco, CA: Jossey-Bass, Krahnke, K., Giacalone, A.R., Jurkiewicz, L.C. (2003).

Workplace dimensions, stress and job satisfaction, *Journal of Managerial Psychology.* Vol. 18, No. 1, pp. 8-21. Retrieved August 21, 2006 from University of Phoenix Library, Emerald database. Fairholm, W. G. (1996).

Workplace Spirituality and Organizational Performance, *Public Administration Review,* Retrieved August 21, 2006 from University of Phoenix Library, Emerald database, Greenleaf, R.K. (1977).

22

Whistle Blowing

The Necessity for New Corporates

Pooja

ABSTRACT

The term 'whistle-blowing' is a relatively recent entry into the vocabulary of public and corporate affairs, although the phenomenon itself is not new. It refers to the process by which insiders go public with their claims of malpractices by, or within, organizations - usually after failing to remedy the matters from the inside, and often at great personal risk to them. Sometimes the cost of such valiant efforts is just too high to pay. The following paper caters to the concept of whistle blowing as an emerging international issue. It provides a deep insight into different cases of whistle blowing around the globe. The paper also advocates for legal protection that should be given to whistle blowers and what has been and need to be done in India and Abroad for the protection of whistle blowers.

Keywords: Whistle-blowing, Agency, CVC, Public Interest Disclosure (Protection of Informers) Bill, Whistle-Blowers Protection Resolution

"If you must sin, sin against God, not against the bureaucracy. God may forgive you, but the bureaucracy never will!"

—U.S. Admiral Hyman Rickover

INTRODUCTION

The term 'whistle blowing' is a relatively recent entry into the vocabulary of public and corporate affairs, although the phenomenon itself is not new. Whistle blowing is a universal phenomenon. The phrase "blow the whistle" dates to 1934 and is a metaphor for a sports official calling a foul and the term whistleblower, itself, only dates to 1970. The origin of term whistleblower derives from the practice of English police officers, who would blow their whistles when they noticed the commission of a crime. The whistle would alert other law enforcement officers and the general public of danger.

To blow the whistle on someone is to alert a third party that a person has done, or is doing, something wrong. So, literally, "whistle-blowing" means that one makes a noise to alert others to misconduct. By blowing the whistle on misconduct in an organization, one alerts the organization to the fact that its stakeholders are being wrongfully harmed, or that they are at risk of harm.

Whistle blowing refers to the process by which insiders 'go public' with their claims of malpractices by, or within, organisations–usually after failing to remedy the matters from the inside, and often at great personal risk to themselves (Nick Perry, 1998). Usually this person would be from that same organization. The revealed misconduct may be classified in many ways; for example, a violation of a law, rule, regulation and/or a direct threat to public interest, such as fraud, health/safety violations, and corruption. It is this willingness to stand up for a principle and court risk openly that distinguishes whistle blowing from such related practices as in-house criticism, anonymous leaks, and the like. The whistleblower is considered a hero or a traitor, a do-gooder or a crank, a role model or a non-conformist troublemaker–depending on one's point of view.

It is true that under normal circumstances, an organization is entitled to total loyalty and confidentiality from its employees. But when there is serious malpractice or when people's lives are at stake–for example, as in corruption and fraud in defence procurement; deaths in 'encounter' of innocent persons; toxic leaks from a chemical factory; non-adherence to flight safety standards by an airline; creative accounting and false declarations by a company; cheating and plagiarism in scientific research–the overriding public interest may lie in protecting the public's right to be told, and the whistleblower's right not to be punished for doing so. Without whistleblowers, one may not get to learn about problems until it is time to mourn the consequences.

Who is a Whistleblower? A whistleblower is a person who raises concern about frauds, corruptions, wrongdoings and mismanagement. For instance, a government employee who exposes corruption practices, within his department is a whistleblower. So is an employee of a private organization, who raises his voice against misconduct, within the company. The misconduct can be classified in several ways, such as:

- Violation of Indian laws.
- Posing direct threat to public interest.
- Violation of health or safety norms.
- Deceptive practices.

A whistleblower may approach an external agency, such as law enforcement officers, media or social groups. He may also report the matter to other members of the organization.

According to Boatright (2003), "Whistle-blowing is the release of information by a member or former member of an organization that is evidence of illegal and/or immoral conduct in the organization that is not in the public interest."

Sekhar (2002) defines whistle-blowing as "an attempt by an employee or a former employee of an organization to disclose what he proclaims to be a wrongdoing in or by that organization."

According to Koehn (2003), "Whistle-blowing occurs when an employee informs the public of inappropriate activities going on inside the organization."

R.M. Green (1994): "A whistle-blower is an employee who, perceiving an organizational practice that he believes to be illegal or unethical, seeks to stop this practice by alerting top management, or, failing that, by notifying authorities outside the organization."

Considering the above definitions together, whistle-blowing can now be defined as the voluntarily disclosure of non-public information, as a moral protest by a member or former member of an organization, outside the normal channels of communications, to outsiders who can correct the wrongdoing opposed to the public interest.

ARGUMENT AGAINST WHISTLE-BLOWING

Given the great harm whistle-blowing does and can cause to both whistle-blower and organization, it is opposed by some, mainly on the grounds of loyalty and confidentiality. According to them, as per the Law of Agency, the agent is expected to act as the principal would have acted himself/herself. The agent is paid (i.e. fee) for the task done by him for principal. The main obligation of an agent is to act in the interest of the principal. In the similar way, an employee is also an agent of his/her organization/employer. Therefore, an employee as an agent has an obligation to work for the benefit of his/her employer as per directions by protecting the confidential information. In nutshell, the employee has to work just like a loyal agent. Since whistle-blowing violates the law of agency, i.e., loyalty, hence it is condemned. Whistle-blowing by violating the law of agency seems to some as disloyalty, i.e., *"to bite the hand that feeds one."*

JUSTIFICATIONS IN FAVOUR OF WHISTLE-BLOWING

The supporters of whistle-blowing also maintain that whistle blowing is not something to be done without adequate justification. The major justification forwarded in favour of whistle blower is that employee has obligation not only toward the employer organization, but to the society as well. They, therefore, view that if the act of whistle blower brings more benefit to the society at large than to for the organization by not blowing the whistle against its wrongdoings, whistle-blowing is well justified.

The major argument of loyalty of an employee given against whistle blowing does not prove that whistle-blowing can never be justified. There is no denying the fact that employees as agents have obligations toward their principals, but at the same time they do also have limits. Blowing whistle against the violation of the law of agency by the principal is, therefore, justifiable even at the great self-sacrifice of the whistleblower. Whistle-blowers also act as one of the least expensive and most efficient sources of feedback about mistakes the firm may be making. The more recent threat is that top executives may themselves be named in the suit for negligence. If CEOs and directors are legally responsible for the illegal actions of organization, even if the actions are unknown to them, they may be more willing to consider all sources of information about possible illegalities, including whistle-blowers. The top executives should rather support whistle blowing rather than harming whistle blowers.

LEGAL PROTECTION MEASURES ACROSS THE GLOBE

The first U.S. law adopted specifically to protect whistleblowers was the Lloyd-La Follette Act of 1912. It guaranteed the right of federal employees to furnish information to the United States Congress. The first U.S. environmental law to include an employee protection was the Water Pollution Control Act of 1972, also called the Clean Water Act. Similar protections were included in subsequent federal environmental laws including the Safe Drinking Water Act (1974), Resource Conservation and Recovery Act (also called the Solid Waste Disposal Act) (1976), Toxic Substances Control Act (1976), Energy Reorganization Act of 1974 (through 1978 amendment to protect nuclear whistleblowers), Comprehensive Environmental Response, Compensation, and Liability Act (CERCLA, or the Superfund Law) (1980), and the Clean Air Act (1990). Similar employee protections enforced through OSHA are included in the Surface Transportation Assistance Act (1982) to protect truck drivers, the Pipeline Safety Improvement Act (PSIA) of 2002, the Wendell H. Ford Aviation Investment and Reform Act for the 21st Century ("AIR 21"), and the Sarbanes-Oxley Act, enacted on July 30, 2002 (for corporate fraud whistleblowers).

The U.S. Whistleblowers Protect Act of 1989 (amended in 1994) protects public interest disclosures by federal employees. An Office of Special Counsel (OSC) was created to aid whistleblowers in the investigation of their disclosures and prevention of retaliatory action against them. It has had only modest success due to a series of hostile judicial rulings undercutting the protection afforded by the Act. More than 40 States have passed similar or even stronger legislation in respect of State employees. After the spectacular collapse of Enron and WorldCom, U.S. Congress passed the Sarbanes-Oxley Act of 2002 granting sweeping legal protection to whistleblowers in publicly traded companies. Anyone retaliating against a corporate whistleblower can now be imprisoned for up to 10 years. The Department of Labour (DoL) is required to complete its adjudication of whistleblower cases within 180 days, failing which the whistleblower may either elect to stay with DoL or seek a *de novo* trial in court. Remedies include reinstatement, back pay with interest, compensatory damages, special damages, attorney fees and costs.

The U.K.'s Public Interest Disclosure Act of 1998 is a unique piece of legislation providing protection to employees in the public, private and non-profit sectors, including those working outside the U.K. Under the law, employment tribunals have power to 'freeze' a dismissal and make unlimited compensation awards. South Africa has followed the U.K. example in providing protection to employees of all organisations through its Protected Disclosures Act of 2000. A number of other countries such as Australia, Canada, South Korea, Argentina, Russia, Slovakia, Mexico and Nigeria have also enacted or are in the process of enacting whistleblowers protection legislation (but only to government employees).

It follows that no measure to curb government and corporate transgressions will bear fruit unless legal immunity and protection against retaliation is given to responsible whistle blowing. It is unreasonable to expect employees to sacrifice their jobs and their future in order to protect the public interest; a few brave souls may do it but the vast majority of employees will not.

PROTECTING WHISTLE BLOWERS IN INDIA

During the past decade, scams, swindles, and rip-offs have become a regular feature of the Indian political and corporate landscape, costing taxpayers, investors and banks crores of rupees. The Securities and Exchange Board of India (SEBI) is considering a proposal to make it mandatory for companies to have a whistleblower protection mechanism. At present, under clause 49 of the listing agreement, it is optional for a company to have such a mechanism, which also has safeguards against victimization of the whistleblower. The proposal is part of a review of certain aspects of clause 49 to effectively deal with instances of fraud in companies.

Already, the Right to Information Act has brought about transparency and facilitated 'whistle blowing'. The Department of Personnel and Training (DOPT) developed the Public Interest Disclosure (Protection of Informers) Bill. The Union Cabinet has also cleared The Public Interest Disclosure and Protection to Persons Making the Disclosure Bill, 2010 to protect whistleblowers and punish those exposing the identity of people disclosing information. It also provides the Central Vigilance Commission (CVC) powers of a civil court to hand down harsh penalty to people revealing the identity of whistleblowers. The bill has provisions to prevent victimisation or disciplinary action against whistle blowers covering central, state and public sector employees. The CVC is an authorized nodal agency for addressing complaints. It has powers similar to a civil court, such as powers to issue summons, order police investigation and provide protection to the whistleblower. However, the CVC is not authorized, by Indian laws to address the complaints regarding matter that are already in court's purview, prejudicial to national security, international relations and proceedings of the Union Cabinet.

IMPORTANT FEATURES OF THE "WHISTLE-BLOWERS" RESOLUTION

- The CVC shall, as the Designated Agency, receive written complaints or disclosure on any allegation of corruption or of misuse of office by any employee of the Central Government or of any corporation established under any Central Act, government companies, societies or local authorities owned or controlled by the Central Government.
- The designated agency will ascertain the identity of the complainant; if the complainant is anonymous, it shall not take any action in the matter.
- The identity of the complainant will not be revealed unless the complainant himself has made either the details of the complaint public or disclosed his identity to any other office or authority.
- While calling for further report/investigation, the Commission shall not disclose the identity of the informant and also shall request the concerned head of the organisation to keep the identity of the informant a secret, if for any reason the head comes to know the identity.
- The Commission shall be authorised to call upon the CBI or the police authorities, as considered necessary, to render all assistance to complete the investigation pursuant to the complaint received.
- If any person is aggrieved by any action on the ground that he is being victimized due to the fact that he had filed a complaint or disclosure, he may file an application before the Commission seeking redress in the matter, wherein the Commission may give suitable directions to the concerned person or the authority.
- If the Commission is of the opinion that either the complainant or the witnesses need protection, it shall issue

appropriate directions to the concerned government authorities.

- In case the Commission finds the complaint to be motivated or vexatious, it shall be at liberty to take appropriate steps.
- The Commission shall not entertain or inquire into any disclosure in respect of which a formal and public inquiry has been ordered under the Public Servants Inquiries Act, 1850, or a matter that has been referred for inquiry under the Commissions of Inquiry Act, 1952.
- In the event of the identity of the informant being disclosed in spite of the Commission's directions to the contrary, it is authorised to initiate appropriate action as per extant regulations against the person or agency making such disclosure.

The accounting regulatory body, the Institute of Chartered Accountants of India (ICAI), has recommended setting up of a whistleblower system within all audit firms. A whistleblower system entails establishing a mechanism for employees to report concerns about unethical behaviour, actual or suspected fraud or violations, directly to the management of the company.

CONSEQUENCES OF 'GOING PUBLIC'

Instances of the whistleblower being fired, demoted or punished in other ways while the organization denies, ignores or quietly buries the disclosure are universal. Apart from the social pressure against turning one's boss or colleagues in, there is the legal bar in the form of the Official Secrets Act and Conduct Rules in the public sector or 'a non-disclosure agreement' in the corporate sector by which employees are gagged from disclosing matters to the public on pain of incurring criminal or civil liability for any breach.

Also most employees do not see it as their role to report wrongdoing unless it is particularly egregious. In contrast, employees who are required by their jobs to report wrongdoing (such as auditors and quality-control supervisors) seem to take this responsibility seriously and report wrongdoing using the internal channels preferred by most CEOs. Whistle-blowers, in fact, seem to be typical employees except that their interest in the public good outweighs their loyalty to the organization.

Whistle-blowers basically question the judgment of managers that is why they are discouraged by managers. Fear of potential whistle-blowers may also discourage managers from taking risks. A question arises in one's mind is that Will there be life after whistle-blowing? For many whistle-blowers there is life after the blown whistle. Although a substantial number of whistle-blowers suffer retaliation, it is apparently possible to create a structure that protects those who report wrongdoing. For example, internal auditors—who are recognized as individuals whose jobs are to report unethical or illegal acts—are less likely to suffer reprisal. However, one cannot minimize the significance of retaliation. Whistle-blowers who fall victim to reprisal tend to suffer in a big way, often losing their job, spouse, home, peace of mind and in many cases life.

STRATEGIES TO PROTECT WHISTLE BLOWERS

Corporate governance should be, first and foremost, about ethics and values.

It is for this reason that good corporate governance requires a system of checks and balances. This must include, amongst other things strong and active independent directors; thorough and competent statutory auditors; rigorous internal audit; appropriate metrics to diagnose the health of the company; transparency and disclosures; and active shareholders. These checks need to be backed up by appropriate laws and strong enforcement by an independent regulator. In trying to protect whistleblowers, we are actually trying to protect ourselves. Many employees may be afraid to speak out even with the legal protection, but its very existence will deter government and corporate wrongdoings to a considerable extent. Afar sighted government must, therefore, encourage and empower civil society organizations, just as it would corporate whistleblowers. In this, the corporate world too has a role: even as it evolves policies to encourage and protect whistleblowers, it must also support those who play that role in the wider societal context.

Under the new law that is being envisaged, the Central Vigilance Commission has been given the authority of a civil court whose decisions will not be challenged. The thinking does not go far enough. The remit of the CVC is very wide. Burdening that institution more can have a slowing-down effect throughout the range of its activities. It might be better to follow American practice in this instance. The US has established the Office of Special Counsel to protect employees, especially whistleblowers, from prohibited personnel practices. This means that employees who violate office norms and discipline to expose wrongdoing in the public interest will be offered protection within the system. In the Indian context, such an authority can be suitably modified in the form of a new institution to deal with issues that are likely to arise. In this country, whistleblowers also need to be protected against dangerous private interests—such as contractors—that typically collude with government officials. Typically, matters may not go as far as murder in the US or in Western Europe, but in America too there are clear provisions to protect whistleblowers in cases involving fraud by contractors who undertake government works. The False Claims Act contains a qui tam or whistleblower provision. It allows citizens (not just insiders) with evidence of fraud against contractors and programmes to sue, on behalf of the government, in order to recover stolen funds. The law goes back to 1863 and was rejuvenated with amendments in 1986. It is the idea of giving private citizens the incentive to team up with government to uncover fraud which animated the amendments. We need something akin to this in India. The bill deals only with protecting whistleblowers within government organizations.

The best solution is to encourage the sort of open organizational communication that allows top executives to learn of the alleged wrongdoing before the dissident goes public with the information. On the other hand, firms found to engage in illegal activities do not necessarily suffer reduced performance in the long term. The public seems to have either a short memory or high tolerance for corporate illegalities. Stock performance often does not suffer substantially when illegal behavior is reported publicly. The most radical solution would be to enact laws that penalize organization members who know about organization illegalities but do not report them. Given all of these considerations, what should managers do about whistle-blowing? Among those who plead for management encouragement of whistle-blowing, only two valid reasons emerge: expediency and ethics. Whistle-blowers should be encouraged because they may provide information about wrongdoing that, if terminated, may result in improved corporate performance (expediency). Even if termination of the wrongdoing does not improve corporate performance, CEOs may encourage whistle-blowing to discourage wrongdoing (ethics). Other methods for discouraging wrongdoing, such as a corporate statement of standards and ethics, seem to be remarkably ineffective. If CEOs wish to create a moral corporate culture, their actions are more persuasive than statements of intent; fair treatment of whistle-blowers may be the most dramatic way to persuade employees to operate ethically.

CONCLUSION

There is no denying the fact that whistle-blowers do a great service to the society at their great risk and cost, even at the loss of life. Hence, whistle-blowers need to be protected to ensure the good governance of organizations. The fact is that while trying to protect whistle-blowers, we are actually trying to protect ourselves. Many employees may be afraid to speak out even when legal protection exists. But, its very existence will deter government and corporate wrongdoings to a considerable extent and, in turn, will ensure good governance. As the type of scenario exists today in India, the chances of enacting legislation for protection to whistle-blowers seem remote. It seems just a matter of time before there will be shift from present culture of zero tolerance of whistle-blowing to a culture of zero tolerance of whistle-blower retaliation. Sooner is obviously welcome.

REFERENCES

Boatright, John R. (2003): Ethics and the Conduct of Business, Delhi: Pearson Education.

Bowie, Norman E. (1980): Business Ethics, New Jersey: Printice Hall.

Chakraborty, S.K. (9086): The Will to Yoga, Vikalpa, Volume III, No. 2.

Dalal, Sucheta (2003): Whistle-Blowing in Banks: How Can It Be Effective?, The 8th Balasubramaniam Memorial Lecture, Corporation Bank Officers Organization, 10 June.

Dandekar, Natalie (1993): Can Whistle-Blowing be Fully Legitimated? Quoted in T.I. White (Ed.): Business Ethics, New York: Macmillan.

Duska, R. (1990): Whistle-blowing and Employee Loyalty, In: T. I. White (Ed.): Business Ethics, New York: Macmillan.

Dealing with—or Reporting—"Unacceptable" Behavior (With additional thoughts about the "Bystander Effect") ©2009 Mary Rowe MIT, Linda Wilcox HMS, Howard Gadlin NIH, *Journal of the International Ombudsman Association* 2(1), online at Ombudsassociation.org

Friedman, Milton (1962): Capitalism and Freedom, Chicago: University of Chicago Press.

Faunce TA and Jefferys S. Whistleblowing and Scientific Misconduct: Renewing Legal and Virtue Ethics Foundations, *Journal of Medicine and Law,* 2007, 26 (3): 567-84

Faunce TA Developing and Teaching the Virtue-Ethics Foundations of Healthcare Whistle Blowing Monash, *Bioethics Review,* 2004; 23(4): 41-55

Green, Ronald M. (1994): The Ethical Manager, New York: Macmillan College Publishing Company.

James, Gene G. (1993): Whistle-Blowing: Its Moral Justification, In: T. I. White (Ed.): Business Ethics, New York: Macmillan.

Koehn, Daryl (2003): Whistle-Blowsing and Trust, In: Laura P. Hartman (Ed.): Perspectives in Business Ethics, New Delhi: Tata McGraw-Hill Publishing Company Limited.

Kohelberg, L. (1981): Essays in Moral Development, Volume I, New York: Harper & Row.

Mary Rowe, "Options and Choice for Conflict Resolution in the Workplace" in Negotiation: Strategies for Mutual Gain, by Lavinia Hall, ed., Sage Publications, Inc., 1993, pp. 105-19.

Nader, Ralph; P.J. Petkas and Kate Blackwell (Eds.) (1972): Whistle-Blowing Report on the Conference of Professional Responsibility, New York: Bantam Books.

Powell, R. (1965): The Law of Agency, London: Pitman and Sons.

Roche, James M. (1971): The Competitive System to Work, to Preserve, and to Protect.

Rowe, Mary and Bendersky, Corinne, "Workplace Justice, Zero Tolerance and Zero Barriers: Getting People to Come Forward in Conflict Management Systems," in Negotiations and Change, From the Workplace to Society, Thomas Kochan and Richard Locke (editors), Cornell University Press, 2002. See also Dealing with—or Reporting—"Unacceptable" Behavior (With additional thoughts about the "Bystander Effect") ©2009Mary Rowe MIT, Linda Wilcox HMS, Howard Gadlin NIH, *Journal of the International Ombudsman Association,* 2(1), online at Ombuds association.org

Sekhar, R.C. (2002): Ethical Choices in Business, New Delhi: Response Books.

The Insiders: Government, Business, and the Lobbyists, by John Sawatsky, 1987.

Whistleblower Protection Enhancement Act of 2007 – Congress pedia California False Claims Act.

Winters *v.* Houston Chronicle Pub. Co., 795 S.W. 2d 723, 727 (Tex. 1990) (Doggett, J., concurring).

Index

Administration of Service Tax, 191
Adopting International Financial Reporting Standard, 210
Advantages:
E-HRM, 120
Aggarwal, Kapil, 207
Aggarwal, Silvie, 229
Arora, Aarti, 55
Argument against Whistle-Blowing, 247
Assessment Centers, 129
Attract New Customer, 201
Aulakh, Rupender, 166
Automated Teller Machine (ATM), 200

Balance Sheet Approach of Compensation Plan, 75
Balachandar, G., 138
Banking Sector Reforms, 196
Beach, Dale, S., 123
Behaviorally Anchored Rating Scales, 127
Benefits:
E-Banking, 201
Human Resource Development Strategies, 172
Better Appraisal and Reward Systems, 82
Brain Storming, 169
British Copyright Act, 1911, 229
Business Ethics, 92

Career Counselling, 170
Assessments, 106
Career Development, Advancement and Opportunities, 96
Career Development Theories, 100
Career Exploration, 103
Career Opportunity Techniques, 105
Central Cooperative Bank, Panchkula, 179
Challenges:
E-Banking, 203
Globalization, 83
Quality Revolution, 83
Changes in HRM, 81
Changing Composition of Work Force, 81
Changing Demographics of Workforce, 66
Changing Profile of Workers, 69
Chaudhary, Nirmala, 138
Cheque Truncation System (CTS), 223
CISCO Systems, 23
Collective Bargaining, 64
Compensation Plan of Expatriates, 74
Competency Mapping, 85
Competitive Global Environment, 174
Computer Skill, 202
Conceptualisation of Human Resource Development, 168

Consequences of Going Public, 251
Consumer Acceptance of Internet Banking, 202
Convenience Stores, 49
Copyright Act, 1957, 231
Corporate Governance, 92
Corporate Sustainability Protocol (CSP), 8
Cost Accounting Method, 128
Cost Savings, 201
Counseling Poor Performers, 125
Credit Cards, 200
Critical Incidents Method, 127
Cross-National Transfer of HR Policies, 71

Dale, Yoder, 124
Dawer, Shivani, 96
Debit Cards, 200
Delphi Technique, 170
Determining Compensation Changes, 125
Development Planning, 82
Development Stage of a Country, 39
Difference in GAAP and IFRS, 217
Disadvantages of E-HRM, 120
Discount Stores, 49

E-banking, 196
E-Cash, 225
E-Cheques, 200, 225
E-compensation, 120
E-employee Profile, 118
E-HRM: 115
  Goals, 116
  Tools, 118
  Objectives, 115
  Scope, 116
E-learning, 119
E-leave, 120
E-performance Management System, 119
E-recruitment, 118
E-selection, 119
E-training, 119
Electronic Clearing Service, 226
Electronic Fund Transfer, (EFT), 225
Electronic Human Resource Management, 112
Elimination of Skill Gap, 174
Emerging HR Trends and Challenges, 78
Emerging Role of HRM, 83
Emerging Trends in Bank Technology, 223
Emerging Trends in HRM, 84
Employee Attitude Towards E-hrm, 116
Employment Practices, 61
Empowerment of Employees, 84
Encouraging Coaching and Mentoring, 125
Encouraging Performance Improvement, 125
Essentials of a Good Expatriate Compensation Plan, 75
Ethnocentric Staffing Policy, 73
Exit Policy, 86
External Environmental Factors, 76

Facilitating Layoff or Downsizing Decisions, 125
Facilitating Promotion Decisions, 125
Factors Affecting the Development of Marketing Plan, 38
Field Review Method, 127
Forced Choice Method, 127
Forced Distribution Method, 127
Ford Motor Company, 9
Future of Industrial Relations in India, 65

Geocentric Staffing Policy, 74
Global Staffing Policies, 72
Green HRM, 89, 91
Green Marketing, 3
Green Packing, 20
Green Practices, 93
Green Product, 4
Green Storage, 19
Green Transportation, 19
Growth of Retail Sector, 46
Gupta, Jyoti, 43

Harvandna, 236
HCL Info. Systems Limited, 21
Hewlett-Packard, 9
History of Services Tax, 190
Home-based Method, 76
HR and IR Coordinated Activities, 58
Human Problem, 76
Human Resource Development, 63, 169
Human Resource Development Strategies, 166
Human Resource Outsourcing, 84
Human Resource Planning, 61
Human Resource Retention Problem, 173
Hyper Marts/Supermarkets, 49

IBM-India, 23
Impact of Globalisation on Human Resource Management, 55
Impact of Industrialization on Environment, 92
Impact on Financial Position of Indian Companies, 207
Improving Overall Organizational Performance, 126
Increase in Education Levels, 81
Increasing Government Role, 82
Indian Retail Scene, 44
Individualised Training and Development, 171
Industrial Disputes, 64
Industrial Relations, 57
Industry Evolution, 48
Influence of Public Sector, 175
Information Technology in Banking Sector, 221
Infosys Technologies Ltd., 23
Innovative MeasuresTowards Green Logistics, 17
Instant Rewards, 86
International Financial Reporting Standards, (IFRS), 211
Internet and Mobile Association of India (IAMAI), 199
Internet Banking, 199, 201, 224
Internet Banking History, 198
Introducing Spirituality in Organisations, 240

Jasrotia, Anu, 122
Job Description, 171
Job Design, 60
Job Satisfaction, 138
Justifications in Favour of Whistle-Blowing, 247

Kanwar, Promila, 122
Kapoor, Priyanka, 78
Kaur, Prabjot, 196
Khanna, Monika, 112
Kumari, Neelam, 152

Lack of Educational Advancement, 174
Lack of Fund for Human Resource Development, 174
Leadership Development, 85
Legal Base of Service Tax, 191
LG India, 9

Management By Objectives, 129
Manisha, 179
Manocha, Tanu, 17
Marketing Plan for Exporters, 26
Marketing Segmentation and Positioning, 33
Matching Academic and Experiential Learning, 108
Meaning of Marketing Plan for Exporters, 28
Measuring Goals, 125
Meenakshi, 78
Mobile Banking, 225
Monotonous, Routine and Repetitive Tasks, 174
Motivating Superior Performance, 125
MRF Tyres, 12
Multi Polar World, 71

New Personnel Policies, 82
New Work Ethic, 82

Occupational Health and Safety, 82
Operational E-hrm, 116
Outcomes of Green HRM, 94

Padala, S.R., 138
Paired Comparison Methods, 129
Panchanatham, N., 138
Pandey, Seema, 89
Participative Management, 64
Performance Tests and Observations, 128
Personal and Comprehensive Career Development, 109
Phone Banking, 200
Pillars of Sustainability, 91
Plastic Money, 200
Polycentric Staffing Policy, 73
Pooja, 244
Price Determination/Export Pricing, 32
Process of Developing Marketing Plan for Exporters, 35
Protect Whistle Blowers, 252
Protecting Whistle Blowers, 249
Providing Feedback, 124
Providing Legal Defensibility for Personnel Decision, 126

Quality and Study Circles, 170
Quotidian and Electronic Meeting, 171

Ranking Methods, 129
Rating Scales, 126
Relational E-HRM, 116
Relevance of Spirituality to Workplace, 238
Reliance Communication Limited, 122
Reliance Power, 6
Research Traditions in Guidance and Counseling, 98
Retailing Format in India, 48
Reverse Logistics, 20
Richa Lomas, 196
Rizwan Ul Zaman Dar, 221
Role of Social Media in Changing Worker, 67

Sahni, Marshal Mukesh, 17
Schuler, Randall S., 123
Sharma, Aakashdeep, 166
Sharma, Neeru, 71
Satellite Banking, 224
School Education, 152
Service Tax in India, 189
Shifts:
  Human Resource Management, 60
  Industrial Relations, 63
Singh, Manmohan, 190
Six-sigma Practices, 86
Smart Cards, 200
Social and Environmental Accountability, 3
Solkhe, Ajay, 138
Spirituality and Worker's Well-being, 239
Spirituality at Work Place, 236
Student–Teacher Relationships, 153
Subramanian, K., 138
Supporting Manpower Planning, 125

Tata Consultancy Services (TCS) Limited, 22
Tata Power, 8
Technological Advances, 83
Technological Developments, 81
Transformational E-HRM, 116
Trends in Recruitment, 81
Types of E-HRM, 116

Vaibhav Manocha, 3
Validating Hiring Decisions, 126
Verma, Mamta, 26

Walia, Sanjana, 229
What HR Managers Can Do?, 86
What is Performance Appraisal?, 123
Whistle Blowing, 244
"Whistle-Blowers" Resolution, 250
Wipro Technologies, 22
Workforce Control System, 76
Workforce Diversity, 84
World Economic Forum (WEF), 21